I0397225

MELTDOWN

MELTDOWN

The Predictable Distortion of Global Warming
by Scientists, Politicians, and the Media

Patrick J. Michaels

CATO
INSTITUTE
Washington, D.C.

Copyright © 2004 by Cato Institute.
All rights reserved.

Library of Congress Cataloging-in-Publication Data

Meltdown : the predictable distortion of global warming by
   scientists, politicians, and the media / Patrick J. Michaels.
   p. cm.
Includes bibliographical references and index.
ISBN 1-930865-59-7 (alk. paper)
   1. Global warming—Political aspects.   2. Science—Political
aspects.   I. Title.

QC981.8.G56M535 2004
363.738′742—dc22

2004057036

Cover design by Elise Rivera.

Printed in the United States of America.

CATO INSTITUTE
1000 Massachusetts Ave., N.W.
Washington, D.C. 20001
www.cato.org

Contents

Epigraph

The prospect of domination of the nation's scholars by federal employment, project allocations, and the power of money is ever present—and is gravely to be regarded. Yet, holding scientific research and discovery in respect, as we should, we must always be alert to the equal and opposite danger that public policy could itself become a captive of a scientific-technological elite.

—President Dwight D. Eisenhower, Farewell Address, January 17, 1961

1. Foreword

$$\frac{S}{4}(1 - \alpha) = \varepsilon\sigma T_e^4$$

Everyone says the way *not* to begin a book is with an equation. But the book you are about to read is going to upset a lot of other common perceptions: facts about climate change, the nature of science and scientists, and the culture that surrounds what everyone seems to think is "the most important environmental issue of our time": global warming. In January 2004, David King, science adviser to British Prime Minister Tony Blair, stated that climate change was a far worse threat to the world than terrorism. Months earlier, Sir John Houghton, head of the prestigious United Nations Intergovernmental Panel on Climate Change (IPCC), said precisely the same.

What this equation means is that human beings have the ability to change the temperature of the surface of the earth. The Energy Balance Equation is in fact simple, though it may look unfamiliar.

S is the amount of energy we receive from the sun. It's divided by four because the earth is a sphere and, as a whole, only one fourth receives the equivalent of direct illumination. Anyone older than thirty was taught in basic science that S is constant, as far as the earth's temperature is concerned. That was wrong. We know now that S varies, and it changes the surface temperature plus or minus about 1°C (1.8°F) on the order of millennia. Humans have no control over that.

α is the amount of energy that is reflected away by the earth. Fresh snow, for example, reflects 90 percent. Because most year-to-year climate variability is a result of changes in winter temperatures, rather than summer ones, warming up the planet a bit could have a big effect on standing snow cover. Subtracting the reflectivity from 1 $(1 - \alpha)$ yields the amount of energy that is absorbed by the earth. Human beings can change that amount in several ways: clearing a forest, building a city, farming, or burning anything with trace amounts of sulfur (which means just about everything). Driving a tractor through a dusty field is an especially good way to make the atmosphere more reflective.

The left-hand side of the Energy Balance Equation defines how much energy goes "in" to the earth, and is clearly influenced by the amount of dust in the atmosphere. A lot of human activity—farming, for example—raises dust (again, picture the tractor moving through a dusty field). The right side is what comes "out."

σ is a constant, "the Stephan-Boltzmann constant" to be specific, that relates temperature to energy.

ε is a measure of how efficiently the earth dissipates heat. Human beings can change that, too. An atmosphere with water vapor or carbon dioxide in it loses heat in its lower layers more slowly than one without. Every molecule of fossil fuel, when burned, yields carbon dioxide. It's going up.

T_e^4 is the fourth power of the temperature of the earth-atmosphere system. Disturbing α or ε will redistribute heat, altering the surface and upper-air temperature. As the chirpy salesperson at the local office supply store says, "We can do that!" Indeed, we've been doing it, at increasing rates, for centuries.

Because almost every human activity seems to have some bearing on it, the Energy Balance Equation is the late-20th century's equivalent of $E = mc^2$ in terms of social significance—which means the political process will be heavily involved in its interpretation.

Thirty years ago, there was much scientific discussion among those who believed that humans influenced the left side of the equation, in which increases in reflectivity cool the earth, more than they affected the right side, which could be altered by increasing carbon dioxide, causing warming.

Back then, the "coolers" had the upper hand because, indeed, the planet *was* cooling. That was especially the case in the Northern Hemisphere, and the three consecutive winters ending in 1979 were, in combination, the worst string of winters in the modern American record.

In science, the default paradigm is often one of continuity. The climate was cooling, so the left side had to dominate. But nature quickly shifted gears. In 1976, a dramatic temperature change spread across the Pacific Ocean, and concurrently the mean surface temperature regime shifted from one of cooling to one of warming. Unprecedented in our limited historical records, that abrupt change in temperature was "discovered" some 20 years later and named "The

Great Pacific Climate Shift." Needless to say, that abrupt shift in the climate caused almost as abrupt a shift in the balance of scientists who predictably followed the temperature toward the right side of the equation.

Computer models sprouted like mushrooms in compost, all fed with increasing carbon dioxide, and all predicting dramatic warming. Not surprisingly, that warming refused to appear in the amount or fashion specified. Consequently, computer models were modified to include both changes in reflectivity and the altered dissipation of heat. Some $20 billion later, those models still don't have it right. While all that money was being spent and all those forecasts tinkered with, nature tipped its hand on climate change: Warming will be modest and can't be stopped anyway.

If the earth's climate was as volatile as it *apparently* is according to the equation, temperatures would fluctuate violently, and the planet would likely be much less hospitable for complex land-based creatures such as mammals. Under those circumstances, we might well have never emerged from the ocean, where temperature changes are more buffered by water's huge thermal inertia.

Instead, along with the other mammals, we humans are thriving— which means there are, no doubt, some pretty strong internal feedbacks and checks that keep the surface temperature within a relatively small range. Some fossil records suggest the earth's carbon dioxide concentration in the geologic past was nearly *15 times* what it is today, and yet the temperature was less than 10°C (18°F) warmer than today. Contrary to current climate hype, this planet therefore cannot undergo a "runaway" greenhouse effect from human emissions of carbon dioxide. We won't double carbon dioxide from its background value until late in this century (if we continue to intensively use fossil fuel, which is a dubious assumption for 100 years from now), and that's a far cry from a 15-fold increase.

Yet a culture of distortion surrounds the global warming issue, clamoring for legislation that would mitigate what politicians characterize as a greenhouse effect gone out of control. The fact is almost every economic activity alters the energy balance equation, so any attempt to mitigate those changes therefore creates cost, which causes political ferment. Powerful people and interests line up in support of or against regulations, pitching their views to a sharply divided electorate. Only 21,000 different votes in the 2000 election would have turned both the presidency and the Congress over to the Democratic Party and Al Gore. Those votes were the difference between the Bush administration's announcement that "Kyoto is Dead," made less than two months after its inauguration, and the continued pursuit of that treaty by a Gore administration. The afterword to this book bears testimony to the degree to which politicians of all stripes have waded into the issue of global warming.

Needless to say, the political climate in which global warming science and research is conducted is a volatile and contentious one, made even more so by the way it competes with other issues, such as cancer research or nanotechnology, for a finite federal outlay.

The distortion of global warming becomes logical and predictable, for this and for many other reasons, including the nature of modern science itself.

That's not a viewpoint that will make a lot of friends for this author. That's okay because I have plenty, anyway. There's my wife, Erika, who loves a guy who is positively addicted to stirring pots and causing trouble. That's not easy. Thanks, QT π! There's my chief researcher, Paul C. "Chip" Knappenberger, who sticks around despite all the controversy and noise. There's my University Research Coordinator, Jerry Stenger, who answers all those data requests to the State Climatology Office as well as tolerating my daily rants. There's Ed Crane, the boss at Cato, a Washington think tank that early on realized the importance of having a resident climate scientist. There's the late Callie the calico cat, a stray that adopted me. And there's my phenomenal and funny editor, Amy Lemley (an asset to any writer), and Steve Gawtry and Dustin Hux, graduate students who helped immeasurably by doing my day job while I wrote this book. Tereza Urbanova from the Liberani Institut in Prague, Molly Elgin from Tulane University, and Kerry Doyle from St. Louis University provided invaluable help and technical assistance at the Cato Institute. E-mail me for letters of recommendation. You've made great friends.

Robert E. Davis, another keen observer of global warming science and politics, wrote the original text for a few amusing subsections of this book, dealing mainly with jellyfish, birds, shark attacks, and human health. Portions of the first section of the chapter on the U.S. National Assessment of global warming appeared in "The Alchemy of Policymaking," published by Hoover Institute and edited by Michael Gough.

There comes a time in one's career when it's just got to be told like it is: Global warming is an exaggerated issue, predictably blown out of proportion by the political and professional climate in which it evolved.

After a brief discussion of global warming physics, facts, and assumptions, this book chants a litany of questionable science, overstated science, poorly reported science, and unwarranted statements by scientists themselves, all on the subject of global climate change.

For example, the role of global warming in melting the world's most iconic ice field, memorialized in Hemingway's *The Snows of Kilimanjaro*, has been terribly overstated. The historic behavior of the North Polar icecap was improperly characterized by scientists whose statements were carried with little question by a newspaper as august as the *New York Times*. The United Nations Intergovernmental Panel on Climate Change dramatically overstated the amount of ice that has been lost from polar seas. The same *Times* left an impression that arctic climate is changing at a rate 10 times faster than it actually is.

Greenland, the largest mass of ice in the Northern Hemisphere, has been reported to be shrinking rapidly. Yet it is largely in balance, not in recession. Where it is receding, the temperature is dropping, not warming. Still, some of the nation's best science writers glibly repeat physically impossible scare stories about a coming ice age.

Voluminous claims of massive extinctions caused by human interference with the climate are almost never tested with even the most rudimentary data, and when they are, such claims can no longer be entertained. Somehow, the peer review process of some of the world's most prestigious academic journals fails to pick up such problems. Instead, we hear this: Jellyfish are exploding, caused by global warming. Jellyfish are disappearing, caused by global warming. Penguins are moving north, as a result of global warming, so far north, in fact, that the coffee fields of Brazil should be frozen— which they obviously are not.

Nature magazine publishes a paper claiming that a change in temperature of less than a degree (C) will cause 15 percent of all species to become extinct. No one ever bothered to check to see whether that was what happened (it didn't) during the last century, when the temperature changed that much.

Sea level has risen because of climate change, but it has risen, at best, only a few inches. In fact, there's no evidence that the rate of sea-level rise has changed at all, despite a surface temperature that has warmed, cooled, and warmed again in the last 100 years. The government of Tuvalu, a Pacific island, claims that it is drowning because of global warming. In fact, sea levels have been falling in that region, not rising. Droughts have, in general, decreased in our major agricultural regions. Rainfall has increased over the same areas. Midwestern corn yields about five times as much as it did before human-induced warming started. Human life expectancy has doubled. Growing seasons have lengthened. Washington's cherry trees bloom earlier, and people say it's global warming, even though there has been no change in temperature in the surrounding country-side. Washington just happens to be an island of hot air in a sea of climate stasis—probably because of all the concrete and the inhabitants therein.

A culture that worships weather disasters hypes Atlantic hurricanes, although they have been steadily weakening since World War II. Tornado deaths are in decline, as is the number of the most damaging whirlwinds. Despite that, cartoonist Tom Toles, in the May 7, 2003, *Washington Post*, writes the opposite in a caption beneath one of his amusing drawings:

> These superpowerful tornadoes are the kind of storm we're likely to see more of with global climate change ... with energy added to the atmosphere, more frequent and intense storms are a probable outcome.

> —Tom Toles, text accompanying editorial cartoon,
> May 7, 2003, *Washington Post*

Deaths in American cities from heat-related causes are in decline, despite the United Nations predicting an increase in heat deaths. There's no detectable change in monsoon rainfall, despite what the United Nations asserts.

Federal climatologists produce volumes and compendia on the basis of computer models that they discover do not work, yet publication proceeds. They speak of a "change point" accelerating global warming with absolutely no evidence that it occurred.

When it comes to climate change, there's a culture of distortion out there. But it shouldn't surprise you. Its development was logical, predictable, and inevitable.

Much has been written about the complex subject of how science and scientists work. After our massive scientific litany, which is the balance of this book (and probably good ammo for any global warming discussion at your next cocktail party), I tender an explanation based on a largely accepted theory of the scientific process interacting with the political sphere. (Readers may want to read that part now, or save the explanation for after we sort the sound science from the junk.)

No one can completely account for the remarkable distortion that has occurred concerning the issue of global warming. But we can try. And we can offer a set of solutions to prevent the misrepresentations from happening with the next great environmental scare, whatever that might be.

2. An Introduction to Global Warming

Global warming is real, and human beings have something to do with it. We don't have everything to do with it; but we can't stop it, and we couldn't even slow it down enough to measure our efforts if we tried.

Figure 2.1 is a chart of various temperature estimates of planetary temperature going back to 1610. That signal date marks Galileo's invention of the telescope. One of the first things Galileo used it for was to view the sun. (That he didn't immediately go blind is testimony to his wisdom: he knew to project the image rather than to look at it directly.) Every few months or weeks he noticed that a black spot, or a few of them, would appear on the sun's surface.

Whether a person believed in an earth-centered universe or a heliocentric one (a view of Jupiter and its moons soon convinced Galileo of the latter), everyone pretty much agreed that the sun warmed the earth. So the appearance of black spots became a curiosity worth recording: Would a darker sun create a cooler planet?

We now know that the opposite is true. A sun with many spots is a hotter sun because the dark regions are surrounded by larger, whiter areas that are more energetic than the quiescent state. Since that discovery, myriad scientists have matched the earth's temperature to the output of the sun. This isn't exactly rocket science. If there were no match, the basic theory of climatology would be wrong, a theory that simply states that the sun is the cause of our climate.

A review of sunspot records is one way to back-calculate the earth's temperature before the general use of thermometers, which dates back to the mid-1800s. But there are other climate "proxies." The width of tree rings, for example, is related to total rainfall and summer temperature. Plants leave fragments, including long-lasting pollen, in the bottom of lakes, and shallow lakes "turn over" every year, creating annual striations, called varves, that can be counted back in time. Shifts in pollen assemblages trapped in varves from

9

Figure 2.1

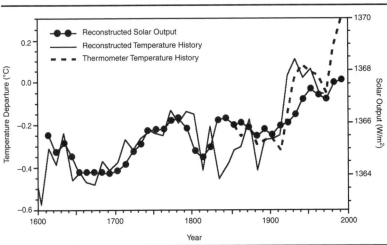

The dotted line is the output of the sun, as measured by sunspots, and the solid line is a reconstruction of temperature histories. The dashed line is the temperature measured by ground-based thermometers. Until the mid- to late 20th century, it was the sun that drove most climate change.

SOURCE: Lean and Rind, 1998.

boreal (spruce, fir, birch—the "north woods" complex) to oak and pine, for example, would characterize a warming climate.

Checking one type of back-calculation against another lends credence to both. For instance, the tree-ring records, shown as the solid line in Figure 2.1, can be matched against the sun's output. The correspondence is quite good. Both records in turn can be compared with the thermometric era (dashed line), and the mutual correspondence is again very good until somewhere around 1970. At that point, the surface thermometer record begins to diverge wildly from the solar history.

Something happened. But what? Why didn't the divergence between solar-derived and greenhouse-enhanced temperatures begin earlier?

First, the early increments of CO_2 were relatively small. After accounting for the known constellation of greenhouse-enhancing gases, only about a third of the total enhancement had taken place by 1950.

THE GREENHOUSE EFFECT

In the absence of an atmosphere, it's pretty easy to calculate the temperature of the earth-atmosphere system. All you need to know is the amount of radiation that the earth intercepts from the sun and the amount that it reflects from its nonblack surface. That number works out to about $-17°C$ ($+1.4°F$).

But obviously, that's not the correct surface temperature. In large part, that's because the gases in our atmosphere selectively absorb some of the sun's incoming radiation as well as another fraction of the heat emanating from the sun-warmed earth. Those molecules, such as oxygen, water vapor, and carbon dioxide, ultimately release that energy, preferentially warming some layers of the atmosphere at the expense of cooling elsewhere.

Carbon dioxide and water vapor are especially adept in absorbing the heat of the earth's surface. When they release (or "re-radiate") that energy, they do so either upward (out to space) or back down. That increase in "downwelling" radiation is what, among other things, keeps the surface of the planet warmer than its temperature would be without an atmosphere. This differential warming is known as the "greenhouse effect," an analogy to a greenhouse, an enclosure that is warmer than the surrounding environment because of different radiational characteristics.

We have known all of this since 1872, following pioneering experiments by British physicist John Tyndall. And since at least 1895, we have known that human beings were increasing the concentration of one minor greenhouse gas—carbon dioxide (CO_2)—largely through the combustion of fuel stored under or at the earth's surface: peat, coal, oil, and natural gas.

The relative roles in surface warming of water vapor vs. carbon dioxide are approximately 10 to 1, which is why CO_2 is considered a "minor" greenhouse enhancer. But if an increment of CO_2 slightly warms the surface, then the vapor pressure of water over the vast oceans of the planet also increases slightly, raising the amount of water vapor in the air. That "positive feedback" is much harder to quantify than it is to qualify, and it is one of the reasons that so many computer simulations of climate give so many different forecasts for 21st-century warming.

(continued on next page)

(continued)

Of course, there are also other greenhouse gases that result from human activity. Methane (CH_4) is especially potent, and it is thought to currently exert an additional warming increment amounting to about 25 percent of the current greenhouse enhancement due to CO_2. Chlorofluorocarbons (CFCs), largely used as refrigerants, have been phased out because of their relation to stratospheric ozone depletion, and concentrations are beginning to drop; but they provide another increment— roughly 10 percent—over the CO_2 fraction. And there are a whole host of other, far more minor greenhouse enhancers that people can produce.

Second, it takes time for the ocean to warm. Consider an analogous experiment: heating a large pot of water by adding infrared energy (i.e., turning on an electric stove). Water has a certain "heat capacity," which is to say it requires a certain amount of energy to raise its temperature a degree. That energy has to be supplied. Water also has a "lag" between the burner-water interface—the bottom of the big pot and the top. The temperature of the entire stovetop "ocean" will only equilibrate after all the heat has been mixed, through vertical currents or through deep horizontal motions. In reality, that pan of water—our ocean—averages miles in depth, and in spots is 35,000 feet (seven miles) deep. Even warming the top few thousand feet takes decades.

Consequently, the combination of slowly increasing the greenhouse effect and a tremendously "fly-wheeled" ocean with massive thermal inertia delays the onset of warming for some time.

Is the warming that began around 1970 largely a result of greenhouse changes? That's a testable hypothesis, and one I looked at very carefully in a paper I published with three colleagues in the journal *Climate Research*. It had to do with the known physics of greenhouse gases and temperature. Early experiments had demonstrated that the response of temperature to carbon dioxide is a logarithm (Figure 2.2), meaning that warming begins to damp off as carbon dioxide increases. Another greenhouse gas, water vapor, absorbs much of the same type of radiation and therefore acts much the same. That similarity has an important implication.

Figure 2.2

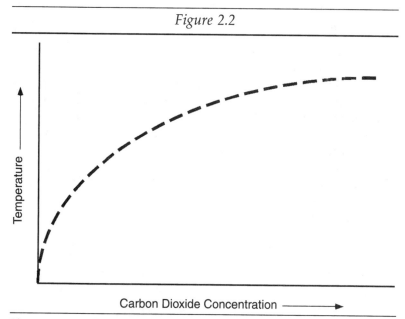

Carbon Dioxide Concentration ⟶

The response of temperature to a change in a given greenhouse gas is logarithmic, meaning that it damps off at increasing concentrations.

If we could find a place in which there is very little water vapor and there was very little CO_2 (before humans burned much fossil fuel), then adding CO_2 to that atmosphere should produce a rapid warming because the temperature response is on the rapidly ascending portion of the greenhouse-response logarithm (see Figure 2.2).

Siberia, in the dead of winter, is an ideal test case. January temperatures hover around $-40°C$ or F (at that temperature, they're one and the same). As a result, the atmosphere has virtually no water vapor. It's been all frozen out. Only an infinitesimal number of molecules evaporate from the snowy and icy surface.

It turns out that by far the largest warmings on Earth are occurring in Siberian winter, just as greenhouse theory predicts (see Figure 2.3 in color insert). And further, we were able to "prove" the greenhouse influence: The more cold and dry air there was, the more it warmed. If the air was moist and cold, there was little if any warming. In the summer we could also run the experiment where the same theory would predict maximum warming in the driest places. Indeed, where adequate data existed, the largest warmings were in or near the Sahara Desert.

So that's the signature of greenhouse warming: a disproportionate warming of dry air. And that signature appears to have begun in the early 1970s. That's when the divergence from the solar temperature begins, and the differential warm-up of the dry air, mainly in Siberia, takes off. That's the recent past, but what about the future?

The Nature of Climate Projections

In 1896, Swedish physicist Svante Arrhenius published the first paper predicting how much the earth's surface would warm from changing concentrations of atmospheric carbon dioxide; his forecasts appeared in the journal *Philosophical Transactions*.

Arrhenius calculated the following:

- A doubling of the background concentration of CO_2 would lead to a net average surface warming of about 5°C (9°F).
- The warming would be greater in winter than in summer, more in the Northern Hemisphere than in the Southern.
- Nights would warm relative to days.
- Warming would be enhanced at high latitudes.

His projections remain remarkable to this day, if only because of their resemblance to the output of current computer models of climate, known collectively as general circulation models (GCMs). Although the median GCM projections for the "sensitivity" of surface-to-doubled CO_2 tend to run at about 3°C (5.4°F), or 60 percent less than Arrhenius's original projections, their geographical, seasonal, and daily distributions of projected warming are remarkably similar.

Why do we need a computer to do what Arrhenius did with a pencil and paper? Arrhenius was calculating expected climate response to a "step change," or an instantaneous doubling of atmospheric CO_2. Note that he never said *when* the temperature change would take place, or how fast it would occur. The answer to those questions, among others, requires much more sophisticated computation because they result from slowly changing atmospheric conditions rather than the unrealistic step change.

In addition, and perhaps more important, Arrhenius' planet was a nondynamic sphere where the atmosphere had no obvious interaction with the surface constitution. In reality, we know that changing climate yields changed ecosystems, and, in turn, those alterations change the energetics of the planetary surface. As an extreme example, consider the difference between the dry, hot Sahara desert and the tropical rainforest. The latter cycles tremendous amounts of moisture into the atmosphere, holding down daytime temperatures and warming the nights. The desert behaves in completely opposite fashion.

Recall that greenhouse effect warmings tend to take place primarily in the driest air. Consequently, you might expect either an expansion or an increased intensity of desertification.

On the other hand, by warming winters and nights preferentially to summers and days, greenhouse warming lengthens the growing season—the time between the last frost of spring and the first frost of autumn. The period in between is the time in which plants actively produce green matter, so global warming is likely, simply from its temperature effect, to make the planet greener, "everything else being equal." There's ample evidence that this type of greening is already occurring, as Boston University scientist Ranja Myneni has articulated in several published papers.

Of course, everything else is never "equal"—making that phrase the largest and most common form of scientific subterfuge. A computer climate model attempts, where possible, to correct for that fact by dynamically changing climate and vegetation. In other words, increased rainfall in some areas, coupled with longer growing seasons, may lead to increased greening, while decreased rainfall in others may lead to browning.

That all seems well and good on the surface, but in fact a computer model is only as good as its understanding of the dynamic process that it must simulate. As an example, we really don't have a very good understanding of the basic flow of carbon dioxide through the atmosphere. After a molecule of fossil carbon is burned, how long does it take before it is ultimately sequestered back in the earth? That depends on assumptions about the rate of uptake by plants, which means their response to weather and climate. It also depends on the rate of decay of dead plant matter littering the world's forest floors. For all those processes, rate estimates vary widely. As a result, the estimates for the "atmospheric lifetime" of a newly released molecule of CO_2 vary from 25 to 150 years, depending what you think is "equal."

Figure 2.4

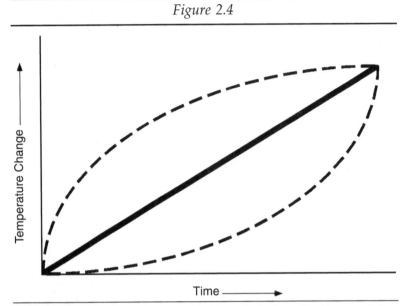

The combination of an exponential increase in carbon dioxide, coupled to a logarithmic response, can be a straight line. As shown in Figure 2.5 (see color insert), climate models converge on this solution.

Climate models do, however, retain a series of core beliefs. One, you may recall, is that the response of temperature to increments of carbon dioxide is logarithmic, meaning that it begins to damp off as concentrations increase. That means that the first increments of carbon dioxide create the greatest warming.

All climate models also assume that the growth rate of carbon dioxide in the atmosphere is exponential, at 1 percent per year (a gross overestimate) meaning that it is going into the atmosphere at ever-increasing rates. The models hold that the CO_2 itself will not damp off, but will rise in concentration forever and ever. That turns out to be a highly questionable assumption, one that may have dramatic implications for future climate change.

However, the interaction of a logarithmic response of temperature to carbon dioxide, coupled to an exponential increase, as shown in Figure 2.4, can easily combine to a straight line.

This behavior is especially apparent in studies known as CMIPs, or Climate Model Intercomparison Projects. Figure 2.5 (see color insert), taken from the first CMIP study, dramatically shows this behavior. (A second study, CMIP-II, added additional complication but essentially gave the same result as shown in Figure 2.6 in the color insert).

So the question becomes this: Which, if any, of these straight lines is correct?

Analogy to Weather Forecasting Models

Environmental conservatives often argue that "weather forecasting models aren't reliable after a week, so why should climate models for the next 100 years be better?" That argument is convenient, but fallacious.

The fallacy: Weather forecasting and climate forecasting models, while retaining much of the same mathematics, are designed to respond to different types of change.

The weather forecasting model is designed to calculate internal changes in the atmosphere given a base external condition, which is the observed weather on a given day. Because of a combination of computational limitations and random behavior, these models run up against a mathematical "wall" around 10 to 14 days out, where the predicted weather patterns, as specified by high- and low-pressure systems and large-scale circulations like the jet stream, no more resemble reality than a pattern that could be randomly picked out of a sample of thousands of days.

In the long-range climate model, or GCM, it is the external conditions that change, as forced by an alteration in the atmosphere's natural greenhouse effect. GCMs then interact this initial alteration with other consequent changes in the atmosphere, such as the vertical distribution of temperature, which in turn produces more "weather-like" effects such as rainfall. In their most sophisticated incarnations, the accumulated weather changes then drive additional alterations at the earth's surface, like the transformation of deserts into forests and vice versa.

As a result, it's unfair to say that climate models must fail because we can't forecast day-to-day weather; what they are attempting is not the same. Rather, they are only trying to predict "aggregate" weather forced by changes in the base atmosphere, which is to say, alterations of the greenhouse effect.

Even so, that is where the climate models fall down—in the "aggregate" weather and its consequences. As one example of many, consider the finding of University of Delaware climatologist David Legates, who has demonstrated that the aggregate precipitation produced by GCMs can easily be off by 50 percent, depending upon location. That GCM precipitation is then used as input to a model for vegetation change, but it is in error. Further, the relationship between precipitation and vegetation is not all that clear—some equally wet and warm environments have radically different vegetation, depending upon other factors, including soil, drainage, and seasonality of precipitation.

The multiplying mess becomes obvious: Because each of these interacting processes is only partially understood, the mathematics for each depends on the choice of the modeling team. As a result, different GCMs produce different patterns, rates, and distributions of warming resulting from human alteration of the atmosphere.

Is there a way to adjudicate this mess? Absolutely, and it involves the same process that confronts weather forecasters when the models for tomorrow diverge from each other. The solution? Look out the window! Literally.

That's exactly what they must do. On any given day, there are about a dozen different weather forecasting models applicable to the United States. Sometimes they are pretty unanimous, but other times they diverge wildly and produce forecasts with radically different implications.

Such a problem often crops up in winter along the Atlantic Coast. The coastal bend from Georgia to North Carolina is a prime breeding ground for strong low-pressure systems because of its proximity to tropical water (east of the Gulf Stream, as close as 50 miles to shore) and to cold air sliding down from Canada. When the jet stream gets in the right orientation, powerful cyclones, known locally as Northeasters, can spin up in a matter of hours, with serious weather consequences.

Virtually every major snowstorm in the Raleigh-Boston corridor is a result of a Northeaster, and the typical band of heavy, disruptive snow is often less than 100 miles wide. Consequently, when the position of the storm in weather forecasting models diverges by more than that distance—a common occurrence—the forecaster confronts a vexing and serious problem: which one to believe, the one that buries Washington, D.C., or the one that says all the action will be out to sea?

That's when the forecaster literally does "look out the window" (or at least at the window of the computer screen) to see which of the many models has handled the *past* 24 hours the best, or which one has handled the last similar situation the best. Unless there's some other compelling reason, that model becomes the model of choice for tomorrow's weather forecast.

Ditto for the climate models. Having established a greenhouse warming for several decades, owing to the strong preference for warming of the cold dry air in Siberia and North America, we can simply take the observed warming, which itself has been highly linear, and project it onto the other forecasts. It becomes very clear that, unless the central tendency for linearity (funded by about $20 billion in climate science research over the years) is dead wrong, then we already know the warming rate to a very small error.

As a result, scientists know quite precisely how much the climate will warm in the policy-foreseeable future of 50 years, a modest three quarters of a degree (°C) (1.4°F) (see Figure 2.7 in color insert). NASA's James Hansen, whom many credit with lighting the fire over the greenhouse issue with his incendiary 1988 congressional testimony, wrote this in the *Proceedings of the National Academy of Sciences* in 2001:

> Future global warming can be predicted much more accurately than is generally realized ... we predict additional warming in the next 50 years of ¾°C ± ¼°C, a warming rate of 0.15°C ± 0.05°C per decade.

That warming rate is about four times less than the lurid top figure widely trumpeted by the United Nations in its 2001 compendium on climate change and repeated ad infinitum in the press. Why wasn't it front-page news that the scientist who was responsible for much of the global warming furor was now predicting, with high confidence, only a modest warming? Hansen went on to write in the following online journal *Natural Science*:

> Emphasis on extreme scenarios may have been appropriate at one time, when the public and decision-makers were relatively unaware of the global warming issue. Now, however, the need is for demonstrably objective climate ... scenarios consistent with what is realistic under current conditions.

With that remarkable statement, Hansen declared that scientists exaggerating to draw public attention to global warming was just fine.

GLOBAL WARMING AND EL NIÑO

One current belief in climate science (which has recently been challenged in an important doctoral thesis by Oliver Frauenfeld at the University of Virginia) is that the biggest weather-maker on the planet is a large oscillation in the tropical Pacific Ocean known colloquially as "El Niño," but more accurately as "ENSO," or the El Niño-Southern Oscillation.

ENSO is certainly one of the major climatic seesaws in the world. Usually, easterly trade winds diverge warm surface water away from the coast of South America, resulting in an upwelling pool of cold water that fuels a fertile anchovy fishery and attendant avian diversity. The pattern is so persistent that sea level in the Western Pacific is usually a foot or two higher than in the east.

The easterly trade winds, literally the largest wind circulation on earth, for reasons that are still speculative, suddenly drop or even reverse direction over the Tropical Pacific. Disrupting the biggest pattern of atmospheric flow that there is affects a lot of weather around the world. This is what happens during an ENSO.

For example, ENSO causes rain in Southern California and tends to dry out the normally soaked Pacific Northwest. By limiting the upwelling of cold water over a huge area off the coast of South America, ENSO events spike planetary temperature. It's most likely that whatever year sets the next "record" for planetary warmth will also be an El Niño year. The current recordholder for surface temperature, 1998, had a whopper El Niño, one of the two or three biggest in the last 100 years.

Science is pretty equivocal about whether global warming will increase, decrease, or do nothing about El Niño frequency or magnitude. Because the 1990s were globally warm and because El Niños were a bit more persistent than average,

(continued on next page)

(continued)

some federal scientists (perhaps pleasing Vice President Gore) attempted to link the two. (Gore visited Florida in 1998 and blamed the large wildfires on El Niño, saying it was a glimpse of what global warming would do to the Sunshine State). But that type of government-science rhetoric seems to have cooled with a return to a more typical El Niño frequency and a Republican president.

Whether or not El Niños increase or decrease because of global warming, the fact is that they have appeared every few years for most of the last 50 million years or so (at least) and, in the span of geologic time, they are about as common as a sunrise. Life goes on and adapts to El Niño cycles as surely as it does to the rhythm of the sun.

The Intergovernmental Panel on Climate Change and Emissions Projections for Greenhouse Gases

Projections of future warming from greenhouse gases largely depend on how much carbon dioxide is produced by the respiration of our civilization. For years, the unchallenged prognosticator of these concentrations has been the United Nations.

In 1988, the UN established the Intergovernmental Panel on Climate Change (IPCC), which describes itself as "an intergovernmental mechanism aimed at providing the basis for the development of a realistic and effective internationally accepted strategy for addressing climate change."

The IPCC conducts occasional "assessments" of the state of climate science, producing one assessment in 1990, another report as a supplement for the Rio Earth Summit in 1992, and subsequent assessments in 1996 and 2002. Those slick, massive volumes are the product of hundreds of scientists and a larger community of reviewers. They include analyses of past climate behavior, projections of future greenhouse gas emission projections, and forecasts of future climate. (The nature of the IPCC is discussed at length in my 2000 book, *The Satanic Gases*, which should be consulted for more detailed information.)

Briefly, the IPCC is as much a collection of government bureaucrats as it is of working scientists. In *The Satanic Gases*, my coauthor, Robert Balling, and I determined that only about 33 percent of the 200+ "lead authors" are in fact climate scientists. Consequently, the "consensus" that these documents achieve is in fact determined by a majority opinion that is not necessarily formally trained in the subject matter. Nor are the IPCC "assessments" "peer-reviewed" in the proper sense.

Normal peer review is a straightforward process. A scientist sends a paper to a major journal, where it is assigned to one of many editors. The editor then sends the manuscript out for review, and the authors must respond. If the reviews are sufficiently critical (as they often are, given that the vast majority of scientific papers are rejected), the paper cannot be published until the points at issue are addressed or rebutted. (At least that's the way it's supposed to work. In reality, editors can and do dramatically increase—or decrease— the likelihood of a manuscript's publication by judicious selection of reviewers and acceptance or rejection of critical comments. It happens all the time, and under duress, I will be happy to show anyone an e-mail from a major journal editor proudly telling me how she does it.)

That's not the way the so-called "peer review" works in the IPCC process. Instead, the selfsame authors of the report decide which reviews to respond to. Many are completely ignored. The result? Tremendous imbalances.

One example, from the 1996 *Assessment*, concerns satellite measurements of temperatures. Those measures are truly global, compared with the rather sparse ground thermometer network, and, at the time, they had shown no warming trend since they had begun in 1979. (Since then, there has been a slight but significant trend established—in large part because of the huge warming spike induced by the 1998 El Niño—yet still far beneath what most computer models have projected for global warming.)

The satellite data are obviously very important, in large part because they are at such variance with ground-measured temperature trends; they were especially so at the time of the 1996 *Assessment*. Yet, in the "Policymakers Summary," a section that is probably the only one most policy wonks (and many journalists) will read, there is not one mention of the word "satellite." In other words, the so-called "consensus of scientists" had decided by so-called "consensus" that the satellite temperatures' inconsistency with ground temperature should not be revealed to the policy world.

The satellite-ground temperature discrepancy is just one example of willful neglect or exaggeration by the scientific community; there are plenty of others.

It shouldn't be surprising, therefore, that a similar dynamic is at play with the IPCC's projections of future carbon dioxide emissions. The IPCC's projections of future emissions are based on what they call "storylines," or seemingly self-consistent projections of future development. There are six:

> "A1." The A1 family includes three scenarios: According to the IPCC, "The A1 storyline and scenario family describes a world of very rapid economic growth, global population that peaks in midcentury and declines thereafter, and the rapid introduction of new and efficient technologies." The three A1 groups are distinguished by their technological emphasis: fossil intensive (A1FI), nonfossil energy sources (A1T), or a balance across all sources (A1B).
>
> "A2." The IPCC states that "the underlying theme is self-reliance and preservation of local identities. . . . Economic development is primarily regionally oriented and per capita economic growth and technological change more fragmented and slower than other storylines." (Author's note: It's a pretty good guess that this one is simply wrong!)
>
> "B1." "The B1 storyline and scenario family describes a convergent world with the same global population that peaks in midcentury and declines thereafter, as in the A1 storyline, but with rapid change of economic structures toward a service and information economy, with reductions in material intensity and the introduction of clean and resource-efficient technologies."
>
> "B2." "The B2 storyline and scenario family describes a world in which the emphasis is on local solutions to economic, social and environmental sustainability."

Someone could write a rather large book criticizing the IPCC's storyline approach. Nonetheless, Figure 2.8 (see color insert) gives the range of UN temperature projections of warming for the next

100 years as a result of these storylines. That range is from 1.4°C (2.5°F) to 5.8°C (10.4°F).

The enormity of this range is disturbing, because it is actually *larger* than the range published in the first IPCC science compendium back in 1990, which was 1.5°C to 4.5°C. The implication is that 12 years and tens of billions of dollars of research funding has resulted in more, not less, uncertainty.

Is that the case? What is the most likely temperature rise, and who can help us to comprehend 245 predictions? For this we look to Stanford University's Steve Schneider. There is little to argue with in his analysis of the absurdly large range of temperature scenarios projected by the IPCC. Writing in the May 3, 2001, edition of *Nature*, Schneider provides insight into the relative *improbability* of the IPCC's high projections of future temperature in a doubled-CO_2 world.

First, a word of explanation: The IPCC's huge temperature range came about when 35 different levels of potential anthropogenic (human-caused) emissions were run through a climate model tuned to seven different climate "sensitivities." A "sensitivity" represents a climate model's prediction as to how much things will warm given a doubling of earth's atmospheric carbon dioxide concentration. The exercise resulted in 245 different temperature predictions ranging between 1.4°C and 5.8°C. Are all equally likely?

A rise of 5.8°C undoubtedly would result in severe consequences. But is it as probable as a rise of 1.4°C, which is a warming that many economists, including the notable Robert Mendelssohn, believes will be a net benefit? A reading of the IPCC on this point provides little or no guidance. Its *Special Report on Emission Scenarios* stipulates, "No judgment is offered in the Report as to the preference for any of the scenarios and they are not assigned probabilities of occurrence. . . . " The vaunted *Summary for Policymakers* asserts, "All [scenarios] should be considered equally sound."

Schneider's explanation? The IPCC, he wrote, was unwilling to assign individual probabilities to its outcomes, "in an attempt to avoid endless disputes" among the participants in a scenario development meeting that he attended and where he unsuccessfully argued for their inclusion as a way of providing scientific credibility.

Because the IPCC refuses to present anything more than a range—as opposed to an actual *distribution* of the 245 possibilities—no one

Figure 2.9

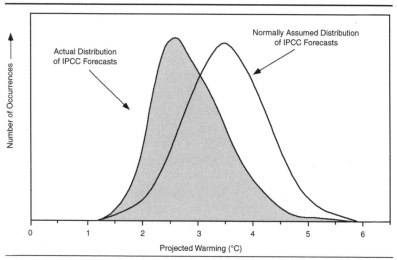

Given the amount of information available from the IPCC in its *Third Assessment Report,* it would be logical to assume the distribution of predictions of future warming would be best represented as a bell-shaped curve. That type of curve would result in an average value of 3.6°C (6.5°F), with half the forecasts being warmer and half cooler. Instead, we now know the *actual* distribution is strongly skewed toward the lower end. The result is an average of 2.2°C (4.0°F), nearly 1.5°C (2.7°F) cooler than the IPCC has led the world to believe.

SOURCE: Schneider, *Nature,* 2001.

is able to assess whether a prediction of 5.8°C is a single "outlier" or is accompanied by other forecasts that are nearly as high. Without that kind of information, readers are forced to assume that the 245 forecasts fall into a "normal distribution" (picture a bell-shaped curve) with an average value of 3.6°C, midway between, being the most common prediction (Figure 2.9). In such a distribution, half the values would be above the mean and half below it. But that assumption is wrong, as Schneider shows.

When Schneider plots the actual distribution of warming forecasts, he finds it is significantly skewed toward the *low end.* In other words, the IPCC's "average" value is in fact higher than the value represented by the average of all the forecasts. Instead of half the forecasts predicting temperatures higher than 3.6°C, only about a quarter do.

Amazingly, just under 50 percent come in at less than 2.5°C, meaning that, absent any further guidance from the IPCC (e.g., their assessment of probability), it is much more likely that future global warming would fall nearer the low end of the IPCC range, 1.4°C, rather than the high end. The IPCC has known that all along, yet they've let a hysterical environmental and popular press run with apocalyptic scenarios touting the huge 5.8°C (10.4°F) warming. And where was the news coverage of Schneider's analysis? Virtually nonexistent.

In wanting us to believe the reason the IPCC hasn't taken a stand on a preferred value of warming for the next hundred years is that they want to "avoid endless disputes," we now reasonably can conclude that the IPCC prefers to play up the possibility of disastrous climate change—the very thing Schneider says scientists are wont to do when discussing climate change (see Chapter 11).

Reality vs. Emissions Projections

Recall that both the climate models and the United Nations Intergovernmental Panel on Climate Change generally assume that the change in greenhouse gases is an exponential function, that is, one of constantly increasing slope. That notion accrues largely from the assumption that global population must grow exponentially and that everyone desires an American (energy-intensive) lifestyle. Those assumptions ignore a lot of reality.

Population projections have dropped dramatically in recent years. As recently as 1980, the UN predicted a global population of 15 billion in 2050, an increase of approximately 9 billion from today's population. Its most recent estimate for 2050 is now 9 billion, or an increase of only 3 billion from today, and a net reduction of the projected increase by 67 percent.

One reason for this drop is the spread of wealth and industrialization throughout much of the world. It is well known (though people differ about the mechanism) that per capita wealth and number of children have a very strong inverse correlation: The richer you are, the more likely you are to have few children. As a result, wealthy nations without large immigration pressures, such as many western European countries, now project population levels in 2050 that are at or below today's levels. The United States would be approaching this situation, too, except for its tremendous immigration, which largely comprises individuals far beneath the national median in wealth, who consequently have a higher than average expected fecundity.

Another development has been the stabilization of carbon dioxide use per capita since much of the world (Africa and a few nations excepted) has transitioned from undeveloped to developing and developed economies. Since the early 1980s, carbon dioxide emissions per capita have become constant or have actually declined. Figure 2.10 (see color insert) shows emissions per capita since 1950, as well as a simple curved trend analysis. The correspondence between the two, indicating that an actual statistically significant decline in per capita emissions is occurring, is a remarkable 94 percent.

If the combined trends of a progressive lowering of future population estimates and a decreased per capita carbon dioxide use continue, then the increase in atmospheric carbon dioxide is likely to be in a transition from exponential (constantly increasing growth rates) to a linear (constant) growth rate.

Has that trend already begun? One way to test it is with a statistical analysis.

It is an easy exercise to analyze whether trends in atmospheric carbon dioxide are increasing exponentially, which the UN assumed to be the most likely scenario, or are merely linear. One way is to pass a linear trend through the data, and then see whether changing that to an exponential function results in a better "fit" of the data, which means a more accurate analysis of the observed increase.

So, let's start in, say, the last 10 years (1993–2002) and run a straight line through the data. Is making it curve upward, in exponential fashion, more realistic? The computer answers a resounding *no*: There is no significant exponential increase that explains more than the straight line. How about beginning in 1992? No. 1991, 1990, 1989, no, no, and no. In fact, we would have to go back to the 1974–2002 period, almost three decades, before there is evidence of significant exponential upward curvature in the concentration of atmospheric carbon dioxide.

Therefore, the assumption used for future behavior by every climate model (and therefore every climate modeler), which is an exponential growth of 1 percent per year, hasn't been right for three decades. The climate modeling community *must* know better! But instead, it chooses to be literally 30 years behind the power curve of reality on the issue of atmospheric carbon dioxide concentration. In fact, only one major modeler, the same James Hansen who first drew attention to this issue, has acknowledged this problem and, accordingly, has dramatically dropped his forecasts of warming.

The observed behavior of per capita carbon dioxide vs. reality is a stark example of the exaggeration of global warming, in which the climatological modeling community and the UN's IPCC continues to assume something that is obviously wrong.

Enormous Implications

The implications of this erroneous assumption are staggering. After all, a constant greenhouse warming trend actually *requires* an exponential (ever-increasing rate) change in atmospheric carbon dioxide. Yet that exponential behavior appears to have ceased nearly 30 years ago! Will global warming therefore slow down in coming decades?

When? The answer may lie in the ocean.

In 2000, oceanographer Syd Levitus demonstrated that warming is now detectable in the top 10,000 feet of much of the world's oceans. One question that has always troubled climatologists is how long it takes a change in the atmosphere and near-surface temperatures to be reflected in that deeper ocean.

To get a handle on this, we could compare temperatures in the thin oceanic surface layer with those in the deep (10,000-foot) column. There has to be some type of lag, and that lag can help to define how long it takes overall temperature to come to grips with what humans are doing to the atmosphere.

Figure 2.11 shows the correlation between global sea-surface temperatures and those from depths of zero to 10,000 feet. Statistical significance is barely achieved in the first 10 years, and then the correlation actually drops to insignificant through about 30 years. Going further back, roughly 35 to 40 years, the correlation between surface and deep ocean temperatures reaches a profound maximum.

This tells us how long it will take for the rate of temperature increase to respond to a damping of the carbon dioxide increase from exponential to linear, which began about 30 years ago (and still has yet to be acknowledged by many scientists!). The peak in the "lag correlation" at 35 to 40 years is strongly suggestive that, contrary to what you have read in every popular account of global

Figure 2.11

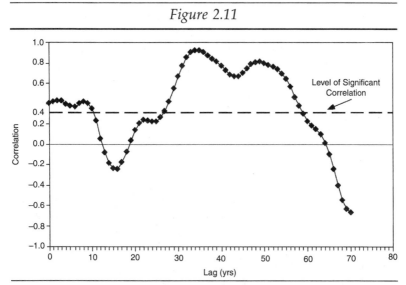

Correlation between surface ocean temperatures and those in the surface-to-10,000-foot depth. The correlation reaches a maximum at around 35 to 40 years. A correlation of ±0.3 is not statistically significant, while ±1.0 is a perfect match between the two sets of data.

warming, the modest rate of surface warming may begin to *decline* in a decade or so. If it occurs, the decline in rate will be slight and will take a decade or two to even be noticed, but that is what results from these observations.

Another View of Emissions Projections

London's *Economist*, which has generally been pretty strident about global warming, hewing to the IPCC line, published a devastating series of articles beginning February 13, 2003, about the UN's approach to future emissions. Ian Castles and Davis Henderson were quite plain that the IPCC was as far behind the times in the economic analyses accompanying its warming "storylines" as it was on the emissions of per capita carbon dioxide. Castles and Henderson indicate that, had the IPCC used currently accepted methods, the resulting warming would be considerably less than what it is currently projecting.

Those two seem to know what they're talking about. Castles was president of the International Association of Official Statistics (a section of the International Statistical Institute), head of the Australian Department of Finance from 1979 to 1986, and the Australian Statistician from 1986 to 1994. Henderson was formerly the chief economist of the Organization for Economic Cooperation and Development (OECD) and is now with the Westminster Business School. Both have been involved in developing appropriate methods for comparing the economy of one country with that of another—a difficult task with different monetary units, standards of living, and the variety of goods and materials produced under different currencies.

There are two customary ways of making such comparisons: The first and simplest is to convert the gross domestic product (GDP) of each country into a universal standard (U.S. dollars) based on the going market exchange (MEX) rate. That is the method the IPCC uses. However, the method suffers from many weaknesses—so many, in fact, that the UN's own Statistical Commission has concluded that using MEX rates results in "material errors," errors that leave the reader with a fundamentally distorted view of the phenomenon being described.

The preferred method is Purchasing Power Parity (PPP). PPP basically compares the cost of the same basket of goods in two different countries. The PPP approach gives a better means of comparison than simply relying on exchange rates, which may fluctuate rapidly and vary from application to application (e.g., tourist rates, bank rates, foreign trade, black market).

Castles and Henderson insist the IPCC should have used the PPP method, and indeed the IPCC now admits as much (after pressure from Castles and Henderson), claiming that its use of MEX rates "was done in full recognition of the fact that the preferred measure of wealth and poverty is to adjust GDP using the purchasing power parity estimates. . . . The reason the SRES report [the report detailing the storylines] adopted a market-based GDP is [that] most greenhouse gas emissions models in the peer-reviewed literature . . . are run based on market GDP."

Okay. And if all the other climate modelers jumped off a cliff, would the IPCC do it too?

As Castles pointed out in a presentation to an IPCC Experts Panel in Amsterdam in January 2003, the IPCC statement seems to claim that certain comparisons between rich and poor countries that are integral to developing the emissions scenarios "were known to be misleading at the time they were made."

Using the MEX rate greatly underestimates the current purchasing power of developing countries and therefore leads to unrealistic future growth rates to make up for that initial inequality. For instance, in the B1 storyline, the GDP of developing countries is forecast to rise 65 times between 1990 and 2100. Using PPP for the same calculation results in a rise of just over 24 times, admittedly still a nearly impossible scenario, but nevertheless, one that is about 2.5 times lower than that using the MEX approach.

Even so, translating either of these figures into carbon dioxide emissions is tricky, as shown by the recent decline in global emissions per person. Even calculating the number of people that will be on earth 50 years from now is a big problem. But, at least according to current (and questionable) logic, emissions will rise with wealth, despite the fact that per capita emissions *and* population projections themselves are both dropping.

It is possible to perform a rough calculation of the effect of using PPP vs. MEX techniques on global temperature projections for the next 100 years. If we adjust the IPCC's six storylines appropriately using IPCC's own climate model as shown in Figure 2.12 (see color insert), the projected temperature rise by the year 2100 is reduced by about 0.5°C, a reduction of about 15 percent with slight variation among the scenarios. But, as shown in Figure 2.7, the UN's projections in general vastly overestimate future warming.

Problems with the IPCC projections don't stop there. Castles and Henderson point out that the future 100-year growth rates of developing countries the IPCC used in its most conservative scenarios are in many instances far greater than has ever been observed by any country in history, resulting in improbable (if not downright *impossible*) scenarios.

Here's a good one: Under the IPCC's B1 scenario family (the family of scenarios that include the lowest CO_2 emissions in 2100), in the year 2100, all of the following countries are projected to have a higher per capita GDP than the United States: Germany, Italy, France, Japan, Russia, the Baltic States, South Korea, North Korea, Malaysia, Singapore, Hong Kong, South Africa, Libya, Algeria, Tunisia, Saudi Arabia, Israel, Turkey, and Argentina. Sound likely?

Currently, the United States ranks second in the world, only behind Luxembourg, in this measure of personal wealth.

31

The work of Castles and Henderson clearly illustrates that the economic savvy of the IPCC is very weak. Further, as we have seen in this chapter, IPCC's scenarios of dramatic warming require the continuation of an exponential increase in carbon dioxide that stopped a quarter-century ago.

All this inevitable exaggeration results from the culture of modern science, where competition for tax monies requires histrionic proposals, engenders a political response, and rewards scientists for going along with the charade. How bad is it? The rest of this book provides the graphic evidence. Readers who think science is a "pure" process, governed by logic and tempered by experiment, are in for a rude awakening.

3. Meltdown? The Truth about Icecaps

The Bush Administration ignores the terror of environmental peril and denies the reality of 2,500 United Nations scientists, who tell us that unless we find ways to stop global warming, sea levels could swell up to 35 feet, submerging millions of homes under our present-day oceans.

—Sen. Joseph Lieberman (D-Conn.), August 30, 2001

The ice masses at the two poles to the north and the south are diminishing. They are melting.

—Sen. Robert Byrd (D-W.Va.), August 8, 2001

The great ice cover that stretches across the top of the globe is about forty percent thinner than it was just two to four decades ago. We find that through our data from nuclear submarines that have been plying the Arctic Ocean.

—Sen. John Kerry (D-Mass.), May 17, 2000

. . . [T]his summer the North Pole was water for the first time in recorded history.

—Sen. John Kerry, May 1, 2001

Predictably, our elected leaders have been sounding the alarm on the melting of the world's ice. After all, scientists have come from all over the world to testify in front of their committees. The scientists leave armed with money. The politicians express with grace how pleased they are to help save the masses. University press offices and trade magazines like *Science* hawk the story. And the media have a field day. Very little is needed to dress up this girl in order to take her out.

But is the North Polar icecap melting at an unprecedented rate? Are huge glaciers of Greenland and Antarctica caving into oblivion, to raise sea levels all the way to the Washington Monument? And what about the poster child of the world's tropical glaciers, high atop Hemingway's mountain? Only a fool would ask those questions today, because we already know the answers, right? We've even seen pictures. Consider Kilimanjaro.

3.1 The Snowjob of Kilimanjaro

> The icecap atop Mount Kilimanjaro, which, for thousands of years has floated like a cool beacon over the shimmering plain of Tanzania, is retreating at such a pace that it will disappear in less than 15 years, according to new studies.
>
> —*New York Times*, February 19, 2001

> These unique bodies of ice will disappear in the next two decades, the victims of global warming.
>
> —Ohio State University, Press Release,
> October 17, 2002

These two blurbs are based on Ohio State University glaciologist Lonnie Thompson's interesting research, culminating in an October 2002 paper in *Science*, in which he predicted the end to Kilimanjaro's glaciers by 2020 or so, according to current trends. His dour pronouncement was repeated in dozens of horrifying news stories that appeared beginning October 17 on networks such as ABC and Web sites such as *Yahoo! Daily News*.

Much of modern environmental journalism displays a pervasive lack of critical insight toward environmental scares and the scientific papers on which they are supposedly based. Those of us who know better find it endlessly fascinating. An inspection of Thompson's own data, also published in *Science*, shows that Kilimanjaro's glaciers would be dying even if Homo sapiens ancestors were still the dominant hominid in the Rift Valley, a few hundred miles to the West. That is to say, humans are not to blame for the glacial recession.

Thompson cited five surveys of Kilimanjaro from 1912, 1953, 1976, 1989, and 2000.

34

Figure 3.1

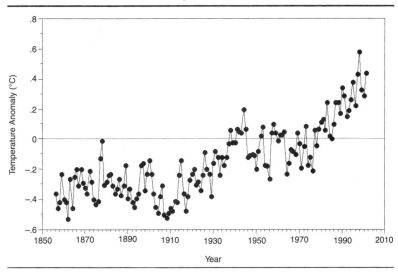

Annual Global Temperature (1856–2001). The global surface temperature history from the United Nations Intergovernmental Panel on Climate Change. Since the warming that began in the mid-1970s, the decline in Kilimanjaro's glacier slowed to its lowest rate since 1912.

SOURCE: http://www.cru.uea.ac.uk.

From 1912 to 1953, global temperature rose (as measured controversially by surface thermometers) 0.4°C (0.74°F) (Figure 3.1). This rise occurred before most of the industrial emissions of so-called "greenhouse" gases, mainly carbon dioxide and methane. As a result, most scientists think the warming of the early 20th century had mainly to do with changes in the sun, which is not the constant star we were taught it was back in middle school general science. In fact, slight changes in solar output have modulated the earth's surface temperature plus or minus about 1.0°C (1.8°F) over millennia.

Kilimanjaro's glaciers lost 45 percent of their areal extent during that era of solar warming. If the glaciers had continued to decline at the pace established in that period, they would be gone by now, even with no additional warming from the emissions of greenhouse gases.

But they're still here. From 1953 through 1976, another 21 percent of the original area was uncovered. This occurred during a period of global *cooling* of 0.07°C (0.13°F). Ohio State's press office could logically have written the following hype in 1976: "Kilimanjaro's glaciers will completely disappear by 2015 if this *cooling* trend continues."

It is patently obvious that global temperatures and the behavior of Kilimanjaro's glaciers are pretty independent, at least on the time scale of decades. Local climate, however, is apparently critical. A glacier cares what happens from its head to its toe, not elsewhere.

The local climate record around Kilimanjaro is confusing. There is very little cohesion between nearby thermometers, which argues more that the data are bad than it does for any local cooling or warming. Poor countries have little income to spend on a quality climate-monitoring network.

Since 1976, another 12 percent of the original mass has disappeared—and despite all the hoopla, a loss of 12 percent represents the slowest rate of decline since 1912. Although the local temperature measurements are clearly questionable, more recent decades' measurements are as close to perfect as possible: In 1979 satellite monitoring began. All scientists—even the most ardent global warming apocalyptics—acknowledge that the satellite is excellent at measuring temperatures at the altitude of Kilimanjaro's glaciers—about 19,000 feet. In fact, it may measure temperature at that altitude better than it does at sea level.

Around Kilimanjaro, satellite data (see Figure 3.2 in color insert) show a cooling of 0.22°C (0.40°F) since 1979, which is exactly the same as the global warming rate between 1912 and 1953 (0.09°C or 0.17°F per decade). Still, Kilimanjaro's glaciers continued to shrink.

In his *Science* article, Thompson noted that the period from 4,000 to 11,000 years ago was warmer in Africa than it is today, and yet Kilimanjaro was much more glaciated because it was also wetter than it is today. Some estimates place today's precipitation at only one half of what it was during the warm period. Obviously precipitation, not temperature, is key to the glaciation of Kilimanjaro.

Did people make it stop snowing? Precipitation in East Africa is highly correlated with El Niño activity in the tropical Pacific Ocean. During the last big one, 1997–1998, how many news stories unquestionably promulgated the notion that El Niños are becoming more frequent because of global warming?

So someone could (and probably will) argue that humans cause global warming, global warming causes more El Niños, more El

Niños affect precipitation, and therefore humans are causing the glaciers to recede. But, if people are causing the warming, and warming is causing more El Niños, then in fact it should be snowing more and more and more on Kilimanjaro—more than it did when it was even warmer, thousands of years ago.

The reporting on Kilimanjaro is a glaring example of a press that lacks critical insight (or even motivation) sufficient to find easily obtainable facts that create a much different impression than a university press release. But this is just one meltdown in glacial coverage.

3.2 Glacier's Glaciers and a Peruvian Meltdown

In the innocent days of early September 2001, in fact two days before 9/11, the nation was perseverating on the personal difficulties of Rep. Gary Condit (D-Calif.) and the disappearance of his friend Chandra Levy. Eager to find something else to talk about, NBC News reporter Jim Avila reached deep into the recycling bin for a way to fill out a portion of the nightly news block. He chose what is fast becoming an annual end-of-summer, back-to-school news story about how glaciers are melting in Montana's Glacier National Park. "The temperature's gone up an average three and a half degrees in the park during the last 110 years," Avila intoned.

A few facts to note: Temperature is measured over reasonably broad areas by the National Climatic Data Center, which divides the country into a couple of hundred "Climatological Divisions." Professionals and volunteers monitor calibrated instruments within each division. Monthly and annual temperatures are calculated by averaging the readings across the division. The history of the Western Montana Climatological Division can be downloaded at http://www.wrcc.dri.edu. Figure 3.3 shows the summer temperature history, which yields *no statistically significant warming whatsoever*. The same is true of the annual record, although it is not as important to a glacier as the summer readings.

If we ignore the first 55 years of temperature history and begin calculating the change since 1950, the result is Avila's 3.5 degrees of warming. But that's grossly unfair to the overall history, which shows *nothing*. The facts are these: Glacier Park's glaciers are melting and summer temperature remains the same as the regional average

Figure 3.3

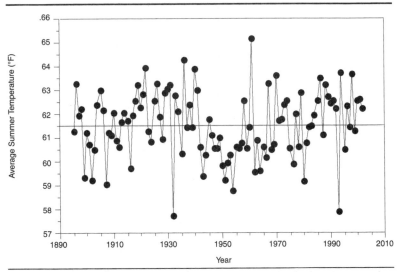

Annual summer (June, July, August) temperatures in the Montana Climate Division 1, which includes Glacier National Park.

SOURCE: Western Regional Climate Center at http://www.wrcc.dri.edu/spi/divplot1map.html.

as it was when the record began 107 years ago, and before the escalation in fossil fuel combustion.

Why didn't Avila, his producer, or NBC's editor in chief check the temperature record for western Montana? If anyone had, he or she would have been forced to conclude that Glacier's glaciers were going to disappear whether or not the planet warmed, because the region itself isn't any hotter than it was a century ago.

Two months earlier, on July 9, the *Washington Post*'s publication of foreign correspondent Scott Wilson's story "Warming Shrinks Peruvian Glaciers" was pretty scary. The story featured Benjamin Morales, whom Wilson described as "the dean of Peru's glaciologists." Describing Peru's glaciers as "the world's most sensitive thermometers," Morales claims, "The temperature was rising very slowly until 1980, and then"—as described by Wilson—"he sweeps his arm up at a steep angle."

Figure 3.4

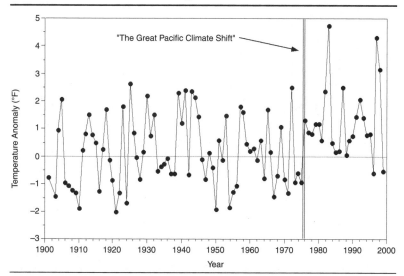

Peru's surface temperature history shows a 1.5°F rise since 1900. But most of it took place during "The Great Pacific Climate Shift" in 1976. Temperature histories before and after 1976 show no statistically significant temperature change. Temperature spikes in 1997, 1983, and 1972 mark strong El Niño events.

SOURCE: http://www.cru.uea.ac.uk.

It's easy to download the UN Intergovernmental Panel on Climate Change (IPCC) data and discover that the surface temperature history for Peru since 1900 doesn't support Morales' arm-waving (Figure 3.4). In fact, since 1980, Peru's temperatures haven't increased at all. The truth is—and you'd think the "dean of glaciologists" would know it—Peru's glaciers have been retreating for at least 150 years.

The IPCC data show that a quarter-century ago, there was a sudden, abrupt jump in temperature. But in the time both before and after that single-year shift there is no statistically significant temperature change. The 1976 temperature jump is the subject of so many scientific papers that it has attained a lofty moniker: "The Great Pacific Climate Shift."

If you are tempted to believe that global warming may be to blame, keep in mind that climate models produce rather smooth temperature increases—not sudden jumps—when increasing levels of greenhouse gases are fed into them. So if you choose to believe that greenhouse gases are to blame for the Pacific Climate Shift, then you've just undermined the computer models upon which predictions of apocalypse rely. You can't believe in both.

To help bolster his story's premise, Wilson cites Ohio State University's Lonnie Thompson who, once again, estimates that many of the world's icecaps could disappear in the next 15 years. At the same time, Wilson acknowledges some unspecified dissent. "Other scientists say this is implausibly fast," he reports. Arming one side of an argument with a famous name and attributing the other side to no one in particular certainly has a way of biasing the readers in one direction!

But, for the sake of argument, what kind of change in temperature *would* it take to melt Peru's glaciers in 15 years?

First, assume air temperature decreases about 2.2°C (4°F) for each 1,000 feet of elevation. Next, assume the average temperature at sea level in Peru is about 22°C (72°F). A quick back-of-the-envelope calculation reveals that it takes a warming of about 11°C (20°F) to raise the average summer temperature above freezing at an elevation of 15,000 feet. That would still leave a *lot* more room—another mile of elevation—for snow accumulation; keep in mind that many Peruvian peaks exceed 20,000 feet. Then, too, rising temperatures might simply displace the snow accumulation to higher elevations. No matter. There isn't a single climate change scenario that calls for this kind of dramatic temperature rise in low latitudes. Not one.

But what seems odd about Wilson's coverage of this story is his tally of anticipated terrible consequences. He points out how, in recent decades, glacier melt has made available more running water, more electricity, and higher agricultural yield and production throughout the region. He then surmises that this may only be temporary, that hard times will return once the glaciers disappear. His reporting would benefit from a quick conversation with a climatologist.

Peru's glaciers are caused by a combination of precipitation and cold temperature. Because the geometry of the Andes isn't likely to change anytime soon, there always will be enhanced "upslope" precipitation (whether it is frozen or not), all year. People in California have adapted to similar circumstances by building dams and storing water and, in the process, creating an agricultural paradise.

Dean Morales opines that same success isn't possible in Peru. The dams would be enormously expensive because they would be located in "dangerous seismic zones." Well, it's difficult to imagine a much more "dangerous seismic zone" than California or Mexico's Sierra Madre Occidental (analogous to California's Sierras and Peru's Andes), where massive irrigation dams have been constructed and operated for decades!

Wilson and Morales seem unable to see what is really happening as Peru's glaciers melt. Peruvians are *adapting*, just as most people do in the face of ever-present change. New hydroelectric plants will bring more power to more people, increase the availability of running water in homes (with significant health benefits), and make possible large irrigation projects expected to raise living standards for the region's more than 160,000 farm families. Granted, advance planning is required so that in years when stream flow is low, water can be released from reservoirs to maintain volume. But such practices are nearly universal.

Not to miss a lick, though, Wilson's coverage of global warming offers the Peruvian trump card: El Niño. As Figure 3.4 reveals, Peru's temperature spikes during El Niño events such as in 1997, 1983, and 1972. Wilson deems El Niño "the culprit" for the rapid glacial melt-ing and states, "Many scientists blame [increased frequency and intensity of El Niño] on atmospheric disruption caused by pollu-tion." Actually, we only know of one real climatologist who makes this claim with stridency, the National Center for Atmospheric Research's Kevin Trenberth. As he stated in the Center's newsletter, "there's got to be a connection," even though no consistent one has ever been found. In fact, some climate models increase El Niños, some decrease them, and some can't even produce them.

Some also keep things the same. The latest version of Britain's Hadley Centre's general circulation model reveals no change in El Niño patterns when it is run under increasing levels of green-house gases.

When confronted by different models with differing results, it's always wise to consult reality. Figure 3.5 shows the five-year running mean of the Southern Oscillation Index (SOI), a common measure of El Niño since 1872. Negative values of the SOI are associated with El Niño events—the more negative the value, the stronger the event. Although the 1990s were marked by a rather unusual period

Figure 3.5

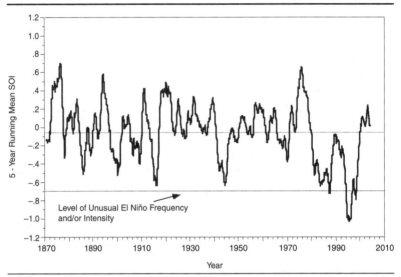

The five-year running mean of the Southern Oscillation Index (SOI)—a measure of El Niño's strength—shows that while there was a bit more El Niño activity than normal during the 1990s, conditions seem to have returned closer to average.

SOURCE: http://www.cpc.noaa.gov.

of El Niño activity, the "naughties" (2000–2010) are seeing a return to normal conditions. Therefore, if El Niños lead to higher rates of glacial melting, their influence should have declined in the past several years.

3.3 Credibility Meltdown in the Arctic Ocean

Here's a wonderful example of scientific doomsaying that ignores a few inconvenient facts. It's also a prime specimen of the echoing of this cheerleading by an unquestioning press outlet about one of the great fears of global warming: the melting of the North Polar icecap.

It started out August 19, 2000, when the *New York Times* reported, on page one, that "The North Pole is Melting" and that "the last time scientists can be certain that the Pole was awash in water was more than 50 million years ago."

The *Times* based its story on the observations of two passengers on a cruise ship, James J. McCarthy, professor of oceanography at

Harvard University and cochair of Working Group II ("Adaptation and Impacts of Climate Change") of the UN's Intergovernmental Panel on Climate Change, and Malcolm C. McKenna, a famous dinosaur scientist with the American Museum of Natural History in New York.

The cruise ship in question was a Russian icebreaker—the Yamal—which wound up at latitude 90.0°N in open water. McKenna took pictures and sent them to the *Times*, which published them. The August 19 article, by John Noble Wilford, then quoted McKenna: "I don't know if anybody in history ever got to 90 degrees north to be greeted by water, not ice."

Harvard's McCarthy said that onboard the Yamal, "There was a sense of alarm. Global warming was real, and we were seeing its effects for the first time that far north."

At that point, someone—the *Times*, McKenna, or McCarthy—should have done a little fact-checking to establish just how unusual ice conditions were up there. A few mouseclicks away on the Internet is the high-latitude temperature record (north of 55°N) of none other than the UN IPCC. Any senior scientist with the IPCC has to know this record by heart.

Figure 3.6 displays winter, summer, and annual temperatures from that record.

From those graphs, it's apparent that current temperatures aren't at all unusual when compared with the broad sweep of this history for the last century. Temperatures in the 1930s and 1940s are clearly indistinguishable from those of recent decades, though few people would suggest that much of the warming 70 years ago was caused by economic activity.

It's likely, then, that that earlier period of higher temperatures also saw summers in which there was open water at the Pole. The record of annual temperatures corroborates that. In Figure 3.6, the period of above-mean temperatures that peaked in the late 1930s (68 years ago) is shaded.

The current warm spell is no different—in length, magnitude, or effect—than what the high latitudes saw long before people could have changed the climate very much.

By August 29, the level of outrage the *Times* had incurred provoked a halfhearted retraction of sorts, hidden on page D-3, where the paper admitted it misstated the true condition of polar ice, noting

Figure 3.6

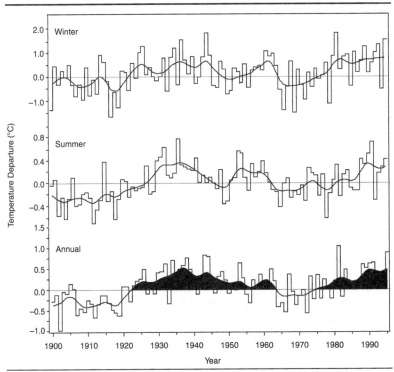

The integrated warming early in the last century—before humans could change the climate very much—is larger than the current warming.

SOURCES: http://www.cru.uea.ac.uk. United Nations Intergovernmental Panel on Climate Change for the North polar region (latitude 55°N or higher); also from Serreze and colleagues, 2000.

that about 10 percent of the Arctic Ocean is open in the summer and that those open areas do in fact sometimes extend to the Pole. McCarthy, the *Times* reported, "would not argue with critics who said that open water at the pole was not unprecedented." How about the truth? Open water is common at very high latitudes at the end of summer.

That's apparent from even a cursory look at the UN's own temperature data or from a study of climate history. Climatologists are pretty sure that polar regions were around 2°C (3.6°F) warmer than

Figure 3.7

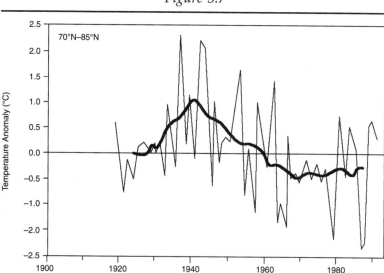

Temperature records starting in 1930 for latitude 70°N and higher, published by Pryzbylak (2000), show a decline since 1940. These latitudes are more representative of polar conditions than those in Figure 3.6.

they are today during the period from 4,000 to 7,000 years ago. That's three millennia in which summer sea ice was likely to be much more scattered than it is today.

There are other independent and recent studies of high-latitude temperatures, such as one published in 2000 by R. Przybylak in the *International Journal of Climatology*.

Przybylak independently examined high-latitude temperature records through the early 1990s and found a very good match with the UN records for latitude 60°N and higher. But when he moved even farther poleward, from 70°N to 85°N, he found a profound cooling trend since 1940 (Figure 3.7).

Is Przybylak right? In 1993, University of Wisconsin climatologist Jonathan Kahl examined then-recently declassified records available from 1958 through 1986. During the Cold War, American pilots dropped sensors from station-keeping B-52s, while the Soviets ordered the politically incorrect onto the polar ice itself for daily measurements. Kahl found a net decline in temperature, with the largest drops in the fall and winter.

Since 1986, at the highest latitudes, Przybylak's data show no change. The fact that Przybylak and Kahl's totally independent records line up so well in their period of concurrence (1958–1986) lends credence to the argument that, at least at the high latitudes that comprise the North Pole, we haven't seen any net warming since 1940.

Whither the *Times*? After no doubt having its ears singed by voice-mail messages noting its obvious errors, inaccuracies, and misleads, it still couldn't quite bring itself out of denial. In the August 29 update, it stated: "The data scientists are now studying reveal substantial evidence that on average Arctic temperatures in winter have risen 11 degrees [F] over the past 30 years." The *Times* went on to quote University of Colorado's Mark Serreze, who had just published a review paper on arctic temperatures in the journal *Climatic Change* (which the *Times* called "Climate Change").

Serreze shows the exact same UN records averaged over the Arctic that appear in Figure 3.6. Note the average winter rise in the last 30 years is around 1.5°C (2.7°F)—not 6.1°C (11°F). Further, as is obvious from the UN's data, 30 years ago arctic temperatures had descended to nearly their lowest value for the last 100 years. Serreze did find a small area in the Arctic that had an 11-degree rise, but that isolated segment is clearly balanced by large areas of cooling, resulting in a modest change in average temperature.

Another arctic record, from Department of Commerce scientist Jim Angell, merits more attention because it comes from twice-daily weather balloons, instruments that are highly calibrated and standardized. A comparison of winter and summer is highly instructive.

Unnecessary as it may seem, we need to stipulate that polar ice does not melt in the winter. That is important. Winter is the time of the year that would or should show the largest warming if the climate models are right. Polar ice does not melt in winter/polar night because it's just too darned cold, at somewhere between −25 and −40°C, on an average winter day in the Arctic and Antarctic, respectively.

Consequently, if you're looking for melting of polar ice, the summer should prove more fruitful than winter. Angell defines his poles as areas poleward of 60° latitude for each hemisphere.

Figure 3.8

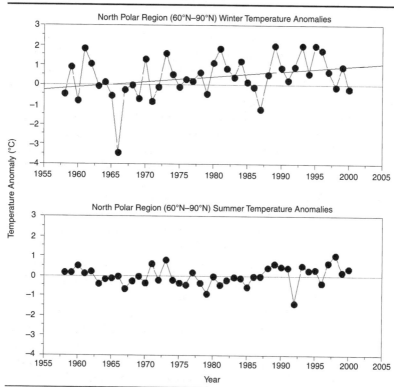

The trend in surface temperatures as measured at the point-of-release of weather balloons for the winter (top) and summer (bottom) seasons in the North Polar region (between 60°N and 90°N). There is a statistically significant warming trend of 2.6°C per 100 years in the winter, when it's too cold for ice to melt, but no significant change in the summer, when melting occurs.

SOURCE: http://cdiac.esd.ornl.gov.

Figure 3.8 shows winter and summer temperature trends in the Arctic beginning in 1958. There is no trend line in the summer data because, in fact, there is no significant trend in warming over the 43 year record. Winters, on the other hand, are warming significantly, at the rate of 2.6°C per 100 years.

North of 60°N is what climatologists call a "source region" for the frigid, deadly air masses that impolitely and routinely barrel

47

equatorward and are given names like "The Siberian Express." This zone is indeed warming up—in winter. But Arctic summer shows no significant change. That means Arctic climate is not changing in a fashion that is likely to melt things very much. That is not to say there will be no trend forever. At the current rate of change, a statistically significant warming should emerge in the summer Arctic somewhere around the year 2020.

Things are quite similar in the South Polar regions (Figure 3.9), where there also is a statistically significant warming of the winter (3.7°C/100 years) and where there is no trend yet evident in Antarctic summer.

3.4 Another Arctic Meltdown!

Arctic Ice is Melting at Record Level, Scientists Say. The melting of Greenland glaciers and Arctic Ocean sea ice this past summer reached levels not seen in decades, scientists reported today.

—*New York Times*, December 8, 2002

The first two sentences are obviously contradictory. So what's the real story?

On December 8, 2002, both the *New York Times* and the *Los Angles Times* carried major articles in their Sunday editions about the latest measurements of a shrinking area of Arctic sea ice and how global warming is to blame. "The shrinking fits in with the trend since the late 1970s and general predictions of global warming," according to the (N.Y.) *Times*. Both papers were reporting from the winter meeting of the American Geophysical Union in San Francisco.

In fact, this year's ice extent probably is not much different from that of summers earlier in the 20th century at a time before there could possibly have been much of a human contribution to the concentration of carbon dioxide to the atmosphere. Carbon dioxide, of course, is the main greenhouse warming gas that is increasing because of our industrial activity.

The newspapers' coverage completely ignored an extremely important analysis of Arctic ice and temperatures by Igor Polykov and others published in the November 18 edition of *EOS*, the official scientific journal of the American Geophysical Union—the same people running the San Francisco meeting. It will hardly come as a

Figure 3.9

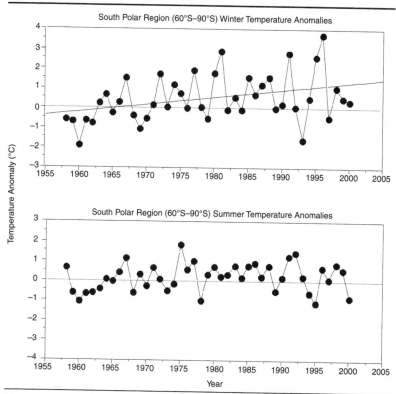

The trend in surface temperatures as measured at the point-of-release of weather balloons for the winter (top) and summer (bottom) seasons in the South Polar region (between 60°S and 90°S). Just as in the North, there is a warming trend in winter temperatures (3.7°C per 100 years), but it is not evident in summer temperatures.

SOURCE: http://cdiac.esd.ornl.gov.

surprise to those who've followed popular media coverage of the climate change issue that Polykov and his fellow researchers found something that doesn't jibe with the dire image of climate change, and as a result they were ignored.

Satellite data cited in the newspaper articles show that in summer 2002 the areal coverage of ice in the Arctic Ocean in summer reached its smallest value since measurements began in 1978. But there are much longer records of ice cover and Arctic temperature, such as

Figure 3.10

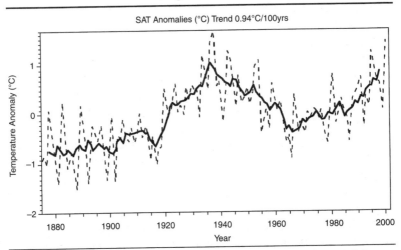

SAT Anomalies (°C) Trend 0.94°C/100yrs

Solid line: Six-year running means of Arctic temperature from Polykov et al. Dashed line: Annual temperatures. Clearly, the 1930s, a time before changes in the greenhouse effect could have caused much warming, were as warm as or warmer than today.

Polykov's history. It goes back a hundred years earlier, to the 1870s, and shows that the current situation is not at all unusual.

Every climatologist knows that the Arctic was as warm as (or warmer than) it is now some seven decades ago. Figure 3.10, from the *EOS* article, clearly demonstrates the warmth of the 20th century. According to Polykov and his fellow researchers—

> Two distinct warming periods from 1920 to 1945, and from 1975 to the present, are clearly evident . . . *compared with the global and hemispheric temperature rise, the high-latitude temperature increase was stronger in the late 1930s to early 1940s than in recent decades.*

With regard to sea ice—

> We examined the long-term observational records of fast-ice thickness and ice extent from four Arctic marginal seas . . . *the analysis indicates that long-term trends are small and generally statistically insignificant.*

How could the people at the American Geophysical Union in San Francisco, all of whom had (or should have) read Polykov's article, have missed this? Or for that matter, where were the science editors of the New York and Los Angelos *Times?*

How do Polykov's data compare with the computer model forecasts for Arctic warming? The researchers specifically address that point. Referring directly to those models, they wrote, "The maximum simulated warming is in the central Arctic, while the observations do not provide evidence of amplified high-latitude warming."

Both newspapers did manage to point out that there is a strong relationship between the area extent of Arctic sea ice and the area's winds. Since the mid-1960s, winds have gradually trended away from patterns that support a lot of sea ice and toward those favoring less ice.

Arctic wind patterns go through natural oscillations. Whereas the 1980s and 1990s favored relatively small ice amounts, opposite conditions dominated the late 1950s and early 1960s. In the warmer early part of the 20th century, the circulation pattern favored open water.

What about the other pole? What's happening in the South is opposite of what's going on in the North. Figure 3.11 shows the satellite-derived sea ice extent for both poles. Notice that while the Arctic sea ice has been declining, Antarctic sea ice has been increasing.

3.5 United Nations Climate Panel Exaggerates Ice Melt

New data from submarines indicate that there likely has been about a 40 percent decline in Arctic sea-ice thickness in summer to early autumn between the period 1958 to 1976 and the mid-1990s, an average of near 4 cm [1.5 inches] per year.

—*Third Assessment Report,* United Nations
Intergovernmental Panel on Climate Change

The nature of modern science predisposes it to groupthink, simply because large programmatic areas, such as global warming, compete with other large groups for finite taxpayer support, a concept elucidated in our final chapters. As if that situation weren't bad enough, what can happen when such a group is convened to express scientific "consensus"? The government never asks individuals to summarize

51

Figure 3.11

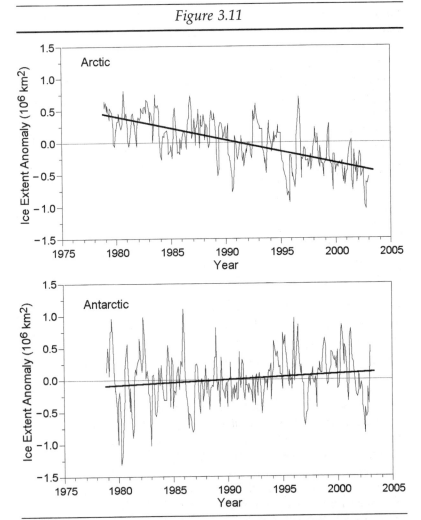

Trend in sea ice extent in the Arctic (top) and Antarctic (bottom).
SOURCE: http://polynya.gsfc.nasa.gov/seaice_projects.html#image10.

large issues; instead, the process is "science by committee." In climate and global warming, the largest of those committees is the United Nations Intergovernmental Panel on Climate Change.

No one who understands the group nature of science funding and science summarization can ignore the dynamics that must occur in such a setting. Does anyone truly expect that the IPCC will suddenly announce that climate change might not be all it's cracked up to be? The IPCC is perhaps the most influential mouthpiece for the climate change community. The "40 percent decline in Arctic sea-ice thickness" quotation that opens this chapter is one of the most quoted lines from the thousands and thousands of pages that comprise the IPCC's most recent compendium on climate change, known as the *Third Assessment Report*. But it is incorrect. It was known to be incorrect before the *Assessment* was published.

The notion that sea ice was thinning rapidly is primarily attributed to data taken from submarine profiles as reported by Rothrock and colleagues in 1999 in the journal *Geophysical Research Letters*, and verified a year later by Wadhams and Davis in the same journal. As a result, "40 percent" loss of ice has become an ice sculpture that is a standard part of global warming lore. And like other similar structures, it may be quite ephemeral.

At the same time, however, other studies said otherwise. They showed that sea ice was affected more by wind than air temperature and that the areas of sea-ice decrease occurred alongside increases in thickness in regions that were not sampled. Ultimately, Holloway and Sou, writing in the *Journal of Climate*, set the record straight once and for all. Predictably, there was no press coverage.

Holloway and Sou determined that, by some happy coincidence, submarines were sampling right along the path where the ice was thinning the fastest. Simply extrapolate that value over the entire ocean, and you've got yourself big headlines. It turns out that the subs missed all the places elsewhere where substantial ice thickening occurred. According to Holloway and Sou, "While modeled thinning at locations and dates [used in Rothrock's study] ranged from 25 percent to 43 percent, [our results for the entire Arctic] showed total thinning by lesser amounts ranging from 12 percent to 15 percent . . . even this lesser amount is quite specific to the timing of the observations."

Figure 3.12 (see color insert) shows the modeled changes in ice thickness (red = thinning; blue = thickening) between the early and late records. Superimposed on the figure are the 29 locations where Rothrock took measurements. Given this sampling pattern, it's hardly surprising that the thinning rate was so overestimated.

Wind and the resulting ocean currents move around quite a bit of ice, making it difficult to take accurate measurements. Holloway and Sou demonstrate that changes in the prevailing wind field from early measurement missions in the 1950s, 1960s, and 1970s differed from the 1990s records, such that the wind essentially moved the ice out of the central Arctic. Holloway writes, "If this is true then the [IPCC-]inferred rapid loss of ice volume was mistaken due to undersampling, an unlucky combination of ever-varying winds and readily shifting ice."

Calculating trends based on so few data points is tricky business, particularly when dealing with something like sea ice that varies so markedly year to year. To demonstrate that, Holloway and Sou took the dates of the missions from the 1950s through 1970s and, using their modeled results, simply shifted each cruise one year earlier. Using these shifting data, instead of a 40 percent decline, they observed thinning of only 11 percent to 15 percent over the same period.

In summary, they wrote—

> Arctic sea-ice volume has decreased more slowly that was hitherto reported. Previous inferences of rapid loss are attributed to undersampling, as varying wind stress forced a natural component of sea ice variability. In particular a dominant mode of variability, moving ice between the central Arctic and the Canadian sector, was missed by the timing and tracks of submarine surveys.

3.6 Is Greenland Melting?

> But I know changes are taking place. The storms are more violent. The floods are more frequent. The droughts are more severe, with far more costly results and more often. The winters have changed. No longer do I experience the snows that I experienced as a boy. The ice masses at the two poles to the north and the south are diminishing. They are melting. The seas grow higher.
>
> —Sen. Robert Byrd (D-W.Va.)

"Greenland is melting! Greenland is melting!" cried a spate of press stories based on two pieces in *Science* magazine appearing in summer 2000. These articles surely call into question the peer review process in the current culture of global warming science.

Most scientists do not intend to deceive. Still, most scientists are people, and even the most objective can and often will write or say things that may not be warranted by objective data and hypothesis testing. That's what the peer-review process is supposed to catch. When a pattern of weak reviews begins to emerge, something bad is happening to science, as discussed at the end of this book.

The first Greenland paper was by veteran glaciologist William Krabill, whose earlier laser-based studies of the West Greenland Ice Sheet—by far the largest chunk of land-ice in the Northern Hemisphere—showed an actual thickening of up to seven feet in the 1980s. That fact may seem counterintuitive, but under global warming Greenland's ice indeed might grow, especially if the warming occurs mostly in winter. After all, warming the air 10 degrees when the temperature is dozens of degrees below freezing is likely to increase snowfall, since "warmer" air is generally moister and precipitates more water, which still must fall as snow at such cold temperatures.

In his 2000 study, Krabill and nine coauthors examined the very brief period 1994–1999. They find, combined with another study published that year, that the largest mass, the ice that's higher than 6,500 feet above sea level, is "rising" at the rate of 0.2 ± 0.2 inches per year. But the land is rising, too—at about 0.15 inch per year. That leaves, in Krabill's estimation, a change of +0.04 ± 0.2 inches per year for this massive icecap, which encompasses the vast majority of Greenland. In the far northern island's coastal regions, ice retreat predominates over about 70 percent of the area studied.

In a companion paper in the same issue of *Science*, Thomas and colleagues wrote, "*The [whole] region has been in balance* [emphasis added], but with thickening of 21 centimeters per year [8.3 inches] in the southwest and thinning of 30 centimeters per year [11.8 inches] in the southeast."

Even so, we can't count the number of press reports blaming melting on global warming, despite the fact that the overall ice is pretty much "in balance." The obvious question: How much has it warmed in southeastern Greenland as the ice melted in that region?

Figure 3.13

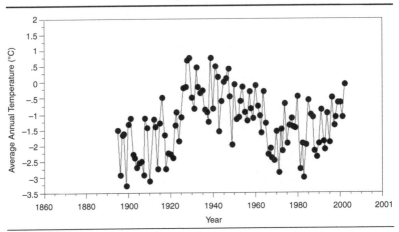

The temperature record from the southeastern Greenland station of Ang-magssalik shows a rapid rise in temperatures from 1900 to 1930—long before the major buildup of atmospheric greenhouse gases—and a gradual decline since.

SOURCE: http://www.giss.nasa.gov.

Figure 3.13 is the best (longest-running and without gap) tempera-ture record from Angmagssalik in southeastern Greenland (latitude 65.6°N, longitude 37.6°W). For 70 years now, a cooling trend has persisted.

What about Nuuk in southwestern Greenland (64.2°N, 51.8°W)? The ice in that region is thickening, and cooling has continued for 70 years also (Figure 3.14). It seems that the ice either accretes or ablates pretty much independent of the temperature.

Krabill and colleagues attempted to relate the melt in the southeast to the temperatures of 1994–1999, the period we have emphasized in the Angmagssalik record (Figure 3.15). They compared temperature anomalies for these years with the average temperature beginning in 1979.

For what it's worth, the annual average temperature at Angmags-salik, based upon the entire 105-year record, is around −1.28°C (+29.7°F), and the average 1994–1999 temperature of about −1.08°C (+30°F) is pretty close to normal. It's about one degree lower than the 1930–1950 temperatures (before human activity changed the

Figure 3.14

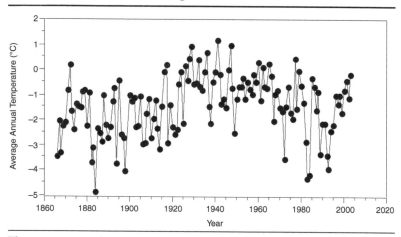

The time series of annual temperatures from the southwestern Greenland station of Nuuk show behavior similar to that of the southeastern coast: namely, the 1930s are by far the warmest period on record and temperatures have declined since then.

SOURCE: http://www.giss.nasa.gov.

greenhouse effect very much). But the period 1979–1999, which Krabill used for averaging, is actually a little colder than its last five years, so the 1994–1999 temperatures appear "warm." In fact, according to Krabill and colleagues—

> Greenland temperature records from 1900–95 show highest summer temperatures in the 1930s, followed by a steady decline until the early 1970s and a slow increase since. The 1980s and 1990s were about half a degree colder than the ninety-six-year mean. Consequently, if present-day thinning is attributable to warmer temperatures, thinning must have been even higher earlier this century.

Major news. Yet there wasn't one news story noting that the "natural" (pre-greenhouse) rate of melting in southern Greenland was higher than it is today! And overall, the largest portion of the ice is at best neutral, as Thomas's companion article makes clear: "On average, the region has been in balance" in recent decades.

What all of that means is that Greenland will have to show a pretty massive melt rate to even equal how much water it lost before

Figure 3.15

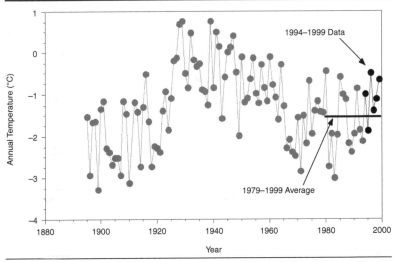

Temperatures during the period examined in the Krabill (2002) study, 1994–1999 (highlighted), are about a degree lower than temperatures during the 1930s, but slightly warmer than the 1979–1999 average used in the study. If Greenland is currently melting, then how much must it have melted during the much warmer period of 70 years ago?

there was a CO_2-producing car in every U.S. garage. And in any event, don't look for it to melt away very fast.

Inexplicably, Krabill told Reuters, "This thinning is a clear indication the global climate is warming up." That's a bit of a stretch, seeing as it is cooling where the ice is melting and has been doing so for seven decades!

So how long do we have left to live? If the icecap lost 0.15 inch per year—the limit given in Krabill's broad range of estimates—it would take about 800,000 years to melt. Between then and now, if history is any guide, we're likely to experience two or three major ice ages, and we will have run out of fossil fuels about 798,000 years before then.

In 2003, another study of Greenland temperatures appeared, by Edward Hanna and John Cappelen. Hanna and Cappelen developed a high-quality data set of Greenland land temperatures from 1958–2001 that were quality controlled to check for errors, biases,

Figure 3.16

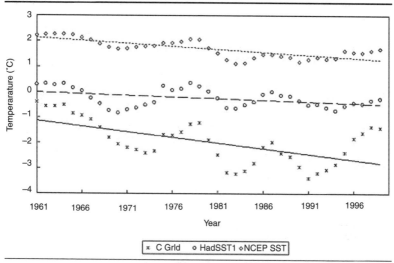

Five-year running average of composite Greenland air temperatures from coastal regions (squares); and two different sources of sea-surface temperatures (circles and diamonds). All three records exhibit significant temperature declines.

SOURCE: Hanna and Cappelen, 2003.

and so on. The eight stations are mostly from coastal southern Greenland—a key area because the edges of the Greenland Ice Sheet, along the coastline, are most sensitive to temperature changes, particularly in summer. Climate models suggest that ice sheet ablation increases by 20 percent to 50 percent for every 1°C rise in temperature.

Their composite record (Figure 3.16), smoothed using a five-year moving average, shows temperatures declining significantly since 1958 (since each year represents a five-year average, the middle year is plotted; the first data point, 1961, is the mean of 1959–1963). Temperatures in southern coastal Greenland have dropped 1.29°C since 1959. Hanna and Cappelen compared this record with nearby sea-surface temperature measurements from two different sources over the same period, also in Figure 3.16. Although the ocean temperatures show less yearly variability (as expected, since water warms and cools more slowly than land, even if the land is very cold), the trend and pattern of year-to-year variation are very similar. So both land and adjacent ocean temperatures have been dropping.

Given that record, why the concern that Greenland is melting? How did Krabill and friends get their more alarming result? Krabill's study focused on 1994 to 1999, six years in the midst of a period of warming in Greenland that began in the early 1990s.

The reality of the overall cooling of Greenland seems to have little influence on what environmental activists will write or what the press will repeat. Consider a Greenpeace press release at the 8th Conference of the Parties (COP-8) of the signatories to the United Nations Framework Convention on Climate Change, held in New Dehli in November 2002, in which their policy director, Steve Sawyer, claimed that a massive sea-level rise brought on by anthropogenic global warming will inundate major world cities (including New York City) by the year 2080 if the world fails to reduce greenhouse gas emissions from fossil fuels.

Greenpeace predicted a massive sea-level rise of 5 to 7 meters (16 to 23 feet) by assuming a *complete* melting of the Greenland ice sheet. If that were to happen, their numbers are essentially correct. But their presumption is wrong: As Krabill's work demonstrates, it is preposterous to suggest that all of Greenland's ice will disappear.

Krabill shows a small net loss of ice in Greenland of about 51 cubic kilometers per year. That loss results in a contribution to sea-level rise of 0.13 millimeter per year. By the year 2080, the current rate of ice loss would result in a total sea-level rise of 10 millimeters—that's one centimeter, or 0.4 inch, a bit less than Greenpeace's forecast.

Greenpeace is fond of talking about the unanimity of the world's scientists and points to the work of the UN's Intergovernmental Panel on Climate Change (IPCC) in support of its assertion. Here's what the IPCC's latest climate compendium (the *Third Assessment Report*) has to say about Greenland's future contribution to global sea-level rise during the next 100 years.

> Projections of components contributing to a sea-level change from 1990 to 2100 . . . using a range of [climate models] . . . give a Greenland contribution of −0.02 to 0.09 meters.

In other words, even the IPCC thinks that Greenland might contribute, at the most, about 9 centimeters (or 3.5 inches) of sea-level rise, while holding out the possibility that its contribution will be negative and that Greenland's behavior under global warming may actually reduce sea level!

Anyone can say whatever they want to about anything. But before any credibility is further afforded Greenpeace on the melting of Greenland, we would hope for a little fact-checking. Exaggerations such as Greenpeace's statements not only damage its credibility, but they also stand in disappointing testament to the lack of credibility of those who publicize them.

One more example of remarkably one-sided reporting on ice occurred on ABC News with Peter Jennings on July 7, 2002, when he spoke of melting alpine glaciers in Italy. The report included lurid videotape of local engineers feverishly working to drain a rising lake that looms over Macugnaga, population 700, an overfill caused by local glacial melting. Officials there worried that the resulting media attention could frighten away tourists. So, despite their efforts to quietly undertake steps that are intended to alleviate a potential threat and preserve their local economy (in other words, to adapt to changing conditions), their next-to-the-worst nightmare comes true: One of the world's largest media outlets made Macugnaga a poster child for the horrors of earth's changing climate.

ABC failed to mention that Alpine glaciers have been melting and receding for over a hundred years in this region. The glaciers surged forward (grew) during the period known as the Little Ice Age—a relatively cool couple of centuries that came to an end sometime in the mid- to late 19th century. As Earth's climate emerged from the Little Ice Age, temperatures warmed and the pumped-up glaciers receded.

Figure 3.17 is an 1850 woodcut of the Argentière glacier, which is about 50 miles west of Macugnaga and above the town of Argentière, Switzerland. Notice how in the mid-19th century it wasn't glacier melt-water but the glacier itself that was so threatening.

Figure 3.18 is a 1966 photograph at the same location. It shows how the entire valley above the town is ice-free. The glacier has receded well up the mountainside.

What makes this photo especially interesting is to realize that 1966 marked the end of about a 30-year cooling trend. The illustrations come from a 1972 book, *Times of Feast, Times of Famine: A History of Climate Since the Year 1000*, by Emmanuel Ladruie, the first book to popularize the notion that climate indeed changes on time scales

Figure 3.17

Argentière Glacier in 1850.
SOURCE: Ladruie, 1972.

relevant to human activity. Of course, the major climatic concern surrounding Ladruie's book was that the earth was cooling rapidly and that the Alp glaciers might re-advance to again threaten the now-safe villages below. The region's temperatures peaked in the early 1940s (before the buildup of greenhouse gases would have had much effect) when temperatures rose 3°F to 4°F higher than they had been just about a hundred years before. Regional temperatures resumed their early-century warming rate soon after the publication of Ladruie's book. Fear of cooling became a thing of the past, and fear of warming replaced it.

Obviously the Alps are warmer than they were, but their alpine glaciers already had been melting for about 150 years before ABC News stumbled onto the situation in Macugnaga. Up to now, local people were free to deal with their situation, take preventive measures, and get on with life. Now they find themselves depicted as victims of circumstances beyond their control. Can you imagine the coverage had it been possible to beam videotape of the looming

Figure 3.18

Argentière Glacier in 1966.
SOURCE: Ladruie, 1972.

glacier in 1850? Given the choice between a stoppable pond, its overflow caused perhaps by human warming, and an inexorable glacier, caused by natural climate fluctuation, which would you choose?

3.7 A Bad Summer for Arctic Melting

Although the modern scientific process whose issues compete for finite support is likely to create a bias for the lurid and the extreme, remember that it is only a bias. Articles can and will appear that argue in the other direction, though the thesis of this book, detailed in Chapter 11, predicts that they must be fewer and further between. Nonetheless, the press reaction will remain predictable. Anything demonstrating that gloom-and-doom forecasts were wrong is liable to be greeted with extreme surprise, even if the truth was self-evident for decades.

The response to a spate of articles on Antarctica published in rapid succession in Antarctic summer (our winter) 2002 is symptomatic of this process. The verbal timidity of the authors, though, was striking.

First, Peter Doran and several colleagues published an online article in *Nature* magazine showing, on average, that Antarctica has been cooling since the mid-1960s, which certainly got the attention of the *Washington Post*, all the way up on page 2 of the January 14, 2002, edition. Staff writer Guy Gugliotta begins his coverage with the lead, "The earth may be in the midst of a planet-wide warming cycle, but in a startling departure from global trends, scientists have found that temperatures on the Antarctic continent have fallen steadily for more than two decades."

Startling? How can a story based on facts known in the scientific literature and publicized elsewhere for a decade be "startling" by any reasonable stretch of the imagination? Even the UN's Intergovernmental Panel on Climate Change says in its *Third Assessment Report* of climate change published in 2001 that there is no net warming in Antarctica.

How new is this? In 1989, 13 years before this "startling" study, the *Journal of Climate* carried an article by John Sansom entitled, "Antarctic Surface Temperature Time Series" that showed no appreciable change in temperature in Antarctica since at least the mid-1960s. In 1995, climatologist Phil Jones published a paper in *Geophysical Research Letters* showing the same thing.

So, Doran's *Nature* article simply supports other temperature records that show—when taken as a whole—how the Antarctic continent has certainly not been warming since mid-1960s (see Figure 3.19 in color insert). The only people, besides the environment writers with little or no training in climatology, who may be taken aback by this "new" finding might be the climate modeling community (which is also composed of remarkably few people formally trained in climatology). Their models generally "predict" that Antarctica should have been warming for decades. Doran et al. timidly suggest, "Continental Antarctic cooling, especially the seasonality of the cooling, poses challenges to models of climate and ecosystem change." Why so timid? Wouldn't it have been better to write, "This finding shows that the recent temperature trends in Antarctica and climate model projections for Antarctica are of opposite sign."

Soon after Doran's article appeared, *Science* published another "shocker" that turns out to be totally consistent with a lack of a big Antarctic warming.

In that one, Ian Joughin and Slawek Tulaczyk reported that glaciers feeding the Ross Ice Shelf are getting bigger, not smaller. Using highly accurate data collected from Synthetic Aperture Radar measurements of the region, the authors are able to improve upon previous estimates of ice stream velocities, as well as annual snow and ice buildup. They find that instead of thinning and losing mass, the region actually is accumulating mass as the ice streams slow and, in some cases, actually stop. This also implies that the West Antarctic Ice Sheet is very stable, allaying fears of a catastrophically rapid rise in sea level. Rather than contributing to sea-level rise, the area around the Ross Ice Shelf actually is acting to reduce sea level.

One week after the Ross Ice Shelf article appeared, global warming science reverted to its more predictable form, with the *Science* report entitled, "Extreme Responses to Climate Change in Antarctic Lakes." Its authors were a team of British scientists led by Wendy Quayle. Quayle examined lakes located in the Antarctic Peninsula—the spit of land that extends from Antarctica toward South America. This is a region that just happens to be about the only place on the Antarctic continent that has warmed during the last 35 years, according to Doran's study.

The title is profoundly misleading. Quayle's research associates didn't even study lakes *throughout* the Antarctic Peninsula, which makes up about 1/50th of the entire continent. Rather, their research focuses on nine lakes situated on Signey Island—a very small place off the peninsula's tip. A more accurate title might have been "Response to local climate change averaged over 1/10,000,000 of Antarctica." But, in any case, Quayle and her team report that lake temperatures have warmed at a rate two to three times faster than air temperatures and three to four times faster than global mean temperature.

What does global mean temperature have to do with lake temperatures on Signey Island, a tip of warming land on an iceberg of a cooling continent? Does global average temperature tell you anything about what to expect at your house from year to year? A more honest approach would have been to characterize this study as examining *local ecological changes* in response to changes in the *local climate* in an environment that is sensitive to change. Signey Island is on the edge of a lot of ice! Small temperature changes produce large impacts on annual ice quantities and, as a result, produce large impacts on the island's ecosystems.

Nothing in Quayle's research findings could possibly be spun into a global warming scare, but that didn't deter the Associated Press.

"A surprise discovery in Antarctic lakes could have important implications for global climate change: As the air got warmer, it set off
a chain reaction that made the water warm three times faster," some
contributing AP subscriber writes. The fact is, these lakes are on a
teeny island that comprises an infinitesimal part of the Antarctic
continent—a place that Doran's concurrent research shows has been
cooling for decades.

3.8 Pulling on the Cultural Heartstrings in the Frozen North

> Inuit elders . . . say they are disturbed by what they are seeing
> swept in by the changes: deformed fish, caribou with bad
> livers, baby seals left by their mothers to starve. . . . While
> scientists debate . . . the Inuit . . . say they are watching the
> world melt before their eyes.
>
> —*Washington Post*, May 28, 2002

Again and again, without even checking the facts, reports such
as this prompt a self-congratulatory political response and seduce
a media that just can't bring itself to notice that the world isn't
coming to an end. Underlying their self-styled empathy is the belief
that people are too poor or too stupid to adapt to our slowly changing
atmosphere. We saw this with the Peruvian glaciers and poor natives
that the *Washington Post* covered in 2001. The follow-up story, on
indigenous people in Canada, appeared in May 2002.

The Inuit have been in northern Canada a long time—10,000 years,
the *Post* said. And "during the past 40 years," the paper notes,
"average temperatures in Canada's western Arctic have risen by 1.5
degrees Celsius [2.7°F] . . . but not in the eastern Arctic, where some
scientists suggest there may even be a modest cooling."

Hmm. About a third of the area is cooling, while the rest is warming. Can't we call it a draw? Or at least business as usual?

We cite business-as-usual evidence in Figure 3.20 (see color insert).
It is *not* a graphic of recent warming, but rather is the temperature
change observed from 1910 through 1945.

Then, from 1945 through 1975, there was a regional cooling that
looks a lot like the reverse of the previous warming; and finally, as
Figure 3.21 shows (see color insert), there's another warming that
looks quite a bit like what happened some 60 to 90 years ago.

Is today's climate unusual for the 10,000 years of Inuit culture? Hardly. It's well known that the region was about two degrees warmer than it is today for three millennia, from 4,000 to 7,000 years ago. If late summer (when marine temperatures reach their annual maximum) witnesses a lot of Arctic open water in today's climate, then surely the Inuit saw virtually ice-free water in September for 30 centuries!

Indeed, the Inuit themselves have adapted to a fairly broad range of regional climate. The mean annual temperature in Iqaluit (on Baffin Island) is some 6°C warmer than at Gladman Point (on King William Island, near where the Lord Franklin expedition disappeared in the 19th century). Both sustain Inuit culture. It is preposterous to say that a culture that is adapted to such a range, which includes substantial biological diversity, will disappear because of a 1.5° temperature change.

There's none of this perspective in the *Post*. Instead, we read, "For the Inuit, climate poses an immediate danger to a way of life." That certainly prompts a number of related questions, namely, about the warming of the early 20th century, about the warm three millennia through which they survived and prospered, and about their current range of adaptation. Yet rather than give the Inuit credit for 10,000 years of adapting to natural climate variability, the *Post* presents them as helpless victims of mainstream cultural prosperity.

3.9 In-Depth Reporting?

> **Mark McEwen:** "Up and down the East coast, it's coming our way, but we will probably see just rain in the big cities."
> **Bryant Gumbel:** "We never get any snow."
> **McEwen:** "Do you think it's global warming?"
> **Gumbel:** "Yes, yes."
> **McEwen:** "Do you, Jane?"
> **Jane Clayson:** "Yeah."
> **McEwen:** "We're unanimous . . . it's global warming."
>
> —*CBS Early Show*, February 2002

People tend to think of New York as a monolithic media outlet (despite the presence of Fox News). But a lot of what we see on CBS and in the *New York Times* does seem pretty similar. A month before their big gaffe on open water at the North Pole (Section 1.3), a July

14, 2000, *New York Times* story, "Study Faults Humans for Large Share of Global Warming," sure could have gone a lot further in the pursuit of "all the news that's fit to print."

On its face, Andy Revkin's article was a clean, qualitative analysis of a *Science* paper by Tom Crowley, now at Duke University. But had he explored the paper in sufficient depth, he would have been compelled to report that it added strong evidence to the data-consistent view that warming in this century is likely to be modest, easily adapted to, and largely beneficial.

Surface temperature records for the 20th century show a warming of about 0.7°C (1.3°F) averaged over the globe. It is well known that much of the warming of the first half of the century is not likely to have been caused by people. Indeed, Crowley's study ascribes about half of century's warming to solar and volcanic changes.

For the sake of argument, let's say about 0.5°C is caused by people. When Crowley inputs that into his computer model, combined with UN estimates for greenhouse and other emissions, he comes up with 1.9°C of warming for the 21st century. Crowley uses a "sensitivity" of global temperature to a doubling of carbon dioxide of 2.0°, which is a bit lower than the UN's estimate of 2.5°.

However, inspection of his paper shows his model to have averaged about 0.2°C too warm during the last 100 years, which means the 2.0° sensitivity is itself too high. The difference reduces his projection for the next hundred years to 1.7°C. But, as noted in Chapter 1, the emissions scenarios used by the UN are easily a third higher than what has been observed in recent decades.

The central tendency of climate models is to produce a constant rate of warming once humans start to heat things. And, like almost every other climate model, Crowley's warming rate for this century is constant, with its slope (rate of change) dependent upon the emission rate. Using a very "conservative" adjustment of, say, 80 percent of the UN emission scenario draws the 21st-century warming down to 1.5°C.

Further, neither Crowley nor Revkin note that during the warming in the second half of the 20th century, which Crowley attributes to human influence, the winter has warmed at over twice the rate of the summer, and that three-quarters of the winter warming is in the most frigid air masses. Greenhouse models all predict that once differentials like this are established, they persist for the duration of the "experiment."

What Crowley's study really does is verify the view of moderate climate change. Too bad the *Times* didn't go deep enough here to find what was really the news "fit to print"!

3.10 Science Fictions

For years, science reporter Sharon Begley has been chasing a peculiar twist on global warming hysteria: that heating the planet will cause an ice age. The shadows of this notion first appeared in her reportage in *Newsweek*'s cover story of January 22, 1996 (see Figure 3.22 in color insert).

A severe snowstorm in Washington, D.C., January 5 through 8, 1996, prompted the associated feature article, in which she wrote that "the blizzard of '96 is just what a greenhouse world would whip up."

As background, Begley interviewed NASA climate scientist James Hansen. He explained to her how such a storm was consistent with "global warming" because global warming heats up the ocean's surface. That evaporates more water. Then, when it's cold, all that water vapor makes more snow. Note that this was during the period when Hansen said that "emphasis on extreme scenarios may have been appropriate," as noted in Chapter 11 on why there has been so much misrepresentation of this issue.

A cursory inspection of the dynamics of mid-Atlantic snowstorms reveals that their limiting factor usually is cold air, not the air's moisture content. The coastal cyclones that cause mid-Atlantic snowstorms typically produce a lot more rain than snow. As a consequence, unless warming causes cooling of the thin wedges of cold air required to make it snow in the mid-Atlantic, it won't snow more.

Had she followed her journalistic instinct, Begley might have asked Hansen to examine the record of mid-Atlantic sea-surface temperatures available to him in a desktop file. They both would have discovered that those records showed no net warming trend in the source region for mid-Atlantic snow for several decades.

This is yet another example of the avoidance of rudimentary fact-checking that has become commonplace in global warming stories.

Begley continued to be fascinated by the notion of a coming ice age brought on by global warming. In a 2000 reprise, Begley's story was a variant on warming-causes-cooling (!). The evidence? Magellanic penguins washed ashore at Rio de Janiero.

The logic was peculiar:

1. Penguins in Rio must mean that the entire South Atlantic Ocean circulation has changed for several thousand miles . . .
2. which might mean that sea-surface temperatures in the North Atlantic "could plunge 20 degrees in 10 years" . . .
3. which would mean global warming could bring on an ice age.

If the presence of those penguins in Rio de Janeiro really reflects a 2,000-mile change in the northern limit of the South Atlantic Gyre—the big circulation of that southern ocean—then the coffee beans of Brazil should be freezing out just about every year. A trip to the grocery store reveals this hasn't happened.

The bizarre assertion that global warming somehow will induce more cooling reared its feverish head again in January 2003 when Harvard University's Paul Epstein and James McCarthy (the same McCarthy involved in the polar meltdown mess discussed in the beginning of this chapter), writing in the *Boston Globe*, claimed that the late-January 2003 cold spell in New England resulted from global warming.

Begley couldn't resist restating this argument in the February 7 edition of the *Wall Street Journal*, seven years after the original *Newsweek* cover. This time: "The juxtaposition of a big chill in the Northeast and near-record warmth globally seems eerily like the most dire predictions of climate change: As most of the world gets toastier, average winter temperatures in Northeastern America and Western Europe could plunge 9°F."

The causal mechanism she invokes is the complete shutdown of the Atlantic Ocean's Gulf Stream. If the Gulf Stream slows or stops (or so the argument goes), then the southern Atlantic will warm while the northern Atlantic cools because the heat will no longer be transported northward by the current. The ostensible result would be very cold and probably snowier winters in the Northeast United States.

Although that argument hangs together pretty well *if* you are willing to assume that climate change will put the brakes on the Gulf Stream, there nevertheless is no evidence in recent northeastern U.S. climate history that any such thing is actually taking place. And, for what it's worth, the winter of 2002–2003 wasn't even exceptionally cold in New England. In absolute terms, it came in at No.

Figure 3.23

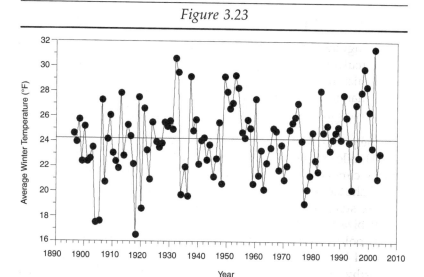

Average December through February temperature for northeastern United States (Conn., Del., Me., Md., Mass., N.H., N.J., N.Y., Pa., R.I., and Vt.) since 1895.

SOURCE: http://www.ncdc.noaa.gov.

19 in terms of the last 108 winters for which we have reliable records. In other words, about one in every six winters was colder than winter 2002–2003. The most recent colder winter was that of 1993–1994.

Figure 3.23 shows the history of winter temperature in the Northeast United States since 1895. There is no statistically significant trend during this 108-year-long winter record. Instead, there's a lot of interannual fluctuations atop decadal-scale variation.

The 1950s were warm (every winter was above the long-term average), and the 1940s and 1960s were cold. If for some reason you think the swing from unseasonably warm to colder-than-normal has been dramatic over the last three winters, check out what was happening between 1932 and 1937! Two very warm winters were followed by three very cold ones, then another very warm one. Imagine the fun Begley, Epstein, and McCarthy could have had scaring the bejesus out of folks back then!

The Northeast's winter temperature history from the National Climatic Data Center shows nothing unusual. Note also that the

71

winter of 2001–2002 was the warmest on record, which is counter to the argument Begley made a mere year later.

Climate change advocates can't seem to allow anything seemingly out of the ordinary to pass without crediting global warming. If it seems unusual (although it in reality is perfectly usual)—be it warm, cold, rain-filled, full of snow or sleet or hail, a terrible tornado or hurricane, drought or flood—someone somewhere predictably will attribute it to "global warming."

4. All Creatures Cute and Furry

One exercise that has become increasingly common at low-level universities and junior colleges concerns endangered or extinct species. Students are invited to appear in costume as, say, a White Tiger or a Passenger Pigeon. A friend of mine had a different idea: She showed up as a *Variola* virus, a.k.a. smallpox, with a sign reading "Glad to have me around?"

In today's college climate, I would predict an A for the tiger and an F for smallpox, which underscores the notion of the "marquee species" extinctions. Dragoon the warm, cuddly, or handsome animals in the support of biodiversity or global warming legislation, and try not to talk about the garden-variety slugs, yucky toadfish, or yard-long tapeworms.

This lesson hasn't been lost on the environmental community, which has adopted penguins, polar bears, and baby seals in service of the Kyoto Protocol. Never mind that bears eat the seals, or that the bears are approaching American-style obesity in garbage-strewn Churchill, Manitoba, far south of the Arctic Circle. It hasn't been lost on scientists that talking about global warming's killing butterflies will get a first-class seat to the next UN confab much quicker than relating climate variability to a decline in skunks—which brings us to the butterfly story.

4.1 Chasing Butterflies

> The end result of these changes could be substantial ecological disruption, local losses in wildlife and extinction of certain species.
>
> —Sen. John McCain (R-Ariz.), January 8, 2003

We've all heard that old saw about how the flap of a butterfly's wings in China can initiate a tornado in downtown East Podunk, or wherever. That's a real stretch from pioneering MIT atmospheric scientist Ed Lorenz's original notion about chaos theory, which is the idea that small perturbations in a fluid can lead to larger ones. But it makes nice copy.

But could the flap of a butterfly's wings lead to the Kyoto Protocol? That's a different matter and a subject of reasonable conjecture, given the great butterfly flap started by University of California–Santa Barbara (now University of Texas–Austin) entomologist Camille Parmesan, with a paper published in *Nature* in the summer of 1996.

Parmesan's paper is a marquee example of the changed nature of the scientific review process on global warming, as even the most obvious questions are muted. When some phenomenon is apparently a result of regional warming, the first instinct a reviewer should have is to check the local climate record. But that didn't happen here.

Parmesan studied Edith's Checkerspot butterfly, which was initially made famous by Paul Ehrlich, the Stanford entomologist who predicted in the 1970s that overpopulation would send the earth's ecosystems into total collapse within a few decades (hint: He was wrong).

In particular she sampled the range of the butterfly, from Mexico to British Columbia, and found that populations were becoming extinct in Mexico, where they are limited by heat, while they were expanding in Canada, where it used to be too cold.

Or so the story went. She then told the *Los Angeles Times* this was "exactly what climate warming models predict," and that her findings were "the clearest indication that global climate warming is already influencing species' distribution." Her work included maps of where the butterfly populations were going extinct and where they were establishing new colonies.

So how much warming is occurring in the place where the most extinction is taking place, in northern Mexico? Figure 4.1 is the latitude/longitude gridbox temperature history available in August 1996 (the date of publication), for precisely that region. The data are part of the overall record that was used by the UN IPCC to estimate global climate change in its three "scientific assessments," in 1990, 1996, and 2001. In British Columbia, where populations are expanding, there also has been no warming over the last 75 years (Figure 4.2).

Maybe that one warm year (1994) at the end of the record caused the extinctions. If so, Edith's Checkerspot is a sensitive beast indeed and probably had a larger extinction in 1871, long before the greenhouse effect began to change in a meaningful fashion.

Figure 4.1

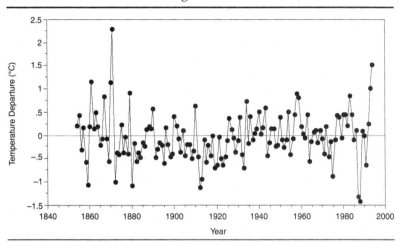

Land-based temperature history from the region of maximum butterfly extinction in northern Mexico.

SOURCE: http://www.cru.uea.ac.uk.

Figure 4.2

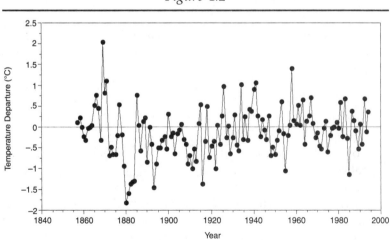

Land-based temperature history from southern British Columbia.

SOURCE: http://www.cru.uea.ac.uk.

75

Or maybe our temperature records are just *bad* and Edith's Check-erspot is a more accurate thermometer. That would mean that we can't say anything objective about cause and effect in global warming.

After I revealed this uncomfortable reality, Parmesan changed her interpretation. When interviewed by Bill Stephens of the *New York Times* in an article that appeared four days later, she said, "I cannot say that climate warming has caused the shift; what I can say is that it is exactly what is predicted by global warming scenarios."

Despite the obvious problem in matching the largest extinctions and expansions to any warming, Parmesan's finding was music to the ears of the reigning global warming politburo, which was the Clinton administration's "U.S. Global Change Research Program" (USGCRP) office.

Within two months, USGCRP whisked Parmesan from the West Coast to present her finding to its weekly "global change" seminar series held in the basement of the House of Representatives. In the Clinton era, USGCRP seminars, with few exceptions, had been the showcase for the allegedly seamless consensus of impending clima-tological and ecological doom and gloom, yet another example of the care and feeding, by scientists and for scientists, of Washington's global warming panic machine.

In Figure 4.1, in the region of maximum extinction in northern Mexico no warming is shown, but it certainly is in the next grid cell to the west. It is along the relatively urbanized Tijuana-Santa Barbara corridor, including San Diego and sprawling Los Angeles. Perhaps *this* warming was global warming!

Apparently not. We can check to see if the warming here was likely to be "local" rather than global by subtracting the more eastern (rural) temperature record from the western (urban) one (Figure 4.3). If there is a general warming, there will be little or no trend in this figure from year to year. Instead, there is an obvious increase beginning in the early 1960s—a clear sign that the warming in the western grid cell is local and not because of general climate change.

This leads to the interesting proposition that the increasing extinc-tion at the southern end of the butterfly's range is a result of the citification of the Pacific Coast. But somehow the headline "Butter-flies Killed by Urban Warming" just doesn't punch as much as jumping to the conclusion that global warming did it.

Then again, were they killed by warming of any kind? The hypoth-esis about "latitudinal gradients" in extinction just doesn't cut it in

Figure 4.3

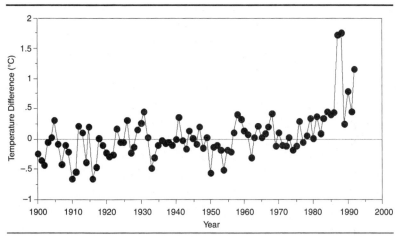

Western district minus eastern district from 1900, the beginning year of Parmesan study. If there weren't a "local" (i.e., urban) warming in one record, the trend line should be flat for the entire record. Obviously that is not the case.

SOURCE: http://www.cru.uea.ac.uk.

the mountain-and-desert terrain of the Pacific Southwest. In Nevada, there were relatively few extinctions, but summer temperatures are a great deal hotter than near the palmy and balmy Pacific Coast. Those butterflies are clearly the ones that should have gotten singed by global warming, but they flap on, undisturbed by and seemingly oblivious to man's pernicious industrial assault.

Parmesan later expanded her work to Europe in a new paper containing a huge international ensemble of lepidopterists as coauthors. They found, not surprisingly, pretty much the same thing she did in her North American work. They gathered survey data from throughout Europe—essentially butterfly aficionados' observations of which species appeared where and when. In some cases, the records went back to 1910; in others, they begin only in the 1960s. Rarely are they continuous.

If, for example, someone today observed a butterfly species in central Finland, and in 1920 there was a record of it in southern Finland, this would be called a northward (i.e., global warming–related) range expansion. The authors tallied presence/absence data for

77

up to 52 species across Europe. They examined only nonmigratory butterfly species, and they eliminated cases of species that required very specific habitats and were intolerant of even modest human habitat modifications.

They found that at the northern edge of the range, 65 percent of the species extended their ranges northward, 34 percent exhibited no change, and only 2 percent shifted south. But at the southern end, 5 percent extended south, 22 percent shifted northward, and a whopping 72 percent remained stable. In sum, though butterfly species ranges are expanding northward, there are almost no southern range extinctions.

If it weren't necessary for scientists to accentuate the negative, the authors should have whooped for joy. After all, the evidence clearly shows that butterfly diversity is increasing! Butterflies are infesting Europe! Everyone loves butterflies.

Instead, Parmesan et al. wrote, "Here we provide the first large-scale evidence of poleward shifts in entire species' ranges." This would have been more accurate: "Here we find the first large-scale evidence that hemispheric warming is associated with an expansion of butterfly ranges and an overall increase in butterfly diversity over a larger area."

Experience with the North American study, in which the largest extinctions were shown to be occurring in areas where there was no warming, can make one suspicious. So a further investigation of this European result might be in order. Figure 4.4 (see color insert) shows Parmesan et al.'s map of range changes in the species *Parare aegeria* across Great Britain. Black squares show the 100 square km. area where populations were found between 1915 and 1939; red squares, 1940 to 1969; blue squares, 1970 to 1997. At first glance, it looks like these species moved northward into central England over the course of the century. Note, however, that these species existed in portions of central England and Wales back in the 1920s and 1930s. Rather than a northward expansion, the time history shows a general expansion over the island.

Northern observations, from Scotland, clearly show butterflies existing during 1940–1969, where no one had seen butterflies before. This is a northern expansion. Interestingly, the species apparently were not observed in northern England at any time, and they are nonmigratory species.

Figure 4.5

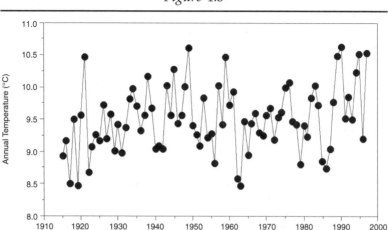

The Manley 1917–1997 temperature history of Great Britain shows no change in net temperature in the past 60 years.

SOURCE: http://www.met-office.gov.uk.

In response to climate changes, Parmesan proposes that the northward migrations are gradual, as subsequent generations slowly spread northward. If that's the case, that butterfly-free zone in the center of the map is a problem. Or is it just that these are very, very subjective, spotty data?

This brings us to the climate, yet again. Central England has one of the world's oldest and most reliable thermometric temperature records, which, compiled by the late Brian Manley, extends back to the 17th century. Figure 4.5 shows the temperature history over the relevant period of record. (This is an ideal time series from a statistical standpoint because one can selectively pick any period of record and show warming or cooling.)

Basically, the region warmed gradually (the last 18 years were about one-quarter degree Celsius warmer than the first 25 years), but there were several cool periods scattered throughout this century. On the other hand, there is no net change in temperature in the last 60 years.

We know that spring comes earlier and fall later over much of Europe and that the planet, in general, is getting greener (see Chapter 7, "A Greener World of Changing Seasons?"). Maybe the butterflies are responding to that, or perhaps there is some other factor. But, given both the North American and European studies, it is apparent that butterflies can and will expand and contract, whether climate does or does not change. In other words, climate change isn't the only explanation, nor is it a sufficient one.

Whatever the reason, it's difficult to see how this butterfly spreading is anything but good news. Nonetheless, the environmental literature promoting the Kyoto Protocol is replete with references to this work. Obviously it is an attempt to use the flap of a butterfly's wings over Europe to try to create economic havoc in America.

4.2 Are Birds Dropping?

After the butterfly extinctions come the birds, at least according to the World Wildlife Fund (WWF) in their Climate Change Campaign begun in 1996. According to their kickoff press release, a new WWF study "details a widespread disruption in migratory patterns as prime feeding and breeding grounds are lost to sea level rise, changes in the timing of seasons, and drier weather."

According to the WWF, "Drier weather . . . could be particularly severe for birds in the Plains states of Canada and the United States [since] half of all North American ducks breed in prairie pothole wetlands that could disappear as a result of global warming."

Perhaps a look at the precipitation trend over the last 100 years in a region covering the north-central United States and south-central Canada, the big migratory flyway, is in order (Figure 4.6). Think whooping cranes, watering down in the prairie potholes that dot the region.

There is a statistically significant *upward* trend in precipitation. Yes, we suppose pothole wetlands *could* dry up because of global warming. It's also possible the World Wildlife Fund *could* stop issuing press releases purporting that things are occurring that are not.

In addition, the WWF claims "global warming could cause more than one million shorebirds . . . who stop at the Delaware Bay to feed during their trip north to leave a week earlier, thereby missing the emergence of the millions of horseshoe crabs from the Atlantic on whose eggs they rely to survive."

Figure 4.6

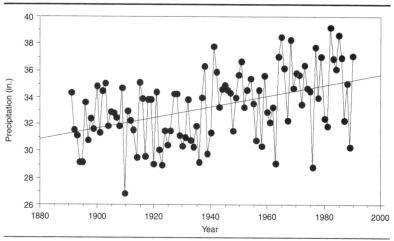

Annual precipitation amount (inches) for the north-central United States and south-central Canada. There has been a statistically significant *increase* of precipitation over this region as the greenhouse effect has enhanced, although the WWF says there should have been a decrease.

SOURCE: http://www.ncdc.noaa.gov.

SPIN ZONE

It's awfully easy to spin any story you want on endangered species and climate change given judicious selection of both weather data and animals. Imagine this hypothetical press release based on WWF's contention about crabs and shorebirds:

Global Warming Good for Crabs!

According to a recent study by *The Center for Truth in Press Releases*, crab populations will swell because of global warming. "Changes in the timing of shorebird migration will cause them to miss the annual emergence of crab larvae into the mid-Atlantic bight," said an unidentified *CTPR* spokesperson. "There's no doubt that the number of crabs will increase dramatically, benefiting the area's watermen, restaurants, and the economy.

One Year Later . . . One year after the WWF kicked off its campaign in the fall of 1997, clear blue skies darkened day after day as one of the largest flights of migratory waterfowl ever counted winged toward their winter home. The 42.6 million fowl that were found nesting eclipsed the 42 million Audubon bird count of 1956. There were so many birds that the countryside was beginning to look like that flannel print inside the sleeping bag you took to Boy Scout Camp! However, during dry years in the 1980s, populations were as low as 25 million, or about 40 percent fewer birds.

We're surprised that the WWF missed this opportunity: "Migratory Bird Droppings Cause Major Health Risk. El Niño Blamed. Some Scientists say big El Niño due to Global Warming."

Bye-bye (state) birdies. How many times does this game get played? An environmental lobbying organization (in this case *two*: the National Wildlife Federation and the American Bird Conservancy) produces some type of not-yet-available-for-release-and-therefore-not-subject-to-critical-evaluation study on the terrible effects of global warming on whatever (in this case, *state birds*), leaks it to the environmental journalist for the local big paper (in this case, the *Washington Post's* Eric Pianin), and suddenly a half-page article of ecological gloom and doom appears on page 3.

The result was the March 4, 2002, issue of the *Post*, headlined, "A Baltimore without Orioles? Study Says Global Warming May Rob Md., Other States of Their Official Birds."

Area sports fans probably felt a flutter of panic until they realized the story was about the state bird, not their baseball team, as they read that

> A new study to be released this week by the National Wildlife Federation and the American Bird Conservancy suggests that the effects of global warming may be robbing Maryland and a half-dozen other states of an important piece of their heritage by hastening the departure of their state birds.

Later,

> The ranges of some state birds could shrink or shift entirely outside the states they represent. That could mean Iowa and Washington state would eventually lose the American gold-finch, New Hampshire would say goodbye to the purple finch, California would lose California quails, Massachusetts'

black-capped chickadee would vanish, Georgia would lose the brown thrasher and Maryland would lose its beloved Baltimore oriole.

Don't worry, you can read all about how to stop this, this time not from the politically tainted Federation or Conservancy, but from the snowbird-pure *Post*. Pianin concluded,

> Environmentalists stress that although the long-term forecast is gloomy, the loss of birds could be averted if government and industry agree on policies for reducing greenhouse-gas emissions and improving the energy efficiency of cars, homes, [and] offices."

He drives home the point of the report with a quick quote from former Clinton administration U.S. Fish and Wildlife Service administrator, Jamie Rappaport Clark, who recently spun through the government-lobbyist revolving door to become senior vice president at the National Wildlife Federation. According to Clark, "This is happening to species of birds we care about, but there's something we can do about it."

This particular report was not as striking as the *Post* might lead one to believe. Although the ranges of the birds that were studied already are shifting a bit, they hardly are shrinking to nothingness (extinction). The real consequence seems to be that birdwatchers may see less of a particular species or two, especially when those species already are living at the southern edge of their range. As climate warms, such species probably will be replaced by warmer-climate species spreading their range northward.

It is a fact that bird diversity increases as one goes farther south, so if things warm up, diversity should go up in previously depauperate more northerly climes. This could suggest an alternative headline: "Birdwatchers May Soon Rejoice, Finding New Species Visiting Feeders."

Whether the climate of the United States has changed during the last century is not a matter of much debate. It was cold around 1900, hotter and drier than now in the 1930s' dust bowl, and cold in the 1970s. Professional climatologists and attentive students realize that climate always is in a state of change. It is no surprise that over time plant and animal species shift along with climate. It's also true that sometimes some species die out as a result of such shifts. At the same time, new ones are evolving. It's a fact that more than 99 percent of all the species that ever existed on Earth are extinct—many as a function of climate fluctuation. One can reasonably expect this cycle of life to continue until Earth finally is incinerated by the Sun.

More of a problem for species today is the loss of habitat as a result of another species—humans—encroaching upon it by modifying the landscape. Fragmented habitats make it more difficult for species to respond to a changing climate. In the case of the vast majority of bird species examined in the WWF Report, the range of habitat is wide and the climate that they tolerate is broad. For most, the effects of even extreme climate change will therefore be adapted to.

4.3 Early to Rise, Early to Croak: Toads, Frogs, and Global Warming

> This is a wake-up call to world leaders—if they do not act to stop global warming, wildlife around the globe will suffer the consequence.
>
> —Jennifer Morgan, Director of World Wildlife Fund's Climate Change Campaign

Few frogs are marquee species, but they're still subject to the very strange scientific review process that confronts global warming stories. Here's another wonderful example of a critical question that should have been asked, but wasn't, in a study of frog calls and climate change.

The August 2001 edition of *Conservation Biology* contained an article claiming that springtime frog-calling around Ithaca, New York, begins 10 to 13 days earlier these days than it did during the 1900–1912 period, which was several degrees colder. "This is the strongest evidence of a biological response to climate change in eastern North America," it concluded.

How did that one get by the reviewers? Gibbs and Breisch examined average daily maximum temperatures from November to June—key months affecting the timing of frog-mating season. They compared records of the earliest calling dates of six frog and toad species during the past century's first 12 years with data collected in the 1990s. Of the six species they examined, four (spring peepers, wood frogs, bullfrogs, and gray tree frogs) began calling 10 to 13

Figure 4.7

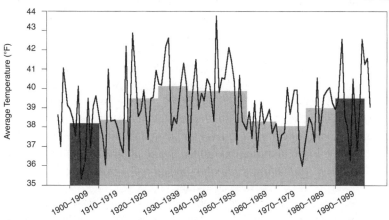

The history of November–June average temperatures around Ithaca, New York, with bars representing decadal averages. Gibbs and Breisch studied only those decades highlighted.

Source: http://www.ncdc.noaa.gov.

days earlier; the other two (green frog and American toad) were unaffected by climate.

Though they're peeping earlier, local "climate warming" won't cause them to croak prematurely, since Ithaca is in the center of their current natural range.

Not so for the mink frog, whose southern limit is about 90 miles north: "Mink frogs would be expected to show predictable, local declines if local climate warming continues," they wrote.

How many examples are there of people making assertions about climate change (butterflies, toads, frogs, state birds, etc.) without bothering to check the data? And absent that, why don't the reviewers of these manuscripts check? Figure 4.7 shows the temperature history from the U.S. National Climatic Data Center for the New York Climatological Division that includes Ithaca. If higher temperatures lead to mink frog losses, then obviously there must have been significant declines in their population during the 1920s, 1930s, 1940s, and 1950s—all decades that were warmer than the period Gibbs and Breisch studied (and a time in which human impact on climate was minimal). Similarly, the chorus of springtime peeping around Ithaca during those warm decades must have begun even earlier.

It's no surprise that the life cycle of those amphibians is closely related to variations in local climate. During the 20th century, there were periods much warmer and much cooler than the 1990s. Amphibians, like most creatures, have survived not only these relatively slight natural climate changes but also have survived far more substantial ones.

In another dissonant convergence of climate change and endangered species, several species of birds, frogs, and toads are disappearing from the highland, cloud-enshrouded forests of Monteverde, Costa Rica, according to a 1998 article in *Nature* magazine by researchers J. Alan Pounds, Michael Fogden, and John Campbell, all from Costa Rica's Golden Toad Laboratory for Conservation. The species' declines are coincident with changes in the patterns of dry-season mist frequency, which has been declining since the mid-1970s.

Sounds like catastrophic climate change is to blame, right? As proof, we have the "lifting-cloud-base hypothesis," which was first proposed by the three authors in a workshop in 1997 and was verified in *Nature* three pages earlier by Stanford's Christopher Still and Steve Schneider (and coauthor Prudence Foster). Here, they compare global climate model simulations in a general circulation model (GCM) for a doubled CO_2 atmosphere with current conditions and note shifts in the height of cloudiness in the dry season that correspond exactly to the decline in toadies.

Isn't this self-referencing system wonderful? Each paper confirms its accuracy by referencing the other.

There are so many fish in this barrel that its almost a shame to waste ammunition! First, we keep hearing about how the planet is going to become moister from global warming and the "enhanced hydrological cycle." In general, based on simple physics, a moister atmosphere will produce more clouds that form at lower elevations and a wetter forest—making for an extremely amphibian-friendly planet.

Second, if we were interested in the climate in some unique montane environment in Central America, the *last* place we'd look for answers is a GCM. GCMs don't even have realistic clouds. Their spatial scale is so large that they can't replicate huge cyclonic storm systems. The only way to use a GCM for this kind of problem is to

Figure 4.8

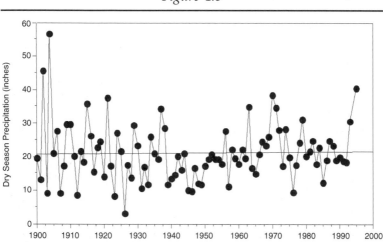

Historical precipitation amounts for Costa Rica.
SOURCE: http://www.cru.uea.ac.uk.

downscale to processes beneath the mathematical resolution level of the model to begin with.

Third, just to show what the reviewers again forgot to mention, we present the 95-year precipitation record from the Costa Rica grid cell from the Climate Research Unit at the University of East Anglia in England that includes mostly land stations from this country (Figure 4.8). There is no long-term change, nor is any change evident since the mid-1970s, when the authors detected an abrupt oceanic temperature change.

Two years later . . . Two years later, R. O. Lawton of the University of Alabama–Huntsville and three colleagues looked more carefully at patterns of cloudiness and cloud heights in this same (formerly) toad-infested woodland. They found not *global* warming but *local* land-use changes were the likely culprit.

Around 1940, a 600-square-kilometer area of forest at the base of the mountain range was cleared for agriculture. The trajectory of the air that rises up the mountainside to form the cloud forests passes over those lowland agricultural fields. Conversion of forests to pasturelands or croplands reduces the amount of moisture in the air but tends to increase the local temperature. If the air moving up the mountainside starts out drier and warmer, it will take longer to cool the air to saturation and form clouds, so the cloud bases will be higher.

The authors show satellite evidence that the deforested regions tend to be relatively cloud-free, even when there is extensive cloud cover over the general area. They also ran a regional atmospheric model and compared the moisture content over the mountain range, assuming a completely forested and completely deforested landscape. In the deforested case, the total atmospheric water content is lower, the cloud base is higher, and the region covered by clouds is less extensive than in the forested case. Lawton wrote, "The model results thus suggest that deforestation in the lowland tropics of the trade wind zone tends to shift the cloud forest environment upward in adjacent downwind mountains."

To adapt an old saw, "All climate change is local." Rather than blaming industrial society for the alleged and future demise of the Golden Toad, perhaps the locals should look no further than the family photo album, since their parents turned the forests into farms and pastures.

Meanwhile, further up the Left Coast . . . Sometime around 1999, there must have been a slug of federal funding for researchers who proposed (i.e., had already concluded?) that global warming was into toads. How else to explain all of these papers appearing at once? Anyway, some of the results were downright shocking. Consider this article, whose title might as well have come from the proverbial *Duh!* magazine: "Animal Species' Viability Linked to Climate." Actually it was *Nature*, April 5, 2001.

Specifically, toads again, this time in the Pacific Northwest. Never mind that the fact that species distribution is related to climate is one of the underlying principles in the science of ecology. (Do Polar Bears Live in the Tropical Rainforest? "Duh!"). There was a flurry of press activity on that research finding, largely because the researchers weren't content to link toad population dynamics to changing climate; rather, they felt compelled to make the leap to human-induced climate change.

Here's what the *Washington Post*'s William Souder wrote on April 9, 2001:

> Researchers say they have evidence that global warming could be playing a role in the decline of the western toad in

Oregon. These findings are the first to link climatic change
with amphibian die-offs in North America, and appear to
demonstrate the kind of ecological chain reaction that scientists have warned will result from rapid global warming.

This was followed by a completely off-topic disquisition about mean
old President Bush and U.S. unilateralism in this apparent "news"
story. What this has to do with toads is a bit unclear, but Souder
went on:

The findings come as U.S. policy on global warming is in
flux. The Bush administration recently reversed a campaign
pledge to seek lower carbon dioxide emissions from power
producers and declared the international Kyoto agreement
to combat global warming dead, angering U.S. allies.

How silly for anyone to think the story was about toads and not
about President Bush!

Anyway, the toad paper was published by J. M. Kiesecker and
two other colleagues, who studied the relationship between the
reproductive success of the western toad and the amount of ultraviolet (damaging) radiation that reached the toads' developing eggs
between 1990 and 1999. Higher levels of ultraviolet exposure led to
a lower number of hatching eggs, according to their findings. When
the eggs are subjected to higher ultraviolet exposure, they postu-
lated, the developing embryos are weakened and they become
increasingly vulnerable to infection by a particular fungus.

The amount of ultraviolet radiation that reached the developing
egg masses was directly related to the depth of water in which the
eggs were laid; the shallower the water, the greater the ultraviolet
exposure. The depth of the water in which the eggs were laid was
related to the amount of precipitation falling over Oregon's Cascade
Mountains between October and the end of March; the less precipitation, the shallower the water, and the greater the damage. All very
logical, so far.

Then the amount of rainfall over the Cascades was related to the
cycle of El Niño/La Niña; the more frequent the El Niño, the less
precipitation.

Unless there was again something very wrong with the attentive-
ness of the reviewers of this paper, the obvious and natural question
would be to ask whether there is a decline in October–March Cascade

Figure 4.9

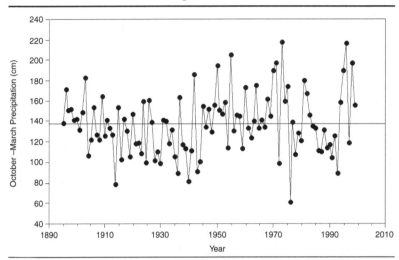

The historical time series of October–March precipitation in Oregon's Cascade Mountains shows that climate varies on time scales from years to decades, and probably even longer. However, since 1895, there has been no statistically significant trend. Since 1910, the trend in precipitation is positive.

SOURCE: http://www.ncdc.noaa.gov.

Mountain rainfall that is related to planetary warming. It's not a very difficult thing to find, about five clicks away at the Department of Commerce's National Climatic Data Center, and it's not many more clicks to enter it into a spreadsheet program and graph it up, as in Figure 4.9.

Now come the weakening links. The authors assert the frequency of El Niño has been altered by human changes to the atmosphere's greenhouse effect. But why stop there? Human-induced climate change therefore is leading not only to an observed population decline in the western toad of the Pacific Northwest but also to a decline in amphibian populations worldwide.

All of this "logic" certainly falls apart if there's no change in the rainfall, but why let facts get in the way of a good theory? There is no long-term trend in the rainfall record that begins in 1895. Since 1910, there is a statistically significant precipitation increase. Following the researchers' logic, that should be salutary for toads.

It *is* apparent that the October–March precipitation totals were below the average for the last century in the late 1980s and early 1990s. (Remember that their study period was between 1990 and 1999.) But, in five of the last six years they were above the average, much more so, in general, than they were below in the previous period.

At any rate, if the low precipitation in the early 1990s was responsible for a large decline in western toad egg viability, just imagine how bad the critters fared during the 1930s and early 1940s, when it was drier still. And never mind that this was before changing the greenhouse effect could have done much to the climate.

This precipitation history illustrates how variable "natural" climate is. The October–March totals fluctuate on a timescale of years, decades. If toad populations are as sensitive to climate as these researchers contend, then toad population "naturally" varies tremendously. Why drag human-induced climate change into it? Toads are sensitive to climate, period.

At any rate there is no convincing evidence whatsoever in this research to support the hypothesis that human-induced changes in the atmosphere's greenhouse effect have negatively impacted the western toad in any fashion that is distinguishable from normal (and measured) rainfall variability. How such an obvious gaffe could have made it through the review process is certainly mystifying.

4.4 Jellyfish, Marquee and Otherwise

The May 6, 2002, *Washington Post* headlined "Jellyfish 'Blooms' Could Be Sign of Ailing Seas." Jellyfish, affectionately known as "rats of the sea," seem to be undergoing a population explosion. Or a population crash, both caused by global warming.

First, the explosion. According to a Gulf of Mexico fisherman quoted in the *Post*, there are now so many jellyfish that "you can almost walk across the water on them." Why?

Well, there are several possible explanations. Overfishing, for one. With fewer nongelatinous fish chowing down, maybe jellyfish are taking over their role, since both often feed on the same prey. As an example, consider the poor little shrimp larvae, food to both jellyfish and commercial fish. Fewer of the latter and you can apparently just follow the jellyfish road between Tampa and the Big Easy.

Another culprit may be the increased nitrogen and phosphorus nutrient runoff from the Mississippi River basin, a prime agricultural region now larded with mega pig and catfish factories. The water becomes eutrophic (overproductive), resulting in oxygen depletion. In this scenario the lowly jellyfish survives and prospers while the finfish die off.

The third explanation, of course, is the ubiquitous "global warming." Don't ask for the logic because there isn't any. There is no correlation that we know of between ocean temperature and jellyfish density, something pretty easy to test. Nonetheless, we read in the *Post*:

> Warming ocean waters as a result of global climate change, and introductions of species into areas in which they are not native, may also play a part.

Notice that not one of the reasons for those jellyfish explosions is natural variability. Surely man has some role; we're simply left with the trivial problem of determining exactly what it is. Still, on the basis of what we've learned so far, the increasing jellyfish population is a problem, right?

Not so fast! The article ends with an opposite take, but one we still can pin on global warming. In this case, jellyfish become a marquee species. There is a place called Jellyfish Lake on the island of Palau in the western Pacific Ocean. The big 1998 El Niño warmed the lake, wiping out the resident rare golden jellyfish. According to Portland State University scientist Dick Dewey, "The situation was seemingly hopeless." Said Dewey: "Palau's reputation as one of the 'seven biological wonders of the world' has been based on this magnificent lake and its jellyfish."

There's a healthy debate in the atmospheric science community over whether El Niños should increase or decrease with human-induced global warming (note that no one ever seems to propose that they will remain the same). But, as in any two-sided debate on this subject, most people only read about one side, in this case the notion that El Niños will become more frequent in a warmer world. Consequently, in the mind of the public, El Niño and global warming might as well be synonymous.

But here's the shocker: When the big 1997–1998 El Niño ended, water temperatures returned to normal, and thousands of tiny golden jellyfish emerged from the bottom of Jellyfish Lake. They now number more than a million. Another jellyfish explosion!

It's a fact that El Niños have been going on for about as long as the Pacific Ocean has been more than 4,000 miles wide. That is a long time, dozens of millions of years. The golden jellyfish have been isolated in Jellyfish Lake for thousands of years. Given that El Niño is the only significant temperature oscillation that occurs in that part of the world, we would bet there may be some adaptation going on. In fact, if the jellyfish hadn't somehow adapted to these temperature oscillations, there probably wouldn't be any Jellyfish Lake, would there?

All of this is really unfair to the Gulf of Mexico jellyfish. Why are jellyfish a cute and furry species in Palau and not in the Gulf? Is it because of their "golden" color? Their famous habitat? This should be remedied immediately, and could be, if we simply renamed the Gulf of Mexico "Jellyfish Gulf—the Eighth Biological Wonder of the World," thanks to global warming.

4.5 Penguins and Polar Bears in Peril

Until the koala is threatened by global warming, the suffering of penguins will go a long way toward raising plenty of cash for plenty of concerned ecogroups. Talk about a marquee species! Penguins are far cuter than any button ever seen. They live in little villages where they take care of each other—a lesson for us all. And they appear to be so vulnerable. The climate is harsh. There's not much to eat. They just stand around as the ozone hole gets bigger, Antarctica heats up like, um, a popsicle in an unplugged freezer, and ice chunks the size of small U.S. states (or large counties in Texas) break off. Surely the warming of their Antarctic habitat can bang the gong of global warming. Technically, penguins are birds (see Section 4.2 "Are Birds Dropping?"), but they're just so special and cuddly that they merit their own pages, along with the polar bears.

Anyway, first, the bears.

A 1997 press release from Greenpeace proclaims, "Arctic Habitats in Danger of Global Warming." Purported warming in the western Arctic of 0.75°C (1.35°F) per decade is shrinking the sea ice, which will "affect" the population of ice algae, the basis of the Arctic food chain.

Greenpeace is typical of what the United Nations calls "non-governmental organizations" (NGOs). In Washington, we call them trade associations or lobbyists. Others include the Sierra Club, World Wildlife Fund, the American Association for the Advancement of Science, and so forth—the usual organizations that use global warming scare stories to generate contributions or to feather the nests of their members, which in turn they use to generate more political pressure, which funds more global warming science, prompting more and more scientists to insist that it is the most important problem in history, prompting the writing of this book. NGOs know the value of marquee species. Algae won't do. Polar bears will. Recognizing that, Greenpeace threw in a warm fuzzy—"Polar bear populations could also be affected." In an ironic twist, the "logic" here is that earlier spring melts would "expose bears to the harsh Arctic environment too early."

Bears are smart. They have adapted in droves to the garbage heaps of Churchill, Manitoba, about 500 miles below the Arctic Circle. They make a journey of several hundred miles each year in search of the delicacies buried therein. That disturbance in diet, accompanied by obvious obesity and fertility, is surely greater than what global warming can reverse.

There are other compelling reasons for bear lovers out there not to worry. As shown in Chapter 3, a critical analysis of Arctic temperatures reveals that the temperature has been rather reluctant to warm much beyond where it was 70 years ago. In that analysis, climatologist Rajmund Przybylak reported, "No evidence of any greenhouse warming in the Arctic over the period 1951–1990 is seen." In his examination of 25 stations north of 60 degrees, four have statistically significant cooling trends while only one has a warming trend. In fact, temperatures have been going down at 19 of the 25 stations.

Although the history of average Arctic temperatures at these stations shows no long-term warming whatsoever, trends can be found in the data if different starting points are used in the analysis—*which is precisely what Greenpeace did.* According to its release, "sea ice in the Arctic Ocean has declined 5.5 percent since 1978." Of course, 1978 is near the coldest point in the record. Starting there had better yield a warming trend!

In terms of budget, Greenpeace can't hold a green candle to the World Wildlife Fund (WWF), the richest environmental NGO in history. The amount of distortion on the polar bear story by WWF is proportionally even larger than that from Greenpeace. Its 2002 report, *Polar Bears at Risk,* claims that these furry creatures currently face major difficulties as a result of human-induced global warming. According to WWF, there are currently 22,000 polar bears in 20 somewhat distinct populations across the Arctic. WWF states that 46 percent of those populations are stable, 17 percent in decline, 14 percent increasing, and 23 percent in "unknown" status. Strange math: Any number divided into 20 yields a multiple of 5—5, 10, 15, on to 100. WWF's map (see Figure 4.10 in color insert) shows 19 populations. No whole number divided into 19 yields 14, 17, 23, or 46 either. Once again, the devil of global warming hype appears to be in the details. We added the current status (according to WWF) of the bear populations to its figure.

Climate models predict substantial Arctic warming, but it is important to note that the reductions in sea-ice coverage are really only substantial right at the end of Arctic summer—in August and September. The sun sets at the North Pole on the first day of fall and doesn't return until the first day of spring. At that latitude, it takes maybe a few days for things to freeze back up, and then it's back to "normal" (i.e., a lot of ice) for another 10 months.

WWF's report disregards a study by Canada's Department of Fisheries and Oceans (perhaps an appropriate source given that polar bears eat fish and swim in the ocean) that examined the relationship between sea ice and arctic temperatures. It concluded: "Overall the possible impact of global warming appears to play a minor role in changes to Arctic sea ice: The Department found rather that changes in wind patterns lead to large-scale redistributions of ice rather than finding an overall decline." (For much more on polar ice, see Sections 3.3 through 3.8 of this book.)

Why, for example, did WWF not map out the regions where populations were changing? Once upon a time, scientists were trained to smell large rats when their fellows omitted such things. Figure 4.11 (see color insert) shows the temperature trends for these regions from 1950 through 1995, taken from Przybylak's 2000 study.

Temperatures in the Baffin Bay region (the area between North America and Greenland) are in *decline* and the polar bear population is in *decline*. The largest temperature *increase* is in the Pacific region between Siberia and Alaska, and nearby bear populations in the

North and South Beaufort Sea (just north of Alaska) have *risen*. Over most of the rest of the area, where temperatures show no significant change, neither do the bears.

When the facts are examined, the relationship between polar bear populations and temperature is the opposite of what WWF says it is.

Penguin's Progress

As documented repeatedly in this book, papers continue to appear that support the notion of disastrous climate change—papers that are terribly flawed in either their methods or their analysis. One or two of these might be accidental, but enough on which to base a long book are not. The truth is that journal editors are fully aware of who believes what about climate change, and there is much more "control" in the peer-review process than a person might naturally assume. Perhaps that context explains the 2001 *Nature* paper titled, "Emperor Penguins and Climate Change," by French scientists Christophe Barbraud and Henri Weimerskirch.

Figure 4.12 (top), taken directly from the *Nature* article, shows average winter and summer temperatures recorded near the Dumont d'Urville Station's Emperor penguin colony in Terre Adélie, Antarctica. Figure 4.12 (bottom) shows a large decline in the number of breeding pairs. But please note: There is no evidence of any warming or cooling, and there's a big penguin decline from 1972 to 1982. Given the paper's title, how many readers would get the impression that the authors uncovered no relationship between penguins and climate?

Perhaps it's worth noting that the period of rapid decline in population coincides with the development of Antarctic "ecotourism," which means people visiting the rookeries as well as buzzing them in airplanes. Remember, the biggest thing these birds have seen in their tens of millions of years of evolutionary history is an albatross. A large airliner or a gaggle of tourists might cause quite a stir, moving them off their nests long enough to induce increased mortality. It's easy to freeze an egg at Antarctic temperatures, and we know which must come first: the egg, not the penguin! That is certainly a more plausible explanation than climate change, because it didn't warm up in or near the colony. (In truth, the jury is still out on this one: The British Antarctic Survey, in 2001, actually flew helicopters over a large penguin rookery and reported only transient disturbance; but an attempt with larger, fixed-wing aircraft was scuttled.)

Figure 4.12

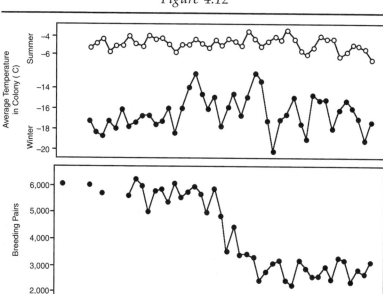

Historical record of winter and summer temperature in the penguin colony (top) and number of breeding pairs observed (bottom).

SOURCE: Barbraud, *Nature*, 2001.

Consider Figure 4.13, a plot of computer-modeled survival estimates of adult male and female penguins against annual sea-surface temperature (SST) departures, using data from 1982–1988. The authors wrote—

> . . . SST accounted for most (89.8 percent) of this yearly variation in survival. Emperor penguins survived less when SSTs were higher. . . . To our knowledge, this is the first time that the consequences of changes in major oceanic parameters on the dynamics of an Antarctic large predator have been identified, and particularly that the proximate and ultimate factors affecting the dynamics of the population have been documented.

How could the reviewers at *Nature* allow such a statement based on only seven years of data, dominated by *one* warm year? Although

Figure 4.13

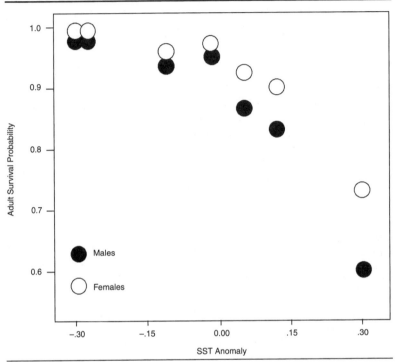

Sea-surface temperature (SST) anomalies vs. survival probability of adult penguins. Notice how this relationship is unduly influenced by the observations from a single very warm year.

SOURCE: Barbraud, *Nature*, 2001.

there are seven data points, they really are not independent measurements because the sea temperature in one year is likely to be pretty close to that of the next year. The statistical correspondence the authors calculate assumes all the observations are independent. The reviewers definitely should have caught this!

As a result, there are really only about two data points, and that simply doesn't supply enough information to any standard of statistical robustness whatever the explained variance between two variables might be when one of the data points is unduly influential. The authors go on to link penguin population changes to sea-ice extent, and conclude that "Emperor penguins may be very suscepti-ble to environmental variability" (Why didn't they just say "global warming"?), and "further long-lasting coupled anomalies are likely to affect their populations."

Then, the predictable press barrage. Here's the coverage from the online *National Geographic News* of May 9, 2001 (beneath a photo-graph of an adult penguin feeding its young):

> ... [r]esearchers have shown that an abnormally long warm spell in the Southern Ocean during the late 1970s contributed to a decline in the population of emperor penguins. ... Terre Adélie experiences a warming period every four or five years that generally lasts about a year. In the late 1970s, however, the warming continued for several years. ... Weimerskirch thinks the unusually warm spell was probably the result of global warming.

But his own data show that isn't true! That is obvious from Figure 4.12, taken directly from his own paper.

A day later, BBC said (beneath the requisite picture of cute pen-guins)—

> French scientists have warned that penguins in the Antarctic could be very susceptible to changes in climate and could be threatened by any long-term temperature shifts. The researchers made their remarks after observing a dramatic decline in the population of one bird colony, which coincided with an abnormal warm period in the Southern Ocean in the 1970s.

Untrue! Again, see Figure 4.12. To the BBC's credit, its reporters did find some British researchers who weren't quite so willing to jump on the global warming/penguin bandwagon. But to the unknowing public, the damage has been done, adding more and more political pressure to reduce carbon dioxide emissions.

Clearly, the authors of the penguin paper, and the editors and reviewers for *Nature*, glibly see a global warming signature in the data that is simply not warranted by the paper's methodology.

One of the fundamental tenets of science is that all results must be viewed with a healthy dose of skepticism. Numerous statistical tests have been devised to overcome that skepticism—to persuade a wary reviewer that a set of results could only very rarely arise by random chance alone. One warm year in a seven-year sample, when there are at best only two or three "independent" observations, provides zero statistical evidence of a climate change impact. The sample is simply not large enough to support any conclusions.

* * * * *

Sure enough, the 2001 flap about penguins also made it to the *New York Times*, which, on June 26 of that year, reported that penguins were in trouble worldwide because of global warming—or at least because of climate changes some people like to link to global warming, things like El Niño and toxic algae blooms.

A colony of Magellenic and Humbolt penguins, whose primary nesting ground is on a narrow peninsula jutting out into the Atlantic Ocean located near the southern end of Argentina's east coast called Punta Tombo, was having a particularly bad breeding year. "The worst ever," Dee Boersma is quoted as saying. Boersma, a researcher whose work is supported by the Wildlife Conservation Society, reports that the colony's population has declined by nearly 30 percent since 1987.

Wildlife Conservation Society researchers blame an increase in El Niño conditions, despite El Niño being primarily a tropical Pacific phenomenon. It has little direct effect in the southern Atlantic Ocean. In fact, 2001 ("the worst ever") was marked by near-normal conditions. Neither El Niño nor its climatic opposite La Niña was present.

Different species of penguins live in a variety of climatic conditions throughout the Southern Hemisphere. Their habitat ranges from Antarctica's frozen shores to the Galapagos Islands' tropical beaches. That means penguins have evolved and adapted to different environments. As these environments change—whether due to changes in climate or for other reasons—the birds' survival depends on their continued adaptation. For example, warmer conditions on Australia's Heard Island, in the southern Indian Ocean, have led to a virtual explosion of marine life, including an increase in the number of King penguin breeding pairs. Where there were only three pairs in 1947, there are more than 25,000 today.

A further demonstration of penguin adaptability can be inferred from reconstruction of long-term temperatures in the Southern Atlantic Ocean (using paleoclimate reconstructions) available in the *Third Assessment Report* of the United Nations Intergovernmental

Figure 4.14

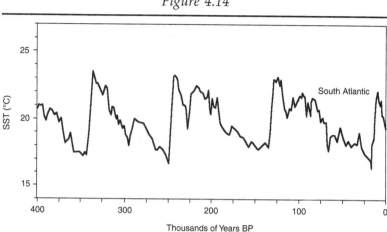

Reconstructed South Atlantic sea-surface temperature.

Source: *Third Assessment Report* of the United Nations Intergovernmental Panel on Climate Change.

Panel on Climate Change. Figure 4.14 shows that there were very large swings in ocean temperature during the past 400,000 years. Because penguins exist today, they must have successfully survived those disruptive climatic events, which certainly would have disturbed the birds' feeding and breeding patterns if temperature/climate changes do so today.

And finally, a good old scientific catfight to coda the penguin story. In 2002, J. P. Croxall of the British Antarctic Survey and several colleagues wrote a review of "Environmental Change and Antarctic Seabird Populations" published in *Science* that included the usual litany of problems penguins face as man continues to recklessly harness energy for the net benefit of global civilization. But in a fairly scathing letter in the April 18 issue of *Science*, penguin expert D. G. Ainley and five coauthors carefully rebut the Croxall arguments about the tenacity of the world's cutest bird.

In general, recent drops in the penguin population have been linked to sea-ice decline, a point Croxall and colleagues highlighted. But Ainley countered that that is only true for the Adélie penguin (the most well-studied of the three penguin species) along the northwestern Antarctic Peninsula, an area that accounts for only about

5 percent of Antarctica's coastline. Elsewhere, despite an alleged widespread decline in sea ice, Adélie penguin populations have in fact been increasing. As sea ice declines, it turns out, longer stretches of coastline become exposed and thus available for the formation of new penguin villages.

Ainley also took umbrage at Croxall's notion of a long-term decline in sea-ice extent. According to Ainley, a widely quoted paper concerning declines in Antarctic sea ice relied on a record of whaling ship positions. But, Ainley points out, reductions in open water whale harvests forced whalers to head toward the coastlines in search of minke whales, which feed closer to pack ice. So the presumed historical trend in sea-ice decline is a phantom. To back up that claim, Ainley cites research that diatoms linked to pack ice retrieved from deep sea cores show that the current winter sea-ice boundary has not changed significantly over thousands of years.

Finally, Croxall made much of Adélie penguin populations' dependence for food on krill, a species some claim is declining in abundance. According to Ainley, that would be a factor only in the northern Bellinghausen Sea region in winter, where sea-ice cover declines indeed have been noted. Even so, penguins primarily feed on krill in summer, along with fish. In winter, when penguins mainly eat fish and squid, krill contribute even less to penguin's diets. As Ainley points out, "the species adjusts its diet depending on prey availability, and diet should not be part of the discussion."

So the bottom line is that these cute little birds are a lot tougher and more versatile than they appear.

4.6 A Universal Migration

The year 2003 began with this shocker: Plants and animals respond to changes in climate! On both coasts (in the *Los Angeles Times* and the *New York Times*) and from many points in between, two articles in *Nature* magazine's first edition of the year received prominent play. According to the assembled researchers, changes in the distribution of species' characteristics are consistent with warming. That species are adaptable to change in their environment is not news. What's shocking, however, is that no one noticed how tiny the reported response appears to be.

In the first article, by Terry Root, the changes work out to an average northward movement of 3.8 miles per *decade*. That's 0.38

mile (or 2,000 *feet* per year). At this rate, the District of Columbia's biological community, for example, can be expected to move all the way to Baltimore by 2102. Is there a disinterested observer who can report to you how woodlands around Baltimore look a lot different than they do in the vicinity of the nation's capital?

Nature would have been the source of a much bigger story if this study had found the opposite to be true—that plants and animals *don't respond* to changes in climate. Were that the case, everything we know about evolution and adaptation would be wrong. So, in effect, the study merely confirms what we already know.

If species failed to alter their behavior in response to environmental changes and simply remained inflexible and inadaptable, they would completely die out every few centuries. In most locales annual climate variation exceeds any recent trend in the mean. That earth is populated with a large array of living organisms is proof positive that inflexibility and inadaptability are not the way things work. Instead, plants and animals actively respond to climate variations and change their behavior. That is precisely what the *Nature* article reports and why it hardly should have generated the coverage it did.

In the second article, researcher Camille Parmesan (the same person who discovered increasing geographic diversity of butterflies in Europe) calculates observed changes in the onset of spring that indicate, at the current rate of change, spring 2103 in Washington, D.C., will arrive at the time it does today in Raleigh, North Carolina.

What appears to have driven coverage of this research is that it indicates what can be expected from a warming climate. Both articles support the observation that the near-surface global temperature is warming. But the surface-based thermometer network has told us that for years. The argument is not whether surface temperatures have been warming for the past 30 years or so (or since the end of the Little Ice Age in the mid-1800s, for that matter). Rather, what is at issue is what *causes* the surface warming and how much warming we reasonably can expect in the future.

An Increasing Warming Trend?

These reports followed a report that appeared three weeks earlier from Reuters claiming a "quarter-century pattern of accelerated warming." The *Los Angeles Times* headline read: "Unprecedented stretch continued this year, the second warmest on record, suggesting the

Figure 4.15

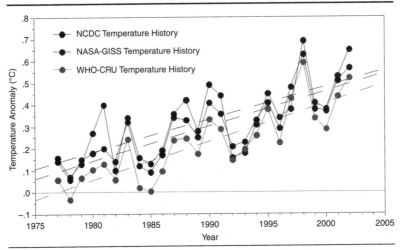

The annual temperature history from 1977 to 2002 from the three primary global temperature data sets: National Climatic Data Center (NCDC), National Aeronautics and Space Administration–Goddard Institute for Space Studies (NASA-GISS), and the World Meteorological Organization–Climate Research Unit (WHO-CRU). Trends in these data sets are linear, not curvilinear as they would be if the rate of warming were accelerating.

planet is heating more rapidly than expected." The problem is that there are no data to support these claims.

Recall that the world emerged from a three-decade-long cooling trend rather suddenly in the mid-1970s with an event that has come to be known as "The Great Pacific Climate Shift," when an enormous volume of warm water bubbled from the central Pacific's subsurface to its surface. Ever since, the world has been in a warming trend.

Figure 4.15 depicts the temperature history contained in the three commonly cited global temperature records since 1977. That's near the beginning of the recent warming. If press reports about *accelerated* warming are correct, those temperature histories should curve upward, not simply head upward as a straight line. Although there is quite a bit of year-to-year variation in the average global temperature (arising from such events as the eruptions of El Chichon in 1982 and Mount Pinatubo in 1991, and the large El Niños of 1982–1983

104

Figure 4.16

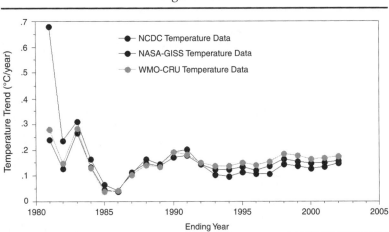

The temperature trends in these three data sets begin in 1977 and end in the year indicated. There is no evidence the trends are increasing.

and 1997–1998), there is no indication that the shape of the overall trend is anything but linear.

Figure 4.16 illustrates these data in a different way. Each point on the graph represents the average annual temperature trend calculated from the temperature data beginning in 1977 and ending at the time indicated on the graph's horizontal axis. For example, the first point represents the temperature trend from 1977 to 1981. The last point represents the trend from 1977 to 2002. Obviously, the more data that go into the trend calculations, the less the trend jumps around from year to year. In other words, the change from point to point on the right-hand side of the graph is much smaller than on the left-hand side. If there were a trend toward accelerating warming, then the data should trend upward. They don't.

Instead, the real story should have been that the earth's climate continues to warm at the rate that began over a quarter-century ago, and that, as predicted by evolutionary theory, there's some evidence that the earth's biota show an adaptive response. Big deal.

4.7 Mad Cows and Englishmen

Late in 2000, H. R. H. the Prince of Wales blamed "mankind's arrogant disregard for the balance of nature" as a source of the storms battering the United Kingdom and Europe, and the outbreak of mad cow disease, according to an Environmental News Service report datelined London November 7.

"Some recent occurrences such as the [mad cow disease] disaster and even perhaps—dare I say it—the present severe weather conditions in our country are, I have no doubt, the consequence of mankind's arrogant disregard for nature. We have to find a way of ensuring that our remarkable and seemingly beneficial advances in technology do not just become the agents of our own destruction," Prince Charles told the Millennium Festival of Medicine meeting in London.

With all due respect, then, a tutorial to the man who would be king and other amateur climatologists:

Climate Axiom No. 1: Single weather events cannot be associated with climate change.

Climate is the sum total of *all weather events* occurring over *long* time periods. Single events, while certainly contributing to the makeup of climate in a particular region, do not—themselves—alter climate. Only *a large number* of events occurring over a long period of time cause an alteration in typical weather patterns. Even the United Nations Intergovernmental Panel on Climate Change disagrees with the prince. From page 5 of its *Third Assessment Report*:

> Changes globally in tropical and extra-tropical storm intensity and frequency are dominated by inter-decadal and multi-decadal variations, with no significant trends evident over the 20th century.

Climate Axiom No. 2: Historical data (and literature) should first be consulted before one asserts discernment of a change in climate. In this case, those data show the annual number of North Atlantic storms has been *declining* during the past 30 years between latitudes 30°N and 60°N, as noted in a 1997 paper by Mark Serreze published in the *Journal of Climate*.

Climate Axiom No. 3: As Niccolo Machiavelli might have counseled his prince, it is imprudent to use a single example in an effort to prove a point when numerous counter-examples exist.

Much is made, lately, of general circulation models (GCMs) that project an increase of storm activity across Great Britain and the rest of Europe. However, they ignore climate models that predict the opposite. Here's what the IPCC said in its 1996 *Second Assessment Report*:

> Clearly there is little agreement between models on the changes in storminess that might occur in a warmer world. Conclusions regarding extreme storm events are obviously even more uncertain.

4.8 A Massive Extinction of Logic

A January 2004 paper published in *Nature* by Chris Thomas and 18 coauthors claiming that global warming will cause a massive extinction of the earth's biota made the front page of the *Washington Post*, in which Thomas minced no words: "We're talking about 1.25 million species. It's a massive number." Thomas et al. performed an interesting exercise in modeling. They used an accepted logarithmic relationship between the area of an ecosystem and the number of species within. Using this function as a starting point, the researchers examined the current distributional area of 1,103 plant and animal species from different parts of the earth, and related that to temperature, rainfall, and seasonality. Then, using the output from various climate models, under scenarios that produced low, mid, and high ranges of future global temperature change, they calculated the area of the regions that were defined by the same climate values as the current species distribution.

As an example, if a particular bird species in Europe is currently found in a region that gets no hotter than 35°C in the summer and no colder than 0°C in the winter, it is assumed that those same climate definitions will bound the species' range in the future. If the range defined by those climatic conditions becomes smaller under projected future climate conditions, the species comes under pressure of extinction. If it stays the same or expands, the species is categorized as not facing increased extinction pressure. It is clear that this methodology can only lead to a reduced number of species (i.e., a growing number of extinctions). In other words, climate change is the sole driver of biodiversity in this calculation.

That assumption, however, is incorrect. Consider the effects on an ecosystem of the mutation of some previously harmless bacterium, a clearly nonclimatic cause of extinction. Or consider that human beings have a habit of literally changing the face of the earth. The

American Midwest used to be a vast and biologically diverse prairie. Now it's largely covered by two species, corn and soybeans. If such a diverse ecosystem can literally disappear without any obvious consequences, species extinction surely rates as yet another exaggerated issue.

But placing the entire onus for extinction on climate, as Thomas et al. did, calls their entire result into question. They calculate percentage species extinctions for a variety of future climate scenarios. One, with a lower limit of 0.8°C of warming in the next 50 years, produces an extinction of roughly 20 percent of the sampled species. That demands a convenient reality check: Surface temperatures indeed *have* risen this amount in the last 100 years. But there is absolutely *no* evidence for massive climate-related extinctions. (You would think the reviewers of that manuscript would have picked that up!)

There are several other major problems:

1. Global climate models, in general, predict a warmer surface and an increased rate of rainfall. In general, as long as there is adequate moisture, the most diverse ecosystems on earth are in the warmest regions, the tropical rainforest being the prime example. Consequently, the general character of future climate is one that is more—not less—hospitable for biodiversity.

2. Temperatures have been bouncing up and down a lot more than 0.8°C in the last several hundred thousand years. But Thomas's methodology implies that there are large extinctions for each and every increment of equivalent change, whether the temperature goes up or down. Warming will squeeze the distribution of species to the north, and cooling will compress it against the tropics.

   It is quite clear that the era from 4,000 to 7,000 years ago was 1°C to 2°C warmer than today, for example, and the rapid climate changes that took place before then, at the end of the last major glacial era, were multiple in nature, both up and down. Before then, there was the dramatic change known as the glaciation itself, when ice covered much of North America. Applying this method to all those changes should cause the extinction of just about every species on Earth!

3. Species often thrive well outside their gross climatic "envelope." The U.S. Department of Agriculture has mapped the

distribution of all major tree species in North America. For almost every species, there are separate "disjunct" populations far away from the main climatic distribution. A fine example is the balsam fir, *Abies balsamea*, whose main distribution is across Canada. But there is a tiny forest of the same remaining in eastern Iowa, hundreds of miles south (and about 10 degrees warmer) than the climatic "envelope" that Thomas et al. assume circumscribes the species. These disjuncts are the rule, not the exception, and are one reason why the most diverse ecosystem on earth—the tropical rainforest—managed to survive the Ice Age.

The "disjuncts" exist because climate is simply not as uniform as it is calculated to be by gross climate models. Variations in topography and landform create cul-de-sacs where species survive and thrive far away from their climatic envelopes. It is more logical to assume that a fractionating climate will produce more disjuncts, not fewer.

4. Thomas et al. make what the famed agronomist Paul Waggoner has called the "dumb people" assumption: that in the face of a massive extinction there will be no human adaptation or mitigation of the prospect. In fact we have been preserving diversity artificially, in the form of parks and zoos, for centuries.

   In addition, the amount of "artificial" genetic diversity is rising dramatically with the technology of modern genetics. It is difficult to imagine, decades from now, that these technologies will not be applied to ameliorate some prospective massive extinction.

Obviously, there is a lot to criticize in that paper. What is surprising is that something with such inconsistencies and unrealistic assumptions made it unscathed through the review process in such a prestigious journal as *Nature*.

5. Spin Cycle: Hurricanes, Tornadoes, and Other Cyclones

> Florida is a land that we call paradise, but it happens to be a peninsula sticking down into the middle of something known as Hurricane Highway. Hurricanes are a part of our life, and global warming foretells, for us, an increased intensity of hurricanes and an increased frequency of hurricanes
>
> —Sen. Bill Nelson (D-Fla.), June 8, 2001

5.1 Love Those Hurricanes!

In the fall of 2002, how did Tropical Storm Isidore, a weenie by hurricane standards, manage to knock Saddam Hussein off the top of the news? That's because, in news currency, the word "hurricane" rhymes with "war."

Given that in almost every year many hurricanes have the potential to hit U.S. shores, it is astounding how few are real monsters. A really destructive storm, Category 4 or 5 on the 1-to-5 Saffir-Simpson rating scale, crosses a U.S. coast about once every seven years or so. The last of the three Category 5s that have hit since good records began in 1872 was Hurricane Andrew in 1992, over a decade ago. But each and every one, monster or not, beneficial or deadly, seems to bump to news story Numero Uno.

There was a signal event that crystallized the relationship between hurricanes and television. In September 1961, big, mean Hurricane Carla blew up southwest of Cuba, somehow managing to avoid the Yucatan Peninsula, a great wrecker of huge storms. As Carla sashayed languorously northwestward through an overheated Gulf of Mexico, the news director for KHOU-TV in Houston, a young fellow by the name of Dan Rather, had an idea. He convinced CBS network headquarters in New York to extend their then 15-minute national news (oh, for a return to those halcyon days!) for an additional quarter-hour while he pontificated (something he was already pretty good at) from the Galveston Seawall.

At that time, few people knew that Galveston was the site of the greatest disaster in American history, when 6,000 to 10,000 people died in the Great Hurricane of 1900. Rather was happy to educate on this matter.

Pathos, bathos, unpredictability, beauty, and death—Carla had it all and Dan had the story. It sold so much airtime that within six months CBS switched to a full half-hour of national news, bringing in Walter Cronkite and hiring Dan Rather away from Houston to the headquarters at Black Rock in the Big Apple.

Though the hurricane severity scale wasn't in existence at the time, Carla actually hit Category 5 right off the Texas coast before stalling around and "weakening" to a Category 4. Mercifully, it chose sparsely populated Matagorda Bay and the small town of Port Lavaca for its big splash. After all the hype, there really wasn't much D&D (Death and Destruction) film to be found.

But this model of hurricane reporting caught on like gangbusters, creating some heroes but mostly spectacular failures (wind just isn't very photogenic) and continually generating more and more and more weather hysteria. Associated advertising revenue created the market for the world's only 24/7 weather show, the cable-TV success known as the Weather Channel. A measure of the uniquely American preoccupation with day-to-day weather is evident from the fact that the Weather Channel-Europe was a smashing failure, and it's going to be mañana, mañana, and mañana before TWC makes money in Mexico or South America.

The drumbeats continued. At the end of September 1985, TV went All Gloria, All the Time, as the Category 4 spun up north of Haiti—Destination: East Coast. Here was a sure repeat of the Great New England Hurricane of 1938, the storm of record for the region that drowned downtown Providence, Rhode Island, under 12 feet of water. Since then, television was invented and has been waiting ever since for a rerun. The 1938 storm was a high Category 3—which is as big as anything is going to be by the time it hits New England, owing to cooler waters north of the Gulf Stream.

Needless to say, Dan Rather was all over Gloria, but he was more all over Neil Frank, the mediagenic director of the National

Hurricane Center. Though there wasn't anything specific in the live interview on September 27, anyone with an ear for tone could pick up the exasperation in Rather's voice that Gloria didn't wreck enough lives and property to merit its coverage. Frank eventually left the center to do television weather in, of all places, Houston, which pays a lot more and has a lot less stress than being the world's chief hurricane forecaster.

Rather was persistent. Sooner or later he'd get his Big One. Exactly three years later, Hurricane Gilbert hit Category 5 in the western Caribbean, at the same time setting the record for the lowest barometric pressure ever measured in the western hemisphere. (Windspeed in a hurricane is inversely correlated with pressure, so you get the idea.)

Gilbert's forecast path wasn't that much different from Carla's, with only a bare brushing of the northeast tip of the Yucatan Peninsula. Next Stop: Houston, as a Category 5 express train, a lead-pipe cinch to be the most destructive cyclone in American history. Rather took the jet to Texas, and also took everyone with him to cover the storm of the century.

Gilbert had other ideas. It did manage to whack Cozumel Island, but hit far enough south on the Peninsula that it lingered most of the day over the Yucatan, emerging relaxed and refreshed into the Bay of Campeche as a mere Category 2. Not to worry, all the computer models and all the Hurricane Center's men rapidly screwed Gilbert together again, perhaps as high as a Category 5, still waiting for a date with Dan.

Didn't happen. Instead of turning north toward CBS, Gilbert continued a beeline for the Mexican coast, burbling across the Bay of Campeche as a garden-variety storm, finally wading ashore at a little town called La Pesca, which appropriately translates as "the Fish." With so much of the news staff trapped in Texas, 28 of the 30-minute national CBS News on September 16 was devoted to a U.S. natural disaster that never happened.

This constant hype has consequences. Everyone now thinks hurricanes are getting worse; that is, everyone except those of us who study them. Some even think it's global warming that is making them worse. So we must stop global warming, and adopt the expensive Kyoto Protocol.

Figure 5.1

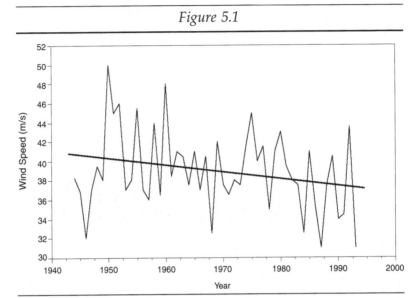

Average maximum winds measured in Atlantic Hurricanes.

SOURCE: Landsea, 1996.

A measure of the disconnection between hurricane hype and reality can be appreciated by looking at Figures 5.1 and 5.2. Figure 5.1 is the average maximum wind measured in Atlantic Basin hurricanes since 1945, which is when "hurricane hunter" aircraft monitoring began. Figure 5.2, which most people would think is some plot relating to hurricane intensity, is actually the number of news stories appearing per month about hurricanes and global warming based on a Lexis-Nexis search.

Increasing Frequency?

With all the talk of global warming potentially increasing the frequency and/or intensity of severe weather events such as hurricanes and tornadoes, the following news may surprise.

When Hurricane Lili made landfall on the Louisiana coast in October 2002, it marked the end of the second-longest period since 1900 that passed between hurricanes making landfall on the U.S. mainland. The penultimate hurricane to hit the United States was Irene, which crossed the southern tip of the Florida peninsula on

Figure 5.2

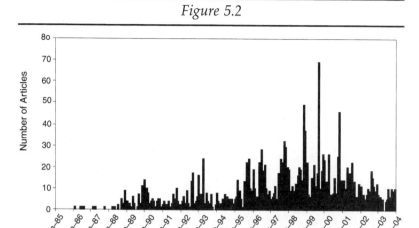

Number of stories appearing per month about hurricanes and global warming.

SOURCE: Lexis-Nexis search.

October 15, 1999—almost three years earlier. The previous record-holder for the longest time between U.S. landfalling hurricanes was the period from August 9, 1980's Hurricane Allen to August 18, 1983's Hurricane Alicia. The only other time that more than two years passed between landfalls was from late September 1929 to early September 1932.

If global warming were increasing the frequency of Atlantic basin hurricanes, and thus increasing the threat to the Gulf and Atlantic coasts, you'd think that long periods between storms would be a thing of the past.

But obviously that is not the case. A century-long look at the annual number of hurricanes that have made landfall on the U.S. mainland (Figure 5.3) reveals nothing that would indicate global warming is having any effect on these occurrences. That is, unless you make something of the fact that the average number of hurricanes per year that hit the United States during 1901–1950 was 1.94, while during 1951–2001 that number dropped to 1.41. That's a full half a storm less per year.

Figure 5.3

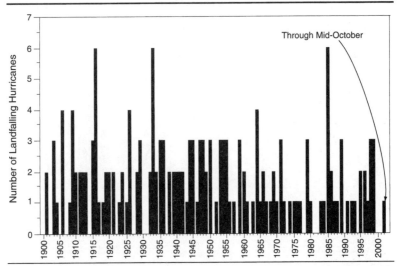

Number of hurricanes making landfall on U.S. shores, January 1900 to mid-October 2002.

SOURCE: http://www.nhc.noaa.gov.

Considering that the damage costs from a hurricane run from hundreds of millions to tens of billions of dollars, a reduction of half a storm a year is nothing to sneeze at.

Whatever the reason, let's hope that this pattern keeps up, especially given the increasing amount of wealth that pours into our coastal communities every year fueled by folks looking for something else to do with their money besides invest it in the stock market.

5.2 Tornado Deaths Declining

> These superpowerful tornadoes are the kind of storm we're likely to see more of with global climate change ... with energy added to the atmosphere, more frequent and intense storms are a probable outcome.
>
> —Tom Toles, text accompanying editorial cartoon, May 7, 2003, *Washington Post*

No doubt about it, May 2003 was a very good month for tornadoes, even by the spinny standards of late spring, which normally has the most twisters. And, even more predictable than the development of severe storms in spring, prominent people in the media would try to to tie them to global warming. Witness Tom Toles's cartoon in the May 7 *Washington Post* that intoned "these superpowerful tornadoes are the kind of storm we're likely to see more of with global climate change."

Perhaps a mere cartoonist deserves a break, even an editorial cartoonist. But how many examples are there of scientists, scientific reviewers, or the media not checking the most rudimentary facts before making assertions about climate change? Tons of tornado data are only a few mouseclicks away, and they show that Toles was dead wrong in his implication that the recent terrible storms show any link to the slight warming of the atmosphere that has occurred in recent decades. In fact, just the opposite may be occurring, despite a perception of increased storminess.

The number of overall reported tornadoes has increased for decades, but the number of deaths has dropped—as has the number of tornadoes in the most damaging classes. Everything else being equal, tornado deaths should have nearly doubled in the last 50 years because of increasing population. Obviously something else is intervening: technology. In an obvious adaptation to the threat of severe weather and climate, the United States has developed the most advanced tornado observation and warning system in the world.

This seems only natural in the nation that experiences far more tornadoes, owing to its peculiar geography, than any other on earth, where the warmth of a truly tropical ocean (the Gulf of Mexico) is separated from the cold of the Arctic by nothing more than a barbed wire fence. Most other midlatitude locations have some type of obstruction—either a cold ocean or a mountain range—between such heat and cold.

The lifesaving technology is radar. Because of a terrible 1953 tornado in Worchester, Massachusetts (far away from the Oklahoma and Texas "tornado alley"), the Weather Bureau (today's National Weather Service) embarked on a crash program to develop a national network of weather radar to provide better warnings. Spearheaded by David Atlas and Ted Fujita (whose "F-scale" rates tornado severity on a 1-to-5 basis, just as is done for hurricanes), meteorologists soon learned that when the radar paints a thunderstorm that looks more like a comma than a blob, there's often a tornado buried in the curliest point.

It took several years for the original radars, known as WSR-57s, to cover the country, but by 1970 the job was pretty much complete. As more radars came online, more and more tornadoes were reported. It's interesting that as this network stabilized, from 1970 through 1990, so did the number of tornadoes, as shown in Figure 5.4.

Around then, a new network began to take shape that was even better at detecting potential twisters. Instead of just painting a picture of a thunderstorm, the new machines, called Doppler radars and designated as WSD-88s, actually measure the change in velocity in a storm by tracking the movement of raindrops. When those drops start to rotate, it's not long before there's a tornado warning. The rotation fields often develop before the comma shape, which means more tornado warnings, faster. Those warnings get people's attention, saving more and more lives. Not surprisingly, the number of tornadoes increased again, this time proportional to the number of WSD-88s, which now blanket the nation.

Any reporter (or cartoonist) doing his homework might have asked if indeed the number of killer storms (categories 3 to 5 on the Fujita scale) are increasing. The fact is that the vast majority of tornadoes are in the weenier classes. Only about 5 percent reach category 3 or higher. As shown in Figure 5.4, there's actual evidence for a decline in the frequency of these storms.

Where does the notion come from that tornadoes must increase because of global warming? Another panel in Toles's cartoon reads, "With energy added to the atmosphere, more frequent and intense storms are a probable outcome." Tornadoes occur because a portion of a normally quiescent thunderstorm begins to spin. That spinning is done in large part by a southerly dip ("trough" in Weather Channel parlance) in the strong westerly winds (the "jet stream," in common parlance) that sometimes penetrates the United States when thunderstorms are common. The jet stream is the result of the temperature contrast between the poles and the tropics. Global warming reduces this contrast (warming the poles much more than the tropics) and reduces the spin.

If tornadoes merely resulted from heating, most would occur in June, July, and August. But tornado season peaks in May. And speaking of heat and tornadoes, why are there so many in Mississippi

Figure 5.4

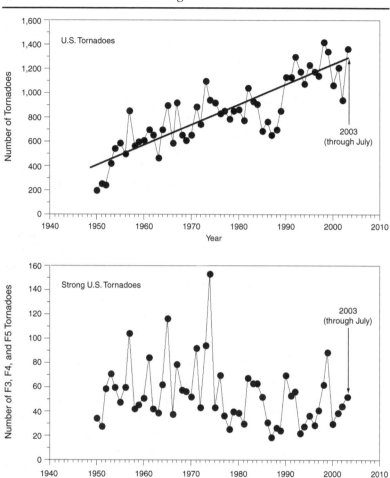

Top: Total number of tornadoes, 1950 to 2002; bottom: total number of severe tornadoes (Fujita Scale F3, F4, and F5).

SOURCE: http://www.spc.noaa.gov.

in February? The key ingredient that spins garden-variety thunderstorms into killer tornadoes—the jet stream—is missing during the hottest part of the year, having migrated north to Canada for the summer. Warm it up, and the migration will start earlier and will move even farther north.

So global warming may actually explain why the number of severe tornadoes is declining. They may be running out of spin, unlike stories attempting to relate these destructive storms to global climate change.

Despite this whirlwind of hype, the number of people killed by tornadoes is also at a very low ebb. The U.S. Department of Commerce began keeping tornado-death statistics in 1950 (Figure 5.5), and it is pretty apparent that the number per year in the second half of the last half of the 20th century (54 per year) is significantly less than in the period 1950–1975 (121 per year).

People who think that humans will not adapt to the gradual climate changes expected in the next century ought to take heart from America's adaptation to the most concentrated wind storms between the sun and Jupiter.

5.3 Spinning Up Hurricanes, Naturally

The thesis of this book, detailed in Chapter 11, is that the way we do science forces exaggeration, and that the scientific community itself recognizes economic gain, as evidenced by their remarkably lenient reviews of highly flawed technical papers on climate change. But there's no hard and fast rule that says this must apply in every case—the thesis merely asserts that there will be a tendency for this to occur more than a tendency for it not to occur.

And that seems true on its face. A person would be hard put to find scientists in prime-time news (at least on the "majors"—CBS, NBC, ABC, and "Public" television) arguing that global warming is inconsequential. And if they appear, as I have, they are often (rightly) cast in the minority, also consistent with this book's thesis. But critics of the lurid notion of climate change can and do appear, and so do articles in the major journals. They're just much fewer and farther between than their counterparts. Here's a prominent example:

A major article in a 2001 issue of *Science* magazine, with the attendant big press coverage, declared that we are now in a climate regime that spells a big increase in major landfalling hurricanes along the U.S. East Coast. *And, for a change, no one blamed global warming!*

Figure 5.5

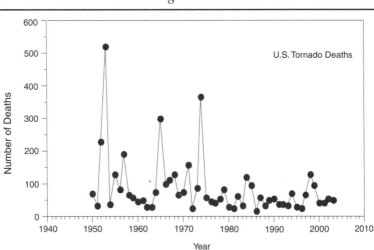

Annual deaths from tornadoes in the United States, January 1950 to July 2003.

SOURCE: http://www.spc.noaa.gov.

Adaptation to Nature's Worst

In 1998, Hurricane Mitch, which had descended from Category 5 over the ocean to a mere Category 1 at landfall, managed to kill perhaps 10,000 people in Central America.

In August 2004, Category 4 Hurricane Charley slammed into the modular-home ghetto of Punta Gorda, Florida, and approximately 9,980 fewer people died. Before the month was out, Hurricane Frances deluged the Florida East Coast with rainfall that would have likely killed thousands in Bangladesh or Honduras. Instead, as noted in the September 9, 2004, *Washington Post*, "Man Defeated Nature" thanks to the massive flood-control system built by the Army Corps of Engineers.

In fact, it was about natural cycles in hurricane activity. Careful examination of long-term records shows quiescent periods followed by more active ones. In their *Science* article, Stanley Goldenberg and three colleagues suggested that a major climate swing recently took

121

place, probably in the mid-1990s, and that we are in for 10 to 40 years of big Atlantic hurricanes—not because of global warming, but just because of the natural variations in hurricane frequency and intensity.

Since 1944, when aircraft reconnaissance made hurricane records more reliable, we have averaged three major hurricanes a year. But, between the mid-1990s and 2001, there has been a noticeable increase in that number (the 1950s were also an active period).

A look at the history of sea-surface temperatures (SSTs) in the Atlantic's main hurricane development region provides a clue (see Figure 5.6 in color insert): From 1930 to 1970, we saw a period of high SSTs and therefore more major storms; the low SSTs from 1970 to 1994 correspond with reduced hurricane activity in that period. One year later—in 1995—we transitioned back toward above-normal sea-surface temperatures. There we have been ever since, which means it's no surprise that we have been seeing more hurricane activity of late.

Observations show those periods of above- or below-normal sea-surface temperatures tend to last for several decades—which leads the authors to conclude we are heading into an extended period of active hurricanes and therefore of greater risk to the U.S. Gulf and Atlantic coasts. This is bad news for the people who were lulled into developing expensive coastal property during the recent quiet period.

Much to their credit, the authors nip the global warming connection in the bud very clearly. In brief, they write—

> One may ask whether the increase in activity since 1995 is due to anthropogenic global warming. The historical multi-decadal-scale variability in Atlantic hurricane activity is much greater than what would be "expected" from a gradual temperature increase attributed to global warming. ... Some studies document an increase in activity [from global warming] while others suggest a decrease. Tropical North Atlantic SST has exhibited a warming trend of ~0.3°C over the last 100 years; whereas Atlantic hurricane activity has not exhibited trendlike variability, but rather distinct multi-decadal cycles.

Could it be that we're simultaneously transitioning into a period of responsible press coverage of global warming issues? Or is this just an anomaly? Judging from the number of exaggerated global warming stories detailed in this book, Goldenberg's candor looks like the proverbial exception that proves the rule.

5.4 A Sea-Plus for *USA Today*

"Boom on the Beach," an article in the July 24, 2004, edition of *USA Today*, seems all too familiar to those of us in the education biz. A professor in a charitable mood might grade it C+, sternly scribbling across the top, "Not your best work." After all, C+ is an unusually low grade for a newspaper that has been more even-handed than most on the subject of climate change.

The core of the article was that there is more and more property damage in recent decades at our nation's beaches. This much is true: More and more Americans live along hurricane-prone beaches (a dubious investment of one's life savings, to be sure). But the article goes on to blame increasingly costly beachfront destruction along U.S. coastlines on "the rising ocean" primarily caused by global warming. "Since 1995," it notes, "there has been a sharp rise in hurricane activity."

Our previous section dealt with that one. The rise seems pretty natural and comes on the heels of some pretty weak hurricane years—in fact, as shown in Figure 5.6, some pretty weak hurricane *decades*.

USA Today's sidebar cites "two major causes" for sea-level rise along the East Coast. Cause No. 1? "The ocean is warming." And No. 2? "The land is sinking." An accompanying graphic shows two beakers of water—one less than half-full and the other full—with the caption, "Water warmed by 10 degrees takes up an extra 0.1 percent of volume."

Talk about the innumeracy of the press! Somehow the picture manages to represent an increased volume of 0.1 percent as more than 100 percent. *USA Today's* graphic only misleads the American public by a factor of 1,000.

Research, available in numerous and easily accessed scientific journals, shows that the global sea-level rise due to warming has at best been a few inches. As for the one-foot rise along the Eastern Seaboard, that's largely because the land is sinking from geological processes. But somehow "Land sinking!" doesn't seem as politically correct as "Sea rising!"—even if it is more accurate.

Figure 5.7

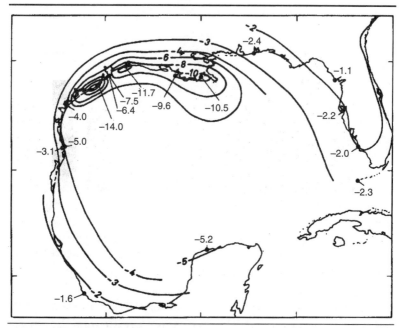

The Gulf Coast has seen a dramatic change in relative sea level over the past century because of falling land level. Along the Texas coast, tide gauge readings show a land subsidence rate of between 0.16 to 0.55 inches per year (4.1 to 15.0 millimeters per year), or about 16 to 55 inches over the course of the past century.

SOURCE: Aubrey and Emery, 1991.

Figure 5.7 shows the rate of apparent sea-level rise along the Gulf Coast during the past 100 years or so. At Galveston, Texas, the change has been nearly four feet because of—you guessed it—land sinking, a result of the extraction of fossil fuels, the area's geology, and the Mississippi River. Only about 7 percent (maximum) of that total can be ascribed to dreaded global warming.

Figure 5.8 shows U.S. hurricane strikes by decades back to 1900. If anything, the 1990s are a bit below the long-term mean. As for hurricane activity since 1995, see the previous section. Global warming? *Nope.*

Figure 5.8

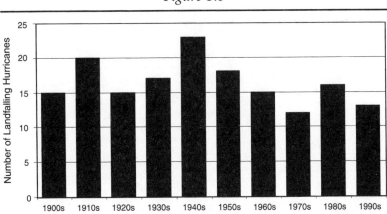

The number of hurricanes making landfall in the United States broken down by decade. By comparison, the decade of the 1990s was unremarkable.

SOURCE: http:www.nhc.noaa.gov.

But who cares about perspective? According to *USA Today*, "Weather experts say 1999 recorded the most violent hurricanes for one year." Here? Where?

The United States got hit by three storms. One was a Category 1 (the weakest of the five categories), and two were Category 3s. The first of these (Hurricane Bret) killed a grand total of two people, both indirectly as a result of a car accident. The other, Hurricane Floyd, was very wet indeed, but didn't pack nearly the power of the 15 Category 4 and 5 storms that hit the United States during the last century.

6. Droughts and Floods: Worse and Worse?

> The floods are more frequent. The droughts are more severe, with far more costly results and more often.
>
> —Sen. Robert Byrd (D-W.Va.), June 8, 2001

> Droughts will be pervasive.
>
> —Sen. James Jeffords (I-Vt.), February 14, 2002

> Warmer temperatures will lead to ... prospects for more severe droughts and/or floods in some places and less severe droughts and/or floods in other places.
>
> —Summary for Policymakers, *Climate Change, 1995,* United Nations Intergovernmental Panel on Climate Change (IPCC)

The UN's remarkable 1995 statement allows anyone to blame any moisture anomaly on global warming. Further, because it was contained in a report from the IPCC, it can be cited as the "consensus of scientists," as the IPCC likes to bill itself. More darkly, anyone who might disagree with such a statement is immediately out of the "consensus."

Here we examine just a few of the resultant blunders relating to floods and droughts.

6.1 Is the United States Wetter Because of Global Warming?

Because of the UN's vacuous statement about warming, droughts, and floods, it's easy for any climate demagogue to stand in front of a flood or drought and blame global warming (or, it might be added, to blame subzero temperatures on global warming, as Al Gore did on January 15, 2004, vetoing the First Law of Thermodynamics).

Here's the logic. Rainfall is increasing in the United States. Global temperatures have risen in the last 100 years. Therefore global warming is increasing U.S. precipitation.

This is a classic mis-mixing of correlation and causation. Let's try an analogy. People who smoke die of lung cancer. A high percentage of smokers carry matches. Therefore matches cause cancer.

Instead of correlation, *causation*—an actual link between two atmospheric phenomena—is much more difficult to prove. In scientific terms, a causal link requires a theoretically logical hypothesis that is consistent with observed data. In fact, science rather poorly understands the relationship between temperature and precipitation—if indeed one exists at all. For example, one line of reasoning goes like this: Warm air when saturated has much more water than does cool air, therefore, when temperatures rise, so should the amount of precipitation. Another goes: When conditions are dry, the sun's energy can go more toward raising the air temperature than toward evaporating moisture, therefore, dryness should lead to higher temperatures. A little thought makes clear that these two notions don't jibe very well.

But both obviously contain some truth. After all, warmth and wetness must in some places coexist to produce the massive tropical rainforests of South America and Africa, while warmth and aridity conspire to create the Saharan and Sonora deserts.

When theories compete, data should serve as the arbiter. Figure 6.1 shows the annual temperature history, the annual precipitation history, and the relationship between the two for the United States since 1895. Notice several things: (1) Temperatures were high in the 1930s and 1940s, low in the 1960s and 1970s, and high again in the 1980s and 1990s. (2) There has been a very gradual, century-long increase in precipitation. (3) There is no relationship between annual temperature and annual precipitation in the United States.

To make these points a bit clearer, Figure 6.2 shows the temperature and precipitation data aggregated into decades. Here it is easy to see that the warmest two decades of the 20th century were the 1930s and the 1990s. It is also easy to see that the 1990s are the wettest decade (warmer temperatures associating with wetter conditions) and the 1930s are the driest (warmer temperatures associating with drier conditions).

So the observations don't seem to be helping us much to determine which theory is dominant. But there is more to look at than just

Figure 6.1

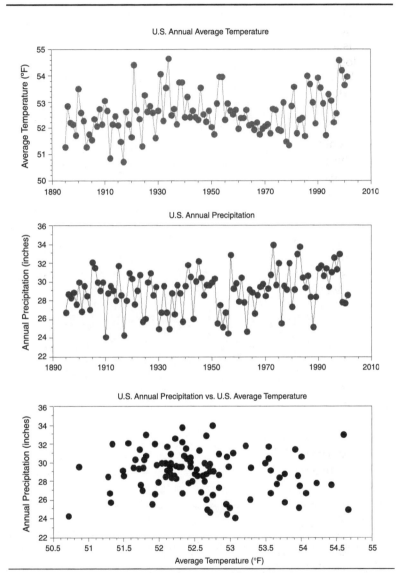

U.S. annual average temperature (top), annual total precipitation (middle), and the relationship between the two (bottom), from 1895 to 2001.

SOURCE: http://www.ncdc.noaa.gov.

Figure 6.2

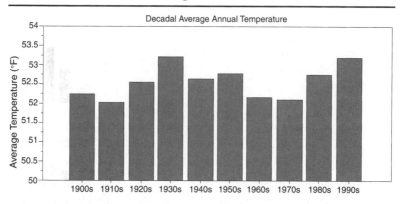

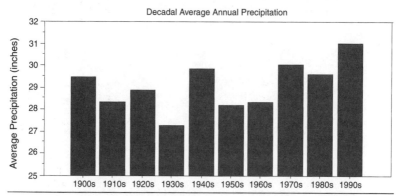

Decadal average annual U.S. temperature (top) and decadal average annual
U.S. total precipitation (bottom).

SOURCE: http://www.ncdc.noaa.gov.

annual precipitation. For instance, what about the possibility that
temperature is not so much related to total annual precipitation, but
instead related to the intensity of daily precipitation events? That
might be implied in the UN's statement about "more intense floods"
in "some places."

To investigate that possibility, count the number of precipitation
events of a particular magnitude that occurred each year at 54 long-
term, high-quality observing stations scattered across the United
States for the period 1910–1993. (The number of stations in this

130

Figure 6.3

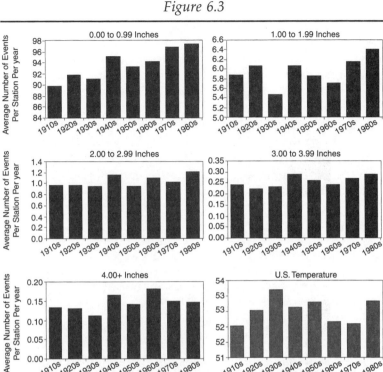

Average number of events per station per year for various daily precipitation-event categories (0 to 0.99 inches, etc.) by decade. For comparison, see the U.S. average annual temperature by decade in the lower right panel.

SOURCE: http://www.ncdc.noaa.gov.

data set with data after 1993 drops off rapidly, so it becomes less representative of the nation as a whole.)

Figure 6.3 shows the results. There is an obvious increase in the frequency of light rain events in the latter decades, and increases in the 1-, 2-, and 3-inch classes are also statistically significant. But there is no change at all in the heaviest category—events of 4 or more inches per day, which are likely to cause flooding. Comparison of these charts with decadal average temperatures, shown in the lowest right, shows no obvious relationship of any of the rainfall classes with decadal average temperatures. Again, these precipitation patterns seem to bear little relationship with temperature.

So where does this leave us? It is clear that there is no relationship between temperature and precipitation in the United States. Some warm decades are marked by low precipitation and a paucity of heavy events, while other warm decades are characterized by high annual totals and an increased frequency of heavy events. Cooler decades show everything in between. Definitive statements, therefore, relating global warming to a change in precipitation here—be they toward more droughts or more floods—are not supported by the observed history. About the only thing we do know is that there has been a gradual increase of about 10 percent in the annual precipitation in the United States over the course of the 20th century, whatever the cause.

6.2 More Droughts and Worse Storms?

> A warmer world is more likely to be a wetter one, experts warn ... but in a troublesome twist, that world may also include more intense droughts, as the increased evaporation parches soils between occasional storms.
>
> —*New York Times*, August 28, 2002

That *Times* article, titled "Forecast for the Future: Deluge and Drought," contained 31 sentences about the awful effects of global warming, 4 sentences allowing that there is another view, and 5 neutral ones.

It started bad and got worse: "Rains have deluged Europe and Asia, swamping cities and villages and killing some 2,000 people, while drought and heat have seared the American West and Eastern cities. .... Many warn that such extremes will be increasingly common as the world grows warmer."

Inspection of the 2001 report by the UN Intergovernmental Panel on Climate Change (IPCC) shows that its climate models tend to predict reduced summer precipitation in Eurasia.

There are many measures of wetness and dryness since climatologists have attempted for decades to provide objective definitions of drought conditions. One of the most popular is called the Palmer Drought Severity Index (PDSI).

The PDSI actually measures both dryness and wetness, and it provides a history of the percent of the United States (lower 48

Figure 6.4

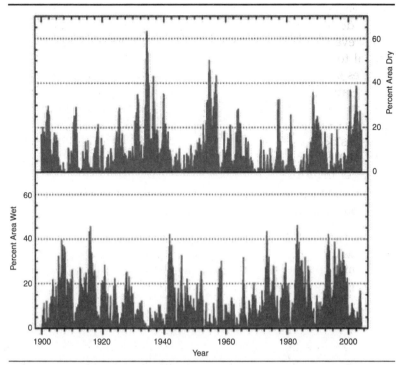

The history of the percentage of the United States experiencing severe to extremely dry conditions (top) and severe to extremely wet conditions (bottom).

SOURCE: http://www.ncdc.noaa.gov.

states) that are unusually wet or dry. This is detailed in Figure 6.4. There's simply no trend in U.S. drought, and there is a slight increase in wetness over the last 102 years.

The August 28 *Times* went on: "Rain is more likely to fall in field-scouring torrents. Government scientists have already measured a significant rise in downpour-style storms in the United States in the last 100 years."

That passage is profoundly misleading. Look again at Figure 6.3. Although there are statistically significant increases in rainfall of less than four inches per day, there is no significant change at all in the four-inch-plus category when averaged across the nation.

Figure 6.5

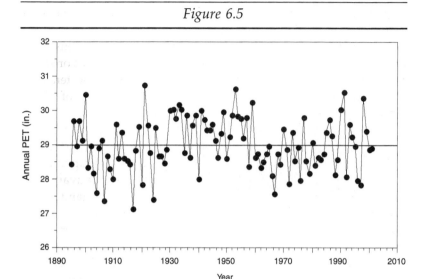

The history of "potential evapotranspiration" for the mid-Atlantic region shows no long-term trend.

SOURCE: Calculated from data available at http://www.ncdc.noaa.gov.

Since when is rainfall of less than four inches per day a "downpour-style storm"?

Hawking drought (and flood) stories has unfortunate consequences. That same week that the *Times* story appeared, Maryland Gov. Parris Glendening blamed an ongoing East Coast drought on global warming. Was Governor Glendening, who repeatedly warned of the perils of global warming during (and after) his tenure in Annapolis, correct? It's obvious that rainfall has increased a wee bit. So, for there to be increased drought at the same time, that increased moisture has to somehow disappear by increased evaporation. That's the basis for the *Times*'s assertion that "increased evaporation parches soils between occasional storms."

Climatologists can calculate evaporation based on temperature and latitude. This is called "potential evapotranspiration" (PET), a mathematical estimate of how much water can be released from a wet surface on an annual basis. We show the history, in Figure 6.5, for Governor Glendening's (and the *New York Times*'s) mid-Atlantic region. Of course, that is highly dependent on annual temperature as more water evaporates in a warmer year.

Note that there's no trend at all, and that the annual values vary about an inch or so. Annual rainfall varies by eight inches or so. Do the math. Governor Glendening was wrong. There's no tendency for increasing droughts in the "Eastern cities" because of higher temperatures leading to increased evaporation.

What about the national PET picture? Is the actual soil moisture increasing, which is obviously beneficial, or are we drying out?

The value of PET can be directly compared with precipitation. If precipitation is greater than PET, there is excess moisture available— excess (or "surplus") water that is free to flow overland or via groundwater to increase streamflow and fill reservoirs. Conversely, if precipitation is less than PET (a moisture "deficit"), then plants have to start taking moisture out of storage (in the soil root zone) so they don't die. Most U.S. farmlands experience a deficit each summer when temperatures peak and rainfall is insufficient to meet this high climatic demand. Irrigation is the most common human remedy.

What's important is not the trend in temperature and precipitation, but the trend in surplus and deficit. Deficits are always high during prolonged droughts. Trends toward more deficit mean that more water is needed for irrigation, reducing the available supply; nonirrigated farms obviously face even more severe problems.

Recently, Greg McCabe and David Wolock of the U.S. Geological Survey examined long-term trends in moisture status—PET, surplus, and deficit—across the continental United States. Figure 6.6 (see color insert) shows the trends in surplus and deficit from 1895 to 1999 and highlights only those climate regions with statistically significant trends. Surpluses are increasing throughout the mid-Atlantic region, much of South Carolina, the Gulf states, portions of the Upper Midwest, and the northern Plains. Over the entire country as a whole, surpluses have increased significantly over the 105-year period. Moisture deficits, however, show no long-term trend. Moisture deficits are increasing mostly in drier regions west of the Mississippi—southern California, Nevada, and Arizona, and portions of the northern Rockies and North Dakota.

Consider this: The moisture surpluses are increasing significantly in 25 percent of the contiguous United States. That bodes well for

Figure 6.7

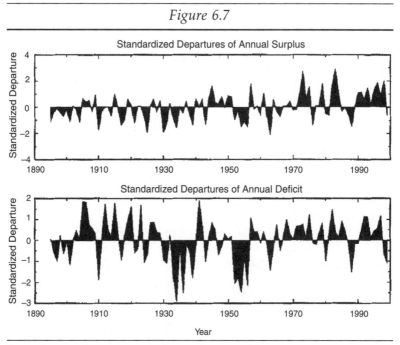

Top: History of moisture surplus in the United States, 1895–1999. Bottom: History of moisture deficit in the United States for the same period. Deficits are greatest when numbers are most negative.

SOURCE: McCabe and Wolock, 2002.

plants and water resources, because most of the surplus serves to increase the water supply. Less than one-third as much area, 8 percent, shows increasing deficit.

Figure 6.7 shows the temporal history of the water surplus and deficit averaged over the entire United States, from the same paper. The top portions show that in the early part of the century, the surplus was often below its long-term average. However, the hallmark of the second half of the century is moisture surplus. The history of moisture deficit is dominated by the big droughts of the 1930s and 1950s, periods when the moisture deficit was very severe. Recent decades have exhibited only a few short periods when the deficit was greater than average. Even though temperatures have increased slightly in recent decades, there is no accompanying tendency for more droughts in the United States.

It remains unclear if those long-term trends are related to increasing greenhouse gases. But an increasing soil-moisture level is critical to agriculture. Of almost equal importance is the well-known fact that higher carbon dioxide levels promote better plant growth and, for most plants, increased water-use efficiency. The future of the United States looks green indeed.

6.3 A Drought of Peer Review

The relationship between economic incentive and the scientific process is truly troubling. The popular perception is that money corrupts science, a common example being the "tobacco industry scientist" who produces reams and reams of paper denying the link between tobacco and death, despite the obvious mound of corpses.

In most areas of science, especially in environmental science, the vast majority of funding comes from the federal government. Recall that every area of scientific interest competes with others for finite sustenance. Remember also that the reward structure in academia, in which tenure equals job security, is highly conditioned by the level of scientific funding that an individual can garner. In that milieu, questions that might seem obvious can often go unasked.

Where those unasked questions create the most obvious bias is in the peer review process, in which a journal editor sends a researcher's submission to select scientists who weigh in on things like the data's accuracy and the conclusions' validity. You would think that process would largely prevent erroneous papers from being published. But it doesn't. For example, I described in some detail in *The Satanic Gases* how one of the most important papers on global warming science, published by Department of Energy climatologist Benjamin Santer and many coauthors, contained a remarkable flaw. Their *Nature* paper claimed a strong correspondence between temperatures in the troposphere—the earth's active weather zone—and projections of climate models. It also appeared, not coincidentally, immediately before the United Nations conference that laid the groundwork for the Kyoto Protocol on global warming.

Here was the problem: The Santer study used weather balloon data from 1962 through 1988. In fact, however, the weather balloon record was actually complete (at the time of the July 1996 publication) from 1957 through 1995, and when the entire record was used, the correspondence vanished.

Why did none of the reviewers at *Nature* notice Santer et al.'s selective data use? Within a very few minutes of reading the paper, my colleague and coauthor of *The Satanic Gases*, Robert Balling (Arizona State University), and I were on the phone to one another. I remember saying to Bob that I could think of absolutely no reason to use only the 1962–1988 data, and I bet him that something very different would result if the entire set were used. After only four hours of effort, my colleagues and I determined that the entire result changed if all the data were used. *Nature* was compelled to publish our finding, and the damage to global warming science resulting from this exchange still reverberates today.

Again and again, however, the peer review process fails. Flawed articles appear in prestigious scientific journals, the media has a field day, and the public is left with mistaken impressions that are hard to dispel. Here's another example of an article whose influence far exceeded its accuracy.

USA Today summarized one such study in a front-page article on January 31, 2003, as follows: "Global warming probably made the recent drought in the USA worse than it otherwise would have been, say the authors of a study published today in the journal *Science*," a synopsis echoed throughout the popular press. In the study *USA Today* is referring to, federal climatologists Martin Hoerling and Arun Kumar ran a climate model with Indian and Pacific Ocean temperature patterns as observed from mid-1998 to mid-2002. When fed those data, their model produced lower than normal rainfall over most of the coterminous United States. Therefore, the authors concluded that "the atmospheric modeling results of 1998–2002 suggest an increased risk for severe and synchronized drying of the midlatitudes."

Now, climate models are simply strings of computer code that attempt to simulate the atmosphere. The key word is "attempt." If their output does not correspond to reality, they require modification. In the parlance of the scientific method, a climate model is a hypothesis in search of validation by observed data. The "hypothesis" in Hoerling and Kumar's paper is fairly straightforward: Global warming enhances drought in the western United States. Indeed, their results indicate that warming should make droughts worse or more frequent over most of the entire lower 48 states. But does it?

Figure 6.8

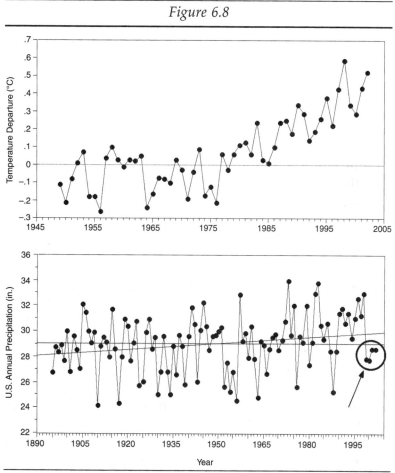

Top: Global temperatures in the last 50 years; bottom: U.S. annual average rainfall. The average of the last four years is less than an inch below the average of the last century.

SOURCE: http://www.cru.uea.ac.uk and http://www.ncdc.noaa.gov.

Figure 6.8 (top) shows the global temperature history for the last 50 years. Remember that the current spate of warming began in earnest in the mid-1970s, and its distribution at the surface of the earth looks pretty much like a "greenhouse" signal. Now look at Figure 6.8 (bottom), which illustrates the U.S. precipitation record from 1895 through 2002. The last four years are the same four years

Figure 6.9

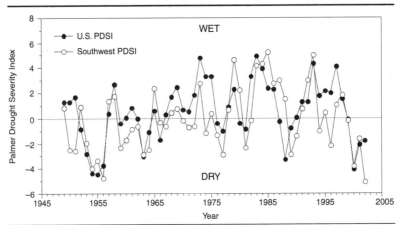

A historical record of U.S. drought as characterized by the Palmer Drought Severity Index for the United States (filled circles) and the Southwest (open circles). There's no statistical relationship to global temperature.

SOURCE: http://www.ncdc.noaa.gov.

that Hoerling and Kumar studied. In the broad sweep of things, they are hardly unusual. The mean U.S. rainfall for the period is 28.20 inches. The average for the entire record is 29.05 inches. The average annual rainfall during the dreaded last four years is 0.85 inch below normal nationally, or a shortfall of 2.9 percent per year. On a national scale, that is hardly noteworthy.

Well, you might argue, it's not the total amount of moisture shortfall that determines a drought—it's a whole constellation of factors, including temperature, groundwater storage, runoff, you name it. So such a small deficit, if perfectly timed, say, in the hottest part of the year, might make for a big drought, and its effect might be accentuated, say the authors, by global warming.

That's what the Palmer Drought Severity Index is supposed to track. Given that Hoerling and Kumar's paper speaks directly to the Western drought that began in 1998, we checked specifically in the U.S. Southwest: Arizona, Colorado, New Mexico, and Utah (Figure 6.9).

Now, if the hypothesis—that global greenhouse warming is intensifying U.S. droughts—has any validity at all, there had better be a

140

Figure 6.10

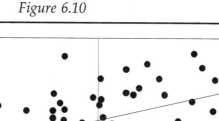

Relation between tropical Pacific temperatures and drought. The strength of this relationship is independent of global warming.

SOURCE: Calculated from data in Fraunfeld and Davis, 2002.

correlation between the Palmer values and global temperatures. There is none.

Why didn't the reviewers at *Science* magazine ask Hoerling and Kumar to do a simple test like this? It must have occurred to *someone!*

What did Hoerling and Kumar really discover? Nothing terribly new. Oliver Frauenfeld and Robert Davis, two University of Virginia scientists, published a paper in the December 2002 issue of *Geophysical Research Letters* that found a very similar pattern of oceanic warming, with warmth in the western tropical Pacific and cold in the East. Further, they found that its magnitude had reached an extreme value, beginning in 1998. (By the way, Frauenfeld and Davis used actual data rather than a model.)

Further, that pattern is actually related to U.S. drought (Figure 6.10). When the eastern tropical Pacific is cold and the western part is warm, the United States tends to be droughty (the lower-left corner of Figure 6.10). Flip the circumstances, and it becomes wet (the upper-right corner of our figure). This relationship is highly statistically significant. But Frauenfeld and Davis could find no relationship between the behavior of this pattern over time and global warming.

Yet *Science* rejected their manuscript out of hand; in fact, the editors there didn't even send it out for review!

It's impossible to determine exactly why that happened, but one essential difference between Davis's and Hoerling's work is that the latter ties the Pacific temperature patterns to global warming and was published (without a test of that hypothesis) and the former could not and was not published.

6.4 A Nation Ablaze?

World on Fire: Saving the Endangered Earth

—Title of 1991 book by Sen. George Mitchell (D-Maine)

Enormous wildfires have been raging in bone-dry regions of the West and Southwest. . . . In Colorado, which is enduring its worst drought in decades . . . the long drought and continued hot weather provided the conditions that enabled this [fire] to explode into an unprecedented conflagration. . . . "Can you say global warming?"

—Robert Herbert, *New York Times*, June 24, 2002

Sen. George Mitchell wrote a very poor seller in 1991 about how global warming was going to burn us all up. In 1998, Vice President Gore positioned himself in front of some Florida forest fires and said such conflagrations were what global warming was going to do to families unless he was elected (ironically, it was Florida where he was torched). Fire is one of global warming's most spectacular selling points.

It is also one of the easiest to dispute. Figure 6.11 shows 10-year averages for acreage burned in the United States. In the warm 1990s, the average was a little around 5 million acres per year going up in smoke. (In the cool 1960s, it was also around 5 million.)

Before the 1942 release of *Bambi*, the cartoon deer who probably spawned more ecological mismanagement and traffic fatalities than any other animal in cinematic history, we used to just let things burn. That's part of the reason why, when we look at, say, the 1930s, about 38 million acres went up each year; an average of 25 million combusted in the 1920s.

This isn't just a straw doe. Consider what's happened since *Bambi*, or in the current era of irrational fire suppression.

Figure 6.11

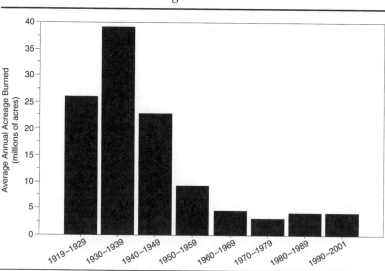

Average acreage burned per year in the United States, by decade.
Source: U.S. Department of Agriculture, Forest Service.

Figure 6.12 shows summer (June–September) temperatures since 1960, and Figure 6.13 is decadal average precipitation over the United States. There is a warming trend, a rise of about 0.9°F in the period. But there's also an increase in precipitation. In the 1960s, we averaged about 28.3 inches of rain per year. By the 1990s that moved up to 30.5, or a rise of 2.3 inches.

It's not very hard to take the temperature, rainfall, and burn data and turn it into a mathematical "model." First, you specify an equation that defines a hypothesis about the way something works.

How about this one:

Acreage burned = X (temperature) − Y (rainfall).

If you have enough data—usually at least 10 "independent" observations of the "modeled" variable ("acreage burned") and for each predictor ("temperature" and "rainfall")—you can run a fairly straightforward statistical calculation that determines the values of X and Y that best describe the hypothesized mathematical relationship between fire, heat, and rain.

143

Figure 6.12

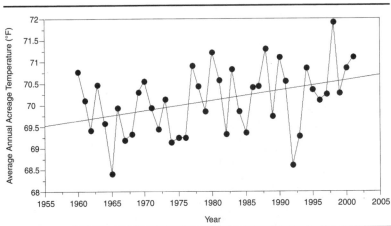

U.S. June-September temperatures since 1960.
SOURCE: http://www.ncdc.noaa.gov.

Figure 6.13

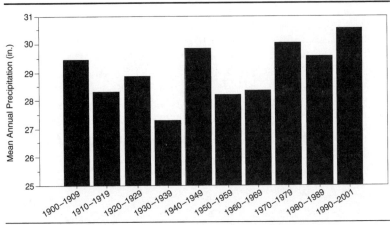

Average precipitation per year in the United States, by decade.
SOURCE: http://www.ncdc.noaa.gov.

The computer calculates that X is approximately equal to 700,000, which means, on the average, that a year that is one degree warmer than normal will have 700,000 more burned acres. Y is equal to

144

Figure 6.14

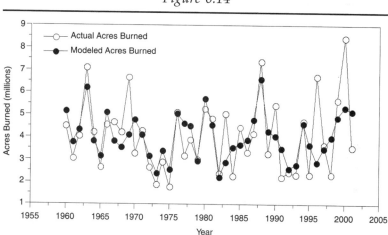

Computer-modeled and observed acreage burned, using temperature and rainfall.

Source: Fire data from the U.S. Department of Agriculture.

400,000. So every inch of rain above normal reduces the annual burn by 400,000 acres. This little "model" explains a bit less than half of the total year-to-year variation in acreage burned in the United States. It's shown graphically in Figure 6.14.

Since 1960, the 0.9 degree rise in temperature means that we are burning 630,000 more acres per year. But, the 2.3-inch rise in rainfall means that we're burning 930,000 *fewer* acres because of the increased moisture. In other words, the total "change" in the climate-related signal according to our model is *minus* 300,000 acres.

Despite our straightforward math, don't draw the conclusion that global warming is therefore associated with *reduced* fire in the United States. That net change of minus 300,000 acres is a needle buried in an annual 5,000,000-acre foreststack. Scientifically speaking, you can't tell the climate signal from the random noise. (And don't assume your perception of more forest fires means that there are more forest fires—remember Dan Rather and the deluge of hurricane coverage he set in motion in Galveston all those years ago. We hear more about it, but that doesn't mean there's more to hear about.)

There's obviously more here than meets the facile columnist's eye. But, in reality, Robert Herbert was only writing what he was (or was not) told by the scientific community, which gains more from fanning the flames of fear than it does from putting them out.

6.5 Let's Just Fry and Die

"The Dumb People Scenario" is how Natural Research Council plant physiologist Paul Waggoner once described the all-too-frequent assumption in the climate change debate that people won't adapt to slow changes in climate. That also seems to be the take-away message coverage of a paper by Stanley Smith and several coauthors in the November 2, 2000, issue of *Nature*.

Smith et al. freely admit that the "well-documented increase in atmospheric CO_2 concentration acts to increase photosynthesis, plant biomass, and plant water-use efficiency in many plant species." Taken together, those changes have the well-documented effect of turning desert into shrublands, as noted by U.S. Department of Agriculture scientist Herman Mayeaux. That should be good news, right?

Of course not! As Mikhail Gorbachev used to say, "That's old thinking!" In the desert, the researchers warn, vegetation runs especially rampant during wet years like those triggered by El Niño events, and increasingly prolific vegetation might give rise to massive western wildfires during ensuing dry years. That's because we humans apparently are "Dumb People," and we simply will allow the conflagrations despite a massive financial incentive (i.e., saving homes) to prevent such activity.

What Smith and his colleagues fail to note, however, is that along with a greening of the American West, there is a decades-long trend toward more desert rain. Figure 6.15, for example, shows a statistically significant increase in Nevada average rainfall over the last 50 years, a change that is representative of the entire Pacific Southwest region of the United States, which shows a larger growth in rainfall than elsewhere in the nation. Increased moisture is likely to be exceedingly welcome in an arid environment. It's the sort of environmental change of which people tend to take advantage.

In fact, people have been adapting for decades to the reality of increasing vegetation, with what are called "controlled burns," an effective adaptation technique that will no doubt be enhanced if Smith's projections of greater growth are accurate. It is unreasonable to assume humans are "Dumb People" who will sit idly by and risk

Figure 6.15

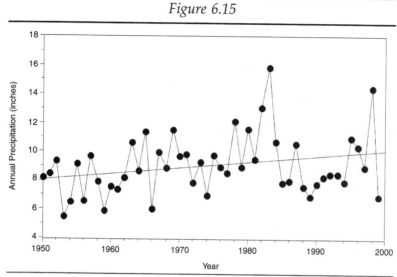

In the last 50 years, Nevada's statewide average rainfall has increased.
SOURCE: http://www.ncdc.noaa.gov.

seeing their desert homes go up in the smoke of uncontrolled wildfires.

The November 6, 2000, edition of the *Washington Post* reports that Smith's findings mean rising levels of CO_2 that "may lead to more fires in North American deserts." If by that the reporter means more controlled burns, that claim is correct. If, however, the implication is that there will be more *wild*fires, then the follow-up report will concern how millions of Westerners were struck by "the stupid stick."

6.6 Changes in the Indian Monsoon

> One new study found evidence that the Asian monsoon, as part of the warming trend, has already intensified.
>
> —*New York Times*, August 28, 2002

> The cloud [of pollution] . . . could cut rainfall over northwest Pakistan, Afghanistan, western China and western Central Asia by up to 40 percent.

147

—CNN, August 2002

What better way to scare the two billion inhabitants of East and South Asia than by threatening the Asian monsoon?

The background article for the *Times*'s assertion was published in July 2002 in *Science* by David Anderson and two coauthors. It looked at the relationship between tiny marine organisms, global temperature, and the monsoon, and found a positive relationship. Anderson et al. then examined the real rainfall data for India, which has one of the world's most reliable records, thanks to the British penchant for weather-watching.

> The trend in all-India rainfall, although positive, is small and statistically insignificant. However, the regional and year-to-year variability is large. Using historical data, Mooney and Pant found no change in the last 200 years in the frequency of extreme drought events.

Clearly, the culture of fear has crept into even our most prestigious scientific journals: That much is evident from the fact that the *Science* reviewers let the notion stand that an "insignificant trend" can be positive ("insignificant" means, in this case, that it cannot be statistically distinguished from no trend at all).

At precisely the same time that the monsoon story hit the news, another scary atmospheric disturbance emerged, the "Asian Brown Cloud" (ABC), a large smear of airborne anthropogenic sleaze emanating from South Asia. According to CNN, it is so bad that it has "scientists warning it could kill millions of people in the area, and pose a global threat."

Not surprisingly, the Asian Brown Cloud story was rushed to publication by the United Nations as a "preliminary report," immediately before their 2002 environmental summit in Johannesburg, South Africa. According to CNN, "The report calculated that the cloud could cut [monsoon] rainfall over northwest Pakistan, Afghanistan, western China, and western Central Asia by up to 40 percent."

Obviously this cloud is nothing new, and it did not appear overnight. Consequently, it might be worthwhile to examine precipitation trends in the aforementioned regions. Figure 6.16 (see color insert) is copied directly from page 144 of the UN's 2001 compendium on climate change (the *Third Assessment Report*). It shows changes in annual precipitation for the last quarter-century around the globe. There's no systematic behavior in any of the regions mentioned (the only place with consistent, but small, increases appears to be North America). Some South Asian places (where the monsoon is important) have increasing rainfall, and some show decreases. Many are staying right around plus or minus 10 percent, which is pretty much the natural variability of rainfall on this time scale.

Absent any evidence for systematic changes in precipitation, how could anyone make the statement that the cloud "could cut rainfall ... by up to 40 percent"? Two words: Climate model. That's right: The UN is looking at a climate model rather than at reality. The UN is doing so despite its own admission in the 2001 compendium that climate models are not reliable for regional estimates of climate change. Page 587 of that report speaks to the "increasing need to better understand the processes that determine regional climate and to evaluate regional climate change information for use in impact studies and policy planning." Further, "to date, a relatively high level of uncertainty has characterized regional climate change information."

The UN's hurriedly released "preliminary report" also blames so-called "erratic weather" on the Asian Brown Cloud, including flooding in Bangladesh, Nepal, and northeastern India and drought in Pakistan and northwestern India. There is not one shred of science behind those contentions. In fact, the United Nations cannot produce any study in the refereed scientific literature that specifically connects the ABC and "erratic weather," or even defines "erratic weather."

6.7 More Floods in New England?

One of the most famous of all climate change papers was published by federal climatologist Tom Karl in *Nature* in the summer of 1995. It found a slight increase in the frequency of two-inch or more rainstorms in summer in the continental United States. Subsequent work, published in the *Bulletin of the American Meteorological Society,* indicated that the tendency for increased heavy rains was concentrated in New England.

After those papers, Harry Lins of the U.S. Geological Survey published an analysis of stream flow records across the nation, and found that the well-known increase in overall U.S. precipitation has

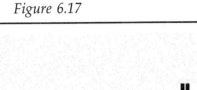

Figure 6.17

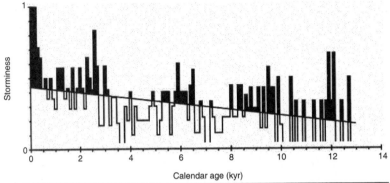

Index of New England storminess during the past 13,000 years.
SOURCE: Noren et al., 2002.

generally resulted in more water during the low-flow times of the year, rather than leading to increased flooding events. In other words, we are getting more rain during the times when rain is scarcer. That means that, by and large, the precipitation increases are beneficial, resulting in more water available for the environment as well as for agricultural, residential, and municipal water users.

A 2002 paper in *Nature* magazine puts much of this in perspective. The apparent increase in storminess, at least in New England, isn't unusual at all. By concentrating on records for the last 100 years, which is about as far back as rain gauge records can be trusted, we're seeing only a small slice of climate history.

A research team led by University of Vermont geologist Anders Noren collected sediment cores from 13 lakes scattered across New England. By analyzing the different sediment layers, the researchers could tell when large flooding events occurred: The sediment became coarser and contained many more terrestrial land plant fossils during flood eras than in times between floods when the sediment was much finer and more uniform. Through analysis of all 13 cores, they were able to construct a rough history of storminess stretching back about 13,000 years. Analysis of this record revealed that New England appears to undergo about a 3,000-year cycle of periods marked by high and low frequencies of flood-producing events (Figure 6.17). The record shows peaks of high storminess at about

11.9, 9.1, 5.8, and 2.6 thousand years ago. These periods also coincide with other stormy periods as revealed in a host of other studies, including those of Greenland ice cores, which indicate a relationship between the climate cycles of New England and those of Europe. As the math would suggest, the record also shows that over the past several hundred years, New England has been trending into another stormy period.

All of this spells difficulties for global warming doomsayers. Here's what the Noren team had to say on the issue:

> Climate models suggest that human activities, specifically the emission of atmospheric greenhouse gases, may lead to increases in the frequency of severe storms in certain regions of the Northern Hemisphere. However, the existence of natural variability in storminess confounds reliable detection on anthropogenic effects. During the past ~600 years, New England storminess appears to have been increasing naturally. This rhythm in storm frequency may explain some of the recently observed increases in extreme precipitation events. If the pattern of millennial-scale variability that we documented through the Holocene [post ice-age] persists into the future, New England storminess would continue to increase for the next ~900 years. Because climate synopses compiled from instrumental records cannot distinguish underlying natural increases in storminess from anthropogenic effect, detected increases in contemporary storminess may not be a reliable indicator of human-induced climate change.

6.8 Is Weather Variability Increasing?

It's a favorite scare story: Climate is becoming more extreme. But as usual, this tale of climate terror doesn't have much supporting data.

Consider a recent paper by climatologists Konstantin Vinnikov and Alan Robock, who looked at a variety of climate indicators to see if they show any tendency toward higher variability over the period 1901–2000. They first calculated the linear trends through their data, and then the departure of each year's observation from the trend line. The resulting anomalies, which statisticians call "residuals," essentially reflect how well the linear trend fits the data.

If the climate were becoming more variable over time, the departures of powers (squares, cubes, etc.) of the residuals from the linear

Figures 6.18a and 6.18b

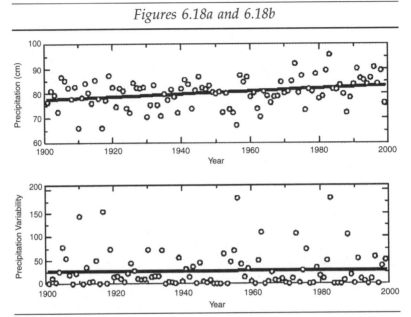

U.S. annual precipitation, 1901–2001 (top); Year-to-year precipitation variability (bottom).

SOURCE: Vinnikov and Robock, 2002.

trend line should be generally larger in 2000 than they were in 1901. So if climate variability really is increasing, there should be evidence in those residual functions. They found no trend in variability. For example, Figure 6.18a shows the linear trend in 100 years of U.S. annual precipitation totals. Precipitation is increasing across the United States at a rate of about 5.8 cm (2.28 inches) per century. But the year-to-year variability of rainfall is unchanged (Figure 6.18b). This is clearly good news: Precipitation is no more erratic from year to year than it was a century ago, but there's more of it.

My research group at the University of Virginia recently published an analysis of U.S. temperatures in the journal *Climate Research*, in which we ranked each day within the year from coldest to warmest and then ran 365 trends—one for each day. For example, the first trend could include data from December 1, 1910, January 15, 1911, February 2, 1912, January 28, 1913, and so on (depending which day of each year was coldest). We then examined each day from the coldest to the warmest.

Figure 6.19

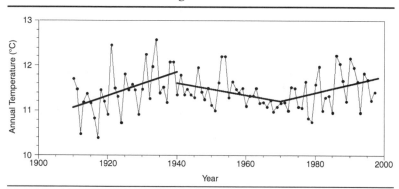

The U.S. temperature history shows three distinct regimes, two of warming and one of cooling.

SOURCE: http://www.ncdc.noaa.gov.

In other words, we were asking if the coldest days have become warmer, and whether the warmest days have become hotter.

Before looking to the results, take a look at Figure 6.19, which is simply the average annual temperature of the lower 48 states, according to data from the U.S. National Climatic Data Center. There's a period of warming from 1910 to 1939, when greenhouse gas levels were low; an unexplained cooling despite continued greenhouse gas increases from 1940 to 1969; and a recent warming.

The behavior of extreme temperatures during the two periods of warming is remarkably different. From 1910 to 1939, maximum temperatures rose more on the warmest days than on the coldest days. Minimum temperatures rose on both warm and cold days (Figure 6.20). The net impact is a tendency toward more extreme heat. Greenhouse gas levels were low in this period.

Compare this with the recent 1970–1997 "greenhouse-gas warming" era. There's relatively little warming on the hottest days but major warming on the cooler days (Figure 6.21). The result is a less extreme, more moderate climate. Is that what greenhouse warming hath wrought?

6.9 CNN in the Classroom: The Great Lakes and Global Warming

From *CNN in the Classroom*, April 27, 2000:

Lesson Plan: Warming Drops Great Lakes to Historic Lows

Objectives

Students will construct and explain theories for the decline in water level in the Great Lakes.

Figure 6.20

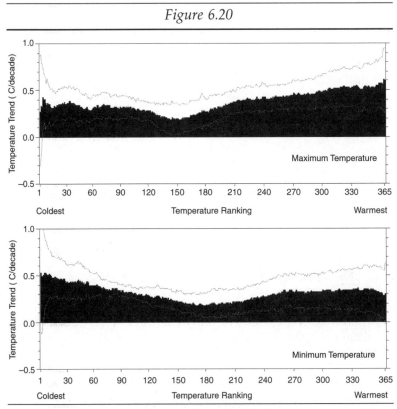

U.S. national average trends through ranked daily temperatures, 1910 to 1939.

SOURCE: Knappenberger et al., 2001.

Procedures

Have students read the CNNfyi story, "Warming Drops Great Lakes Toward Historic Lows."

You have to wonder whether the fact-checkers at CNN missed a bit of data that would have spoiled a good propaganda attempt in the classroom. But, again, what would prompt them to find it? Certainly not the constant cheerleading from the larger scientific community about the evils of global warming!

At the time of this "Lesson," Great Lake levels were indeed well below their long-term averages, approaching, in some cases, the

Figure 6.21

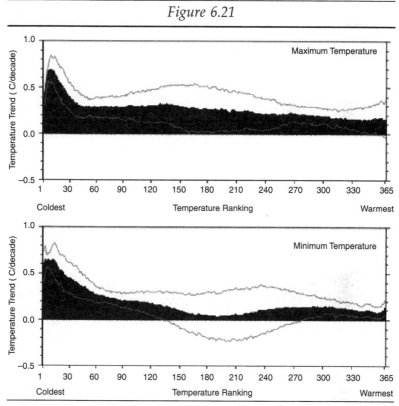

U.S. national average trends through ranked daily temperatures, 1969 to 1997.

Source: Knappenberger et al., 2001.

record low levels set in the 1930s and 1960s. Such low water creates significant effects. As lake levels drop, commercial and recreational activities are adversely affected—cargo ships have to carry lighter loads, hydropower plants can't run at full capacity, and marinas have to dredge new channels and boat slips. The decline in lake levels is related to warmer and drier conditions that had persisted in the Great Lake region during the previous three or four years. CNN is clearly stating the following as fact: Global warming is reducing the level of the Great Lakes. The truth is, although four years is a long enough period to capture CNN's attention, a much longer period is necessary to relate changes in lake levels to global warming.

Figure 6.22 shows the annual history of water levels in Lake Superior and Lakes Michigan-Huron. Notice that variations occur over all time scales, from years to decades to centuries. Over the long term, the water level in Lake Superior has shown a slight rise since the middle of the 19th century (top) while the waters in the Michigan-Huron basin show a great degree of fluctuation but no trend over the past 70 to 100 years (bottom). A decline did occur from 1860 to 1920 (i.e., it ended 80 years ago), but that was long before humans had done anything appreciable to the earth's natural greenhouse effect.

Figure 6.23 shows the 100-year temperature and precipitation history for the state of Michigan—the "Great Lake State"—surrounded by water on all but its southern borders with Indiana, Ohio, and Wisconsin. Precipitation has increased about 10 percent since the late 1880s (Figure 6.23, top). The increase has been smooth and steady, despite the fact that changes in the atmospheric greenhouse effect were very slight in the first half of this record.

The Michigan temperature history similarly shows no relation to global warming. Although the last several years have been warmer than the long-term average, there is simply no trend (Figure 6.23, bottom).

Consequently, the Michigan climate history provides absolutely no evidence that current lake levels are a result of warming, despite "CNN in the Classroom."

As shown in Figure 6.22, a mere 17 years ago, in 1986, the Great Lakes were at or near record-high levels. In the 1920s, Lake Superior was lower than ever measured since. Here's the classroom lesson: *Water levels in the Great Lakes vary. A lot.* It's a pretty good wager that the near-shore ecosystems are pretty well adapted to these fluctuations, too—otherwise they wouldn't be there! Variations in water levels help maintain the diversity in the coastal marshes— some of the most diverse and productive ecosystems in the world— as different plant species become successively established in low-water years, and drowned out and replaced in high-water years. Steady lake levels, however, would slowly lead to less diversity and a much less dynamic ecosystem.

Roger Gauthier, supervising hydrologist with the U.S. Army Corps of Engineers in Detroit, elegantly sums up the issue: "The

Figure 6.22

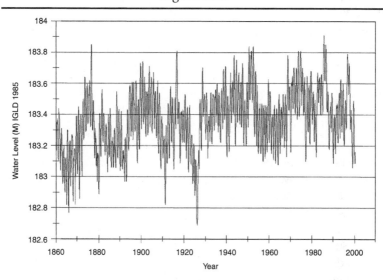

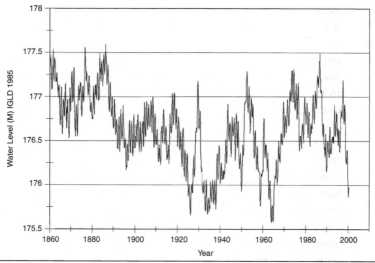

Lake Superior's water level has shown a slight rise since the middle of the 19th century (top), while the waters in the Michigan-Huron basin show a great degree of fluctuation but no trend over the past 70 to 100 years (bottom).

SOURCE: http://www.glerl.noaa.gov.

Figure 6.23

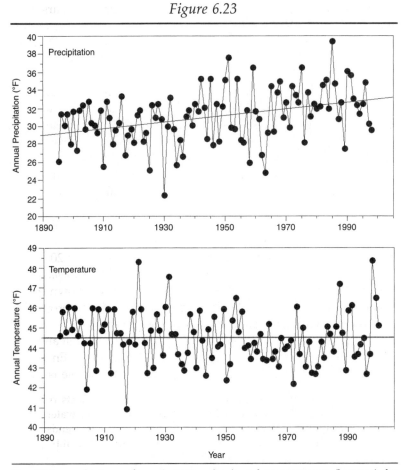

The 100-year history of precipitation (top) and temperature (bottom) for the state of Michigan, an area representative of the Great Lakes region as a whole.

SOURCE: http://www.ncdc.noaa.gov.

lakes are not bathtubs. The water levels have been changing for thousands of years. We have to accept that and adjust to it." After all, we might add, nature certainly has. These fluctuations will occur into the future, but there is no observational evidence to suggest that global warming is influencing their levels a lick.

One good thing about natural variation is that it occurs often enough to prove (or disprove) a point. For instance, things around the Great Lakes turned around within one year of the CNN story. During April 2001, the Lake Superior basin received 271 percent of its normal rainfall, which triggered a massive snowmelt resulting from an especially deep snowpack (something that should diminish with global warming). The resultant rise in water level was the fastest ever observed in April (see Figure 6.24 in color insert). On April 1, 2001, Lake Superior was 8.3 inches above its all-time low, and by mid-May, it was only 4.2 inches below its long-term average, a rise of 14.4 inches in six weeks. How, you have to ask, could anyone ever sort out the long-term signal of global warming in such month-to-month noise?

Despite the CNN hype, all this variation appears to be quite natural, and should be contrasted with the gloom-and-doom projections made in the infamous compendium released around the 2000 election, *The U.S. National Assessment of the Potential Consequences of Climate Variability and Change.* That document merits its own special section (Chapter 10) in this book, in which we examine its projections of the Great Lake fluctuations in the coming century.

Throughout the climate change issue, the most steadfast and least alarmist federal entity has been the U.S. Army Corps of Engineers. Here's what they said, on April 5, 2001, about this whole issue:

> While scientists continue to speculate about the effects of climate shifts, global warming, and long-term cycles on water supply in the Great Lakes basin, recent water-level trends illustrate that levels continue to exhibit a natural variability.

6.10 Rather Bad Weather!

> Coastal states such as Alaska will see massive impact, including flooding of coastal villages. Brook trout may lose 50 percent of their habitat. Drought will be pervasive. Heat-related deaths will increase 100 percent in cities such as New York, Philadelphia, Cleveland, Los Angeles, and others.
>
> —Sen. James Jeffords (I-Vt.)

Remember the incessant stories from the summer of 2000 about the terrible drought gripping the nation's breadbasket?

Dan Rather led off the June 13 edition of CBS Evening News with—

> Good evening. This could be a summer to survive. . . . An ultra-drought builds in the West, Southwest, Midwest, and Southeast.

To say the least, this was Rather wrong, so wrong at the time of his broadcast that viewers should be urged to fact-check every weather and climate catastrophe story CBS ever runs.

Quite simply, there was no "ultra-drought." By June 13, Illinois (which is in the Midwest) was halfway through what turned out to be the fourth-wettest June since the long-term records begin in 1895. By June 24, the entire state of Illinois, 90 percent of Missouri and Wisconsin, and half of Iowa were reporting abnormally moist soil conditions. Now, there's a headline: "Midwest experiences abnormally moist drought!"

These surpluses did not build up overnight. The 7 a.m., June 13 U.S. Drought Monitor—a joint publication of the U.S. Departments of Agriculture and Commerce and the National Drought Mitigation Center, widely available on the Internet—reported—

> Midwest: The pattern bringing rainfall across Minnesota, northeastern Iowa, northern Illinois, southern Wisconsin, and the Lower Peninsula of Michigan continued as in previous weeks.

How did CBS News miss that?

To his dubious credit, Dan Rather long has recognized the media salability of weather-hype stories (as noted in Section 5.1), beginning with 1961 Hurricane Carla. In 1997–1998, he blew the El Niño into apocalyptic proportions, though it turned out to be a net benefit to the United States, as reported in the *Bulletin of the American Meteorological Society* by Illinois climatologist Stanley Changnon.

So CBS's hype of the "ultra-drought" of 2000 isn't anything new at all. Rather, it's a tedious repetition of the same weather exaggeration that has plagued the news from Black Rock since Carla.

Here's what actually happened while those lurid reports were on. Figure 6.25 (see color insert) shows the Crop Moisture Index, an objective mathematical measure of shallow-soil moisture status, for the week ending June 24, 2000. Note that the world's breadbasket—

a.k.a. the Midwest—is green. On this map and in reality, green indicates abundant moisture. The bright red regions—where the index is below −3.0 (extremely dry)—are around Death Valley, California; Needles, Arizona; and east-central Arizona, depicting drought in the desert (which is certainly something that rhymes with bringing coal to Newcastle).

7. A Greener World of Changing Seasons?

The vegetation poles of the greenhouse debate are defined by the greener and the browner people. The former think that a world warmed by carbon dioxide is a greener place with more abundant food, while the latter worry about advancing deserts and starvation. On first principles, it seems pretty hard to side with the browns here. As noted in earlier chapters, the prime characteristic of greenhouse heating is a warming of the winters, and, in particular, of the coldest air of the winter.

During late fall, cold air masses in the Northern Hemisphere sometimes migrate southward and eastward from Siberia or northwestern Canada, bringing an abrupt end to the growing season with the first freezing temperatures. Similarly, the last of these in the spring initiate the beginning of the growing season with the final freezing temperature before summer. Warming these, which has occurred preferentially (see Chapter 2), will tend to lengthen the growing season.

Chapter 6 provided considerable evidence for an increase in rainfall in the world's most important agricultural zone, the United States. And, as also shown in that chapter, increases in temperature have been so small compared with the increases in rainfall that indeed the surface of the planet is wetter than it used to be. It's hard to imagine how, once started, this happy differential—where increasing rain more than compensates for increasing temperature—would suddenly reverse.

If the defining characteristics of greenhouse warming are warmer winters, more rain, and longer growing seasons, what's so bad about that? Plenty, apparently.

7.1 Warm Winters: How Good News Becomes Bad

Sometimes, the killjoys at the *New York Times* just can't seem to leave warm enough alone. So, after a spate of wonderfully balmy days in February 2002, an article appeared entitled "When Good Winters Go Bad."

A person could get the impression that the *Times* wanted people to feel guilty about the fine weather the city had recently experienced. The first half of its story describes how much everyone was enjoying the toasty, late February weather—lunchtime strolls in the park, spring flowers blooming—even the number of cases of wintertime depression were down. But then came the hammer: "Climate scientists see a dark cloud behind that kind of reaction to the weather." Here's the logic, from the *Times* article:

> "In thinking about human responsibility for future generations and ecosystems, the spirit of living for today can lead to a sense of acceptance and passivity, [Harvard Medical School psychiatrist] Dr. [Eric] Chivian said, "and that could have disastrous consequences."
>
> "It illustrates a kind of helplessness, that there's nothing we can do about this, the best we can do is count our blessings and enjoy life as it comes," he said. "Yes, it's nice to enjoy every day, but these are things we can control, and that we've got to control, or people coming after us will say we squandered an opportunity."
>
> Even asking people whether a pleasant winter alters their thinking about climate makes some scientists uncomfortable. A changed climate will in fact have winners and losers, those scientists say, and New York, in some ways, might well benefit. But to think only of the parochial consequences is exactly the sort of self-centered short-term thinking, they say, that created the problem especially from the burning of fossil fuels in cars and electric power generators.
>
> "As we're enjoying consumer society, most of us don't think about the negative consequences of having too much enjoyment in life," said Dr. Dan A. Oren, an associate professor of psychiatry at Yale University School of Medicine. "I suspect that the average citizen, including you and me most of the time," he said, "does not feel the guilt that ought to be there."

Perhaps Drs. Chivian and Oren should pause to consider some of the benefits of the modern world, made possible by fossil fuels—longer life spans, more food, better medicine, and so on—and then balance the guilt that they would suffer if society would have given all that up by embarking upon a path not reliant on fossil fuels (hint: we'd still be awaiting the Industrial Revolution) against the guilt that they suggest we should have over the perils of global warming.

Actually, the competition down I-95 (a.k.a. the *Washington Post*) may have set the bar for reporting on this subject a few months earlier on December 17, 2001. The article was by Michael Powell. Powell's article concerns the impacts of climate change on New England and as best as can be told from his reference to reports "commissioned by Congress," he was apparently using the *National Assessment* of global warming (see Chapter 10). Scientists on a panel appointed by the Environmental Protection Agency, Powell wrote, "conclude that global warming is already occurring, noting that, on average, the Northeast became two degrees warmer in the past century,"

Yet, on page ii of the introduction to "Preparing for a Changing Climate: The New England Regional Assessment Overview" (a portion of the National Assessment) we read, "Overall, the region has warmed [from 1895 to 1999] by 0.7°F." Powell's coverage exaggerates the warming to a level *nearly three times greater* than what actually has been experienced, something that could be discerned without even reading the body of the report!

Powell's coverage also ignores the fact that during the past 70 years, temperatures in the Northeast actually have declined. As Figure 7.1 shows (using data freely available from the National Climatic Data Center), the warm-up that is responsible for the 0.7°F rise since 1895 occurs in the period from 1895 to 1930—more than 70 years ago and during a time when the concentration of greenhouse gases in the atmosphere had scarcely risen beyond their preindustrial level.

Point-by-point, here are some of this article's other problems:

"[By the end of this century] New York could have the climate of Miami."

Although this may be an interesting illustrative concept, New York City could *never* have Miami's climate. Miami is located at latitude 26°N and is surrounded by a warm tropical ocean. Nearly all of Miami's weather results from systems that originate over (or in association with) the Gulf of Mexico or the tropical Atlantic Ocean. Such an oceanic influence moderates Miami's climate so that its

Figure 7.1

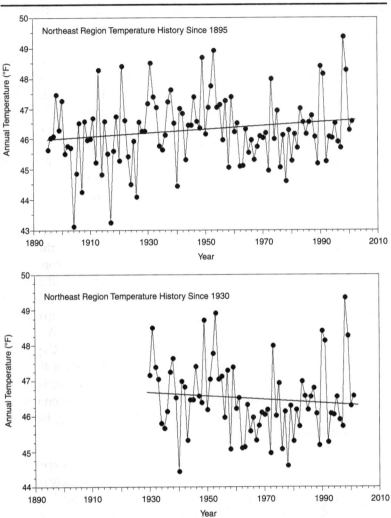

The temperature trends in the Northeast Region. The temperature history since 1895 shows a rise of 0.7°F, but this entire rise occurred before 1930. From 1930 to 2001, the trend is slightly negative.

SOURCE: National Climatic Data Center.

summers are not too hot (with an average July maximum temperature of 89.0°F and record July maximum temperature of 98°F), and its winters never too cold (average January minimum temperature 59.2°F and record January minimum temperature 30°F).

New York City, on the other hand, sits at the eastern edge of a continental land mass at latitude 41°N. Since weather systems at this latitude primarily move from west to east, the vast majority of the city's weather originates over the continent. Continental systems are quite different than tropical systems. They tend to be much drier and therefore have a much greater range in temperature. Average July maximum temperature at LaGuardia Airport is 83.9°F and the record July maximum, 107°F. In January, New York City's average minimum temperature is 25.5°F, with a record of −3°F. In other words, New York's winter values are some 30 degrees below those of Miami while its July record maximum value exceeds that of Miami.

For New York City to enjoy a climate like Miami's, the entire circulation system of the atmosphere and ocean must completely break down and be reorganized. The trade winds would have to shift about 1,500 miles northward and all of the city's weather come from the east. More important, New York City would have to become surrounded by hundreds of miles of soup-warm ocean. A cursory look at North American geometry can dispel that notion. Cape Hatteras and the eastward extension of the Carolinas shunt the Gulf Stream off to the east. North and west of there, the water is chilly, south and east it is steamy. Even the wildest speculators on climate change will agree that global warming is *not* going to move North Carolina.

"By 2080, storms with 25-foot surges could hit New York every three to four years, inundating the Hudson River tunnels and flooding the edges of the financial district, causing billions of dollars in damage."

Suffice it to say that never in recorded history has a 25-foot storm surge hit New York City. As a matter of fact, no place on earth experiences 25-foot storm surges at a frequency of three to four years. It's difficult even to imagine such *otherworldly* conditions conjured from what Powell earlier refers to as the "middle-of-the-road and sometimes contradictory predictive models" on which the report is based. (It's easy, though, isn't it, to predict doom and gloom

80 to 100 years out? In that realm, anything, even the impossible, seems possible until you sit down to analyze it.)

"The brilliant reds, oranges and yellows of the maples, birches and beeches may be replaced by the browns and dull greens of oaks. [Within 20 years] the changes could potentially extirpate the sugar maple industry in New England."

If one accepts the outlandish proposition that New York City someday can experience Miami's climate while 25-foot storm surges routinely pound the Northeast coastline, then yes, New England's sugar maple industry probably will be pulled up by the roots and destroyed completely, only to be replaced by such vibrant industries as rampart building, skin diving, and sugar cane-raising.

But a couple of tourism bureaus might want to look into what amounts to a pretty bad slam on forests farther south. If the autumn colors generated in the oak, pine, gum, and maple woodlands of North Carolina's and Virginia's Blue Ridge move to New York and points north, then the Taconic State Parkway soon will experience the bumper-to-bumper traffic of the Skyline Drive and Blue Ridge Parkway. Color note: Oaks manifest a sharp red-brown (not dull green) leaf coloration toward the end of the leaf-gaping season.

In fairness, we can cut Powell some slack. His reportage relied on the U.S. National Assessment of global warming, a federal publication. But, we have to ask, what has become of the good old suspicion of the government that used to be a trademark of the *Post*?

7.2 Warming Winters in Europe: Human Influence or Random Change?

For the last half-century, Europe has been getting warmer—a trend that's evident in nearly all of that region's high-quality weather records. How much of this is a result of human influence and how much is a result of natural changes in climatic patterns that don't relate easily to increasing trace gas levels in the atmosphere?

Research by J. Otterman et al., published in *Geophysical Research Letters*, argues for a strong "natural" component. In winter, most of Europe is right in the middle of the westerly wind belt. The difference between warm and cold winters is directly related to changes in wind patterns. During cold winters, northwesterly winds dominate, bringing with them colder air masses from the North Atlantic Ocean.

Conversely, warm winters are more influenced by westerly and southwesterly winds that transport warm air masses from the warmer waters of the subtropical Atlantic over Europe.

So Otterman et al. examined the frequency of winter southwest winds from 1948 to 2002 over the Atlantic at key locations west of Europe. They found the strength of this flow into Europe from the Atlantic to be increasing at most study locations from 1948 to 1995 (see Figure 7.2 in color insert). That has to result in warmer winters.

But couldn't it also be a result of global warming? Perhaps, but the trend falls apart at all stations after 1995 (see Figure 7.2 in color insert). Although this is admittedly a short period of time on which to base major conclusions, the data since 1995 are inconsistent with the prior observations.

Otterman et al. went on to examine a circulation index called the North Atlantic Oscillation (or NAO). The NAO is calculated from the pressure differences between two semipermanent climate features in the Atlantic—a low-pressure zone around Iceland and a large "high" around the Azores. (When this feature extends westward, as it often does in the summer and fall, pumping up tropical air over the East Coast, it's called the "Bermuda High.") When the pressure difference between these two pressure cells is large, the NAO is termed "positive," westerly winds are strong, and European winters are warm. When the NAO is "negative" (meaning that the high- and/or the low-pressure zones are relatively weak), Europe typically can look forward to cold winters. The NAO increased significantly from 1950 through 1995, with an especially strong acceleration after 1980. But in 1995, this trend reversed, as we would expect, based on the southwesterly wind results. According to the authors—

> The strong trend in the southwesterlies, to which we attribute the bulk of the temperature rise until the 1996 winter, could possibly be a consequence of circulation changes associated with the global warming.... However, the 1996 downturn ... is not consistent with [the] steadily increasing trend implied by the global warming. *Attributing the 1950–1995 rise in European winter temperatures to global-warming-related circulation changes appears unwarranted* [emphasis added]. The 1948–1995 trend in the southwesterlies, and their contribution to the winter warming in Europe, should thus be considered to a large degree an aspect of the NAO.

Where were the major media on this story? Missing in action.

7.3 Longer Growing Seasons in the United States

Here's another big one where the media went AWOL.

The growing season is getting longer across most of the United States. That's the primary implication of a study by David Easterling of the National Climatic Data Center. Easterling examined daily weather records from the U.S. Historical Climate Network (HCN) from 1948 to 1999. The HCN is a prized record in the climate community, as it was specifically designed to include only stations with as little effect from urbanization and site disturbance as possible.

Easterling examined the history of the dates of first fall frost, last spring freeze, and the frost-free period in between (a.k.a. the growing season). He organized the data into climate regions and examined the statistical significance of the resulting trends. For most of the continental United States, the growing season is getting significantly longer (see Figure 7.3 in color insert). The lengthening is most pronounced in the western states (in California and Nevada, for example, the growing season is getting 5.4 days longer each decade!). There is no statistically significant change in the Midwest or the Southeast.

A longer growing season, coupled with higher carbon dioxide levels, suggests a continuing feast for American agriculture.

Another study, by Indiana University's Scott Robeson, also shows that spring is springing sooner. About one week's worth, in fact. Robeson looked at long-term records from Illinois and found that the last spring freeze is occurring about a week earlier, averaged across the state, than it did 100 years ago.

Both Robeson's and Easterling's findings are highly consistent with greenhouse theory, which predicts that dry air should warm much more rapidly than anything else. The cold air masses that cause the final freeze in spring can only reach sufficiently low night temperatures if their dewpoint (the temperature at which moisture will condense out) is near or below freezing. Dewpoint is a measure of the total amount of moisture in the air, so air masses with low dewpoints are very dry. Those are therefore the ones we expect the greenhouse effect to warm the most, and it is not surprising that Robeson found a slight lengthening on that end of the growing season.

Even so, this rather good news might seem worth reporting, yet apparently it was not.

7.4 Washington's Cherry Bomb

> The peak blooming date is dependent to a large extent on spring temperatures. Warmer springtime and nighttime temperatures tend to lead to an earlier bloom date. Both warmer average springtime temperatures and warmer nighttime temperatures are predicted to occur with global warming.
>
> —Dr. Janine Bloomfield and Sherry Showell,
> Environmental Defense

In March 2000, blossoms on the cherry trees surrounding the Tidal Basin and Jefferson Memorial in Washington, D.C., popped open about a week earlier than usual, prompting the recycling of that perennial news story that the premature profusion of pink is a dread result of global warming.

This hearty perennial received front-page coverage (above the fold) in the March 22 edition of the *Washington Post*. The *Post* offered two explanations, but neglected to click the mouse the requisite five times to determine which one was right.

First paragraph:

> Washington's fabled cherry trees, along with scores of other flowering plants in the region, are blooming, on average, a week earlier now than they did 30 years ago. The reason, according to a new study from Smithsonian Institution scientists is "global warming"—or at least warmer winter and spring nights.

Fifteenth paragraph:

> "It might not necessarily be global warming," said Vernon E. Kousky, a research meteorologist at the National Weather Service's Climate Prediction Center. "It's a safe bet that it could be the 'urban heat island' effect," whereby the accumulation of heat-holding asphalt and concrete raises the local average temperature, particularly the minimum temperature.

Not a paper to seem parochial, the *Post* also reported that flowers in London's Kew Gardens are doing the same darned thing. Those two urban capitals have something in common. But it has little to do with global heat. Cities tend to grow up around their weather stations, inner-city commercial cores, museums, and government buildings. Bricks and concrete retain the heat of the day and are especially adept at warding off late spring and early fall chills. This means that an urban growing season will increase its length whether or not the "globe" is warming.

GESUNDHEIT!

Soon after all the cherry hype in Washington, the 2000 election season began, along with the marching order to emphasize issues dear to Al Gore. President Clinton's Secretary of Agriculture, Dan Glickman, obliged by hyping a prominent U.S. Department of Agriculture (USDA) study trumpeting how his scientists discovered that levels of ragweed pollen are rising because of the increasing atmospheric concentration of carbon dioxide.

Not just ragweed. Most plants (including the world's major food crops) are doing better because of carbon dioxide fertilization. That fact is attested to in literally thousands of articles in the scientific literature. It has been estimated that crop yield has increased by about 10 percent as a consequence of anthropogenic carbon dioxide emissions, by an individual no less august than Sylvan Wittwer, former head of the Board on Agriculture for the National Research Council.

One might naively believe that the U.S. Department of Agriculture might sing the praises of something that helps agricultural produce flourish. Farmers need expend absolutely no additional effort to reap this benefit—a benefit documented by USDA researchers, including other research by the USDA scientist, Lewis Ziska, whose study resulted in Secretary Glickman's press release. The enhanced CO_2 is present rain or shine, at high temperature and low. USDA research demonstrates how carbon dioxide protects crops against the vagaries of climate, how plants grown under elevated CO_2 conditions better withstand stresses from drought, high temperature, insect predation, and lack of nutrients than do those grown at lower CO_2 concentrations.

Is it really any surprise, then, that ragweed enjoys those same benefits, increasing its growth rate and pollen yield?

(continued on next page)

(continued)

Although allergy sufferers might consider this a negative consequence, consider the alternative. Because ragweed responds like most plants do to its environment, if ragweed went into decline, that likely would be a sign that everything else was in decline as well. Although modern medicine is able to substantially reduce allergy suffering, it has yet to find a cure for hunger. A world where plants and crops grow better, on balance, is a world that is better fed and healthier, where there is less suffering and greater plant and animal diversity.

That Secretary Glickman ignored an abundance of USDA research to focus narrowly on a study he concludes "may help us better understand the troubling impact of high carbon dioxide levels on our environment and health" is yet more evidence that hyping global warming is political.

So much for the USDA's mission statement under his tenure: "To enhance the quality of life for the American people by supporting production of agriculture." If Glickman were to carry out that mission he'd have led a rally celebrating atmospheric CO_2 enhancement of plant growth and crop yields.

This is clearly the case for the District of Columbia and its close-in suburbs. Although downtown D.C. temperature records have warmed in a fairly steady fashion for the last 50 years, Dulles Airport—25 miles northwest—began its warming much later. That is, once all those government-serving industries and dot-coms began to spread out along the Dulles Access Road, thanks to the relatively favorable tax policies of Virginia (vs. Maryland). Much farther down the road in Charlottesville, Virginia, where the weather station is located in an observatory far from the sprawl of town-and-gown, temperatures haven't changed a lick.

Anyway, the *Post* could have easily discriminated between the "global warming" and "urban warming" explanation for early bloom of D.C.'s cherries.

All an enterprising investigative reporter need do is log on and type http://climate.virginia.edu.

The mean temperature of the Commonwealth of Virginia, of which Washington, D.C., is an excised part, hasn't changed at all in the 20th century.

Indeed, the entire southeastern quarter of North America has not experienced the type of warming evident in our nation's capital and other urban locales. Whatever it is that is warming Washington, it's a truly local effect embedded within regional temperature stasis.

At the dawn of the new millennium, more D.C. people were complaining about $2-a-gallon gasoline than they were griping about global warming. But even that price didn't discourage consumption in spring 2000 to any appreciable degree. Evidence? The massive traffic jams along Independence and Constitution Avenues in our Nation's capital. Why all the cars? People gawking at the precociously bloomed cherries.

7.5 Spinning Universities

As noted way back in Section 3.1, "The Snowjob of Kilimanjaro," university press services aren't beneath spinning its own faculties' global warming research into larger (and more alarming) cloth than its threads might warrant. Late in 2000, one good spin about food supply and global warming from the University of Florida seemed especially noteworthy.

The Institute of Food and Agricultural Services (IFAS) at the University of Florida led a December 2000 press release with "Temperature increases anticipated as part of global warming appear to significantly reduce rice yields, a finding that has worrisome implications for the third of the world's population that relies on rice as a primary staple." Well, there you have it! Or do you?

The press release, it turns out (once you do just a little digging), concerns results from yet-to-be-published research conducted by a graduate student whose work achieved the unsurprising outcome that rice grown in chambers with different temperature conditions has a lower yield in warmer chambers. That is an entirely predictable laboratory result. All else being equal, higher temperatures can be expected to produce lower yields. So the researcher tested the hypothesis and confirmed it. But who is responsible for extrapolating from that a consequence for global food supply? In the real world, *all else is not equal*. In truth, there will be a large number of confounding effects on future rice production. Ascertaining the impact of these intermingling variables will likely provide a very interesting professional career for any enterprising student.

Only one variable is mentioned in the press release: rising temperature. More heat-tolerant varieties might be developed. Washington State University botanist Maurice Ku is currently researching a strain of heat-resistant rice that is demonstrating increased yields of up to 35 percent. (Talk about more food to feed the world!)

But the central curiosity in the reportage of the University of Florida research is how it identifies "global warming" as a threat to world food production without mentioning what ostensibly causes the world to warm: a higher atmospheric concentration of carbon dioxide. This is all the more curious because tons of peer-reviewed research performed by IFAS scientists mentioned in the press release finds that rice grown under conditions of higher CO_2 shows large increases in photosynthetic rate, water-use efficiency, and a decreased rate of evapotranspiration. The conclusion? "Rice grown in the next century may use less water, use water more efficiently, and be able to tolerate drought better under some circumstances."

Even the increased temperature/decreased yield relationship isn't straightforward. In a 1995 literature review, Sylvan Wittwer concluded that, worldwide, rice culture is more constrained by low temperature than by high. Wittwer stated that a temperature increase may produce a net expansion of regions where rice can be grown successfully.

Recent research on observed climate trends in China by German professor Axel Thomas, including regions of heavy rice production, concludes, "Regional climatic change appears to have had a beneficial effect for several regions in China that have to cope with an increased demand on water resources by a growing population and industry as well as an intensified agriculture."

Ascertaining plant responses to varied climatic conditions is important work. But as the University of Florida press office amply demonstrated, it's easy to distort this through the prism of global warming alarmism.

7.6 For Peat's Sake: News in the Balance

Let's call the closer for this section "news in the balance." Even when balanced coverage appears in a big journal, the subsequent news coverage isn't.

The January 11, 2001, edition of *Nature* contained two articles on the interaction between enhanced carbon dioxide (CO_2) and ecosystems. One is a "Brief Communication" from Chris Freeman of the University of Wales and two coauthors. It is two-thirds of a page long. In it the authors claim that the increased frequency of drought accompanying global warming will stimulate an enzyme in peatlands and bogs. This pumped-up enzyme will, in turn, accelerate decomposition of organic matter and further increase the atmosphere's carbon dioxide content. The second article by Shuijin Hu of North Carolina State University and four coauthors spans three pages, which makes it a hefty piece for *Nature*. They measured the effect of increased carbon dioxide on the below-ground storage of organic matter in grasslands and found that a higher atmospheric concentration of CO_2 raises the rate of storage and accelerates the drawdown of CO_2 from the atmosphere.

Seeking climate news that's fit to print, the January 11, 2001, edition of the *New York Times* was all over both articles, sort of. The page A-16 headline reads, "Droughts Might Speed Climate Changes. Study Says Warming Helps Northern Soils Release Carbon Dioxide." Six of the article's 27 paragraphs (22 percent of the article) refer to the North Carolina research showing increased carbon sequestration. Nineteen paragraphs (or 70 percent) describe Freeman's work. Two more paragraphs of text (7 percent) provide background. Almost as many column inches are dedicated to a picture of Freeman as concern his research.

There's no other way to say it: This is biased coverage. The ratio in length of the scientific information contained in the two *Nature* articles favors the carbon drawdown research by 4:1. The *Times* ratio (including the picture) more than reverses the ratio and favors the *possibility* of increased CO_2 by 5 to 1! In other words, with regard to potential climate change, the *Times* favored the "bad" news over the "good."

It's not only the coverage that is curious; so is the reportage. The *Times* quotes ecologist Sandra Brown of the Winrock Institute, a group that advocates sustainability, to say that increased drought—which is required to bring Freeman's scenario forward—is likely. "The best predictions I've seen say it will be a warmer and drier climate," Brown is quoted as saying.

I called Dr. Brown. She began our conversation with "Let me tell you I am not a climatologist." She repeatedly told me she did *not*

Figure 7.4

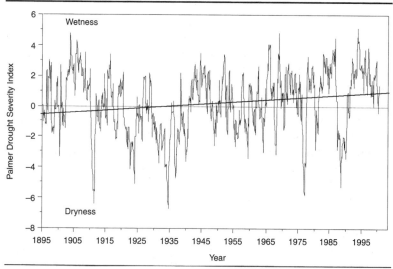

The Palmer Drought Severity Index for Minnesota, our peatiest state, shows a tendency for wetter, not drier conditions.

SOURCE: http:www.ncdc.noaa.gov.

tell the *Times* that "the best" predictions were for increased aridity. "I never said the best," she said at least three times. "I hate it when these people misquote."

Brown pointed out how the recent U.S. National Assessment (see Chapter 10) used two climate models, and how one predicts increased rainfall while the other predicts a decrease. "I am also very skeptical of the gloom-and-doom scenarios," she added.

How about a reality check? What does the Palmer Drought Severity Index for Minnesota—the peatiest among the lower 48 states—have to tell us? Despite a hundred years of an increasing atmospheric concentration of carbon dioxide, there is absolutely no evidence for an increase in drought in Minnesota (Figure 7.4). In fact, it's wetter.

8. Global Warming, Disease, and Death

> Diseases such as malaria and dengue fever will spread at an
> accelerated pace.
>
> —Sen. Bill Nelson (D-Fla.), June 8, 2001

> Heat-related deaths will increase 100 percent in cities such as
> New York, Philadelphia, Cleveland, Los Angeles, and others.
>
> —Sen. James Jeffords (I-Vt.), February 14, 2002

Obviously, many politicians are concerned that global warming
will cause the spread of tropical diseases and increased heat-related
mortality in America's cities. Their logic is pretty simple—which
makes it easy to scare the populace. Tropical illnesses, by definition,
occur in hot environments. Given that global warming must make
things hotter, these diseases must therefore spread, right? And, as
evinced by the hundreds of people who died in the big Chicago
heat wave of July 1995, the hotter our cities get, the argument goes,
the more the elderly, poor, and infirm die. That's certainly the
impression you get from the dour pronouncements of politicians
and the items the press selects from the scientific literature. But here
are three nice examples of things that didn't make it into the news.

8.1 Global Warming and Malaria?

> Insects are bringing illnesses like malaria and dengue to
> higher altitudes in Africa, Asia and Latin America. It was
> also reported . . . that continued global warming will cause
> the spread of these diseases and also encephalitis and yellow
> fever to higher latitudes
>
> —Paul Epstein, Harvard School of Public Health,
> *San Francisco Chronicle*, September 28, 1996

Are observed changes in malaria occurrence a result of climate
change? That the climate change in East Africa is altering the range,

179

population, and survivability of malaria-carrying mosquitoes is a simple, if suspect, assumption. Oxford University's Simon Hay investigated the hypothesis that something else is the cause. In his research, Hay found no relationship between warming and the spread of malaria.

Plasmodium falciparum (the parasite that causes malaria) can be transmitted when average temperatures exceed 15°C (59°F) and rainfall exceeds 152 mm (6.0 inches) for two consecutive months. Using those criteria, Hay plotted the number of months in which malaria could be transmitted at four East African sites where recent malaria increases have been observed (Figure 8.1). The only site with a statistically significant increase in malaria is Kabale (Uganda), and even there the biggest increase occurred in the 1960s, not recently.

Hay also examined temperature and precipitation trends. As an example, Figure 8.2a shows mean, maximum, and minimum temperatures at Kericho (Kenya), since 1970; Figure 8.2b shows the monthly rainfall. Obviously there's no change. Results were similar at three other highland stations. As the paper succinctly states—

> The absence of long- and short-term change in the climate variables and the duration of *P. falciparum* malaria transmission suitability at these highland sites are not consistent with the *simplistic notion* [emphasis added] that recent malaria resurgences in these areas are caused by rising temperatures.

So why is malaria increasing? There are myriad reasons. At Kericho and in the Usambara mountains of Tanzania, there has been an increase in antimalarial drug resistance. In southern Uganda, recent increases seem linked to weather changes, perhaps associated with the recent El Niño. In other locations, population migrations and the breakdown of the health service infrastructure have made people more susceptible. According to Hay, "Economic, social, and political factors can therefore explain recent resurgences in malaria and other mosquito-borne diseases with no need to invoke climate change."

Hay's research team ends the paper with a call for health researchers to be more responsible and question implicit assumptions about climate change:

> The more certain climatologists become that humans are affecting global climates, the more critical epidemiologists should be of the evidence indicating that these changes affect malaria.

Figure 8.1

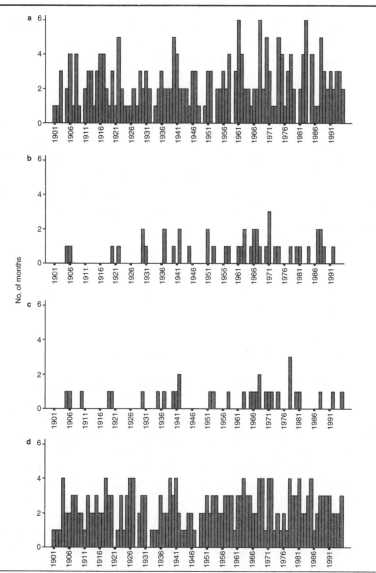

Number of months per year in which *Plasmodium falciparum* malaria could be transmitted, from 1901 to 1995, at (a) Kericho, Kenya; (b) Kabale, Uganda; (c) Gikonko, Rwanda; and (d) Muhanga, Burundi.

SOURCE: Hay, *Nature*, 2002.

Figures 8.2a and 8.2b

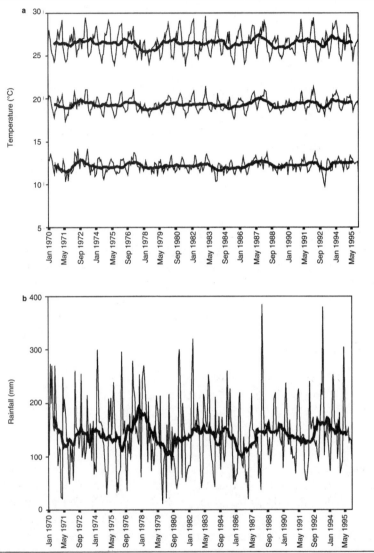

(a) Maximum, mean, and minimum temperature time series for Kericho, Kenya; (b) total monthly rainfall time series for Kericho, Kenya; all data have a 13-month moving average superimposed to show the long-term change (or lack thereof).

SOURCE: Hay, *Nature*, 2002.

8.2 West Nile Virus, Mosquitoes, and Global Warming

Summer of '03: West Nile Virus Looms as Threat to Humans and Wildlife

—environmentaldefense.org, July 7, 2003

West Nile virus outbreaks have been related to a combination of heat and drought followed by heavy downpours. And that kind of weather pattern, according to The Intergovernmental Panel on Climate Change, is likely to occur more often with global warming.

—Dickson Despommier, Ph.D., Columbia University, and Janine Bloomfield, Ph.D., Environmental Defense

According to the Centers for Disease Control (CDC), West Nile virus has resulted in a few dozen deaths in the United States since it first appeared in the United States in 1999. Dead birds are typically the harbinger that the disease has moved into a particular area. The CDC does not consider West Nile, which was first discovered in Uganda in 1937, to be a serious health threat in the United States.

Nonetheless, its presence today has all the makings of a global warming scare story:

- The disease wasn't here in 1998, but it was in 1999.
- Recent years have been warm.
- Mosquitoes are the disease vector, and mosquitoes thrive in a warm climate.

What more do you need?

Harvard School of Medicine's Paul Epstein fell into this trap in a 2000 editorial printed in the *Washington Post*. Epstein noted that the West Nile cases that appeared in New York followed a period of changeable weather—"The prolonged drought and intense heat lasted until the pendulum swung ferociously in the opposite direction, bringing torrential end-of-August rains." Sounds scary and dramatic! (Atmospheric scientists have another, somewhat less compelling term for this—a cold-front passage.) But in Epstein's world, this is just the type of situation that sets the stage for the emergence of a new disease:

It was extreme weather events that allowed the West Nile virus to be launched with a vengeance in this hemisphere in 1999. Now, with the virus well established on America's eastern seaboard, wide swings in weather—the projected hallmark of global climate change—threaten to encourage mosquito breeding and spawn new outbreaks in the future.

(With regard to increasing weather variability in the United States, take a look at Section 6.2.)

Is there really anything to the possibility that mosquito-borne disease patterns might change as the planet warms? Will mosquitoes buzz merrily about in a blood-sucking frenzy across our DDT-free planet? The most thorough and balanced review on mosquitoes and climate change was penned in 2001 by the CDC's Paul Reiter in *Environmental Health Perspectives*. It's a thorough and fascinating read for anyone who wants to know everything about diseases derived from mosquito bites.

As with so many other topics in this book, this one is filled with relationships that would be considered unexpected at first blush. For example, you might naturally expect more disease transmission with high temperatures since they reduce the time required for incubation of the pathogen within the mosquito. But egg-laying and biting—both high-risk activities if you're a mosquito—should also accelerate, and that could lower the survival rate and thereby *reduce* transmissions.

Rainfall produces pools of stagnant water that can serve as mosquito breeding sites. Yet heavy rains have a flushing effect, removing mosquitoes from those areas. Drought can eliminate standing water (fewer mosquitoes), but also cause flowing water to stagnate (more mosquitoes). Then again, drought can also encourage more people to capture and store water in cisterns that can serve as breeding sites. Clearly, the relationship between rainfall and mosquito breeding is complex.

Given that it's effectively impossible to predict mosquito-borne disease transmission based on climate, what are the known factors that are important? Reiter identifies several influences:

Population growth and urbanization. Rapid increase in the population in malarial areas of the tropics and subtropics and the urbanization of these regions greatly increase the likelihood of disease spread.

Human mobility. Increased use of roads and air travel, especially to and from developing nations, allows diseases to extend their reach—from, for example, lesser developed nations where potable water and even window screens are scarce and malaria more prevalent.

War, civil strife, and natural disasters. Mass movements of people promote malaria transmission, and unrest often affects the infrastructure, such as damaging water distribution networks. Further, high concentrations of displaced people in camps is a classic scenario for high disease incidence.

Resistance to insecticides. Since pesticides kill off the weaker individuals in a population, the remaining individuals are stronger and pass this physiological resistance along to their descendants.

Air conditioning. Not only does air conditioning prevent people from dying during heat waves, but it also dampens mosquito enthusiasm. People basking in the comfort of air conditioning are less exposed to mosquitoes, and if those pests gain entry to one's humble abode, they have a tough time surviving in the low temperature and humidity. (Again, even something as simple as window screens can improve matters by limiting exposure.)

And those are just a few of the factors that influence the transmission of mosquito-borne diseases.

Here's another example that demonstrates how complex this problem really is and the difficulty of prediction. The species *Aedes aegypti* is responsible for the transmission of yellow fever. After World War II, a major effort was put forth to eradicate *aegypti* from the Western Hemisphere via DDT. Despite tremendous early success, because of insufficient persistence and the presence of a few small *aegypti* pockets, by the late 20th century the species had spread beyond its original range. Then, in the United States, an Asian species named *Aedes albopictus* appeared via an incoming shipment of used tires and has since completely displaced *aegypti*.

According to Reiter,

> This displacement of one species by another illustrates a major flaw in the popular debate on climate change. Biotic responses to climate change cannot be predicted on the mere basis of climate envelopes. The distribution of a species is determined by its interaction with other species and by many

other behavioral and ecological factors. It is therefore naive to suggest that species will move to higher latitudes and altitudes simply on the basis of temperature change.

Plumping for Diseases

There is often a major disconnect between what a scientist may write in a scientific journal and what a reporter may write about that same article after interviewing the author, based upon that interview and not on the journal article. It may not be the fault of the reporter: Perhaps the researcher gets excited about the sudden media attention and inflates or exaggerates what is being written about. In other instances, perhaps the reporter believes only gloom and doom will get the story by the editor and uses only the "sexiest" quotes while omitting the researcher's scientific caveats or statements of uncertainty that seemingly diminish the story's impact. Whatever the reason, such stories appear with remarkable frequency. To wit:

The June 21, 2002, edition of *Science* contained a review article by Drew Harvell of Cornell University and six coauthors titled, "Climate Warming and Disease Risks for Terrestrial and Marine Biota." As a review, the article was a compendium of many researchers' previous work and therefore included little that was scientifically new. Rather, its purpose was to assemble recent findings on how climate affects diseases and how conditions for disease transmission *might* change if current climate trends stay on track. Here are some excerpts:

> Associations between climate and disease do not necessarily imply causation.

> Difficulty in separating directional climate change from short-term variation has made it challenging to associate climate warming with disease prevalence or severity.

> Whether [vector-borne disease] expansions are due primarily to climate change or other anthropogenic influences (e.g., habitat alteration or drug-resistant strains] is controversial, as is predicting future distributional changes in disease prevalence. . . . In fact, expansion of antimalarial resistance and failed vector control programs are probably as important as climate factors in driving recent malaria expansions.

> We found no unequivocal examples of natural changes in severity or prevalence resulting from directional climate warming *per se*.

The paper is filled with caveats like those, as scientific writing should be when it is about something as nebulous as how climate might potentially affect disease. After all, it amounts to nothing more than speculation when so many factors completely unrelated to climate are far more important than climate change itself in determining why a given animal or plant is infected by a particular disease.

But news reports on this paper were radically different. From the Associated Press, we heard: "A warming climate will allow disease-causing pathogens to thrive in places they once could not live, posing a new risk for species as diverse as butterflies and humans, oysters, and lions, a study suggests." Notice the emphasis on expressed certainty ("will allow"), and the buried attribution admitting that the study only suggests the possibility.

AP then quotes Andrew Dobson, the fifth coauthor of the report, as sounding much more certain and definitive than he does in his own article: "Climate change is disrupting natural ecosystems in a way that is making life better for infectious diseases." Dobson says, "The risk for humans is going up." Even lead author Drew Harvell appears to have found it difficult to resist, saying, "Just a one- or two-degree change in temperature can lead to disease outbreaks."

The plain truth is that climate plays an extremely minor role in the transmission of pathogens. Everything else being equal, given a small change in climate, some diseases will spread somewhat and others will recede somewhat. But to assume everything else will be equal is a poor scientific assumption. Think about technology, antibiotics, genetic engineering and sanitation, to name a few things that sure aren't "equal" over time and distance. Change in climate is so small by comparison that it is nearly irrelevant. What is not small is the dissonant convergence between media hungry for dramatic news and researchers eager for a place in the paper or on TV. In today's climate, that's a major scientific disease vector.

8.3 We're All Gonna Die!

> On a warmer planet, intense heat waves alone are by 2050 likely to result in increases in death by cardiac and respiratory ills of several thousand a year—especially in urban areas and among the elderly and very young.
>
> —*Wall Street Journal,* October 19, 1999

[Based upon data from several North American cities,] the annual number of heat-related deaths would approximately double by 2020 and would increase several-fold by 2050.

—United Nations' Intergovernmental
Panel on Climate Change, 1996

Death has a way of focusing attention—as in some government report claiming that, by the middle of this century, thousands of Americans will die every summer from global warming. Such forecasts are based on projected increases in the "apparent temperature" (also called the "Heat Index"). It's summer's partner to winter's nefarious "wind chill index" that tells us how cold a naked person feels. The Heat Index is actually more credible. Based on a combination of air temperature and moisture, it estimates the level of discomfort a person feels during the warm season. For example, an air temperature of 100°F coupled with a relative humidity of 45 percent makes it feel like 115°F (see Figure 8.3 in color insert).

Apparent temperatures have been linked to human health impacts. Heat Index values in excess of 105°F produce heat exhaustion in a sizable portion of the population, while a smaller, more susceptible cohort can suffer from heat stroke. When apparent temperatures exceed 130°F, widespread heat stroke becomes likely. Although most people who suffer from heat exhaustion can recover fairly quickly when they are dehydrated, with heat stroke, in which the body's core temperature reaches 105°F and the sweating mechanism shuts down, about 15 percent of victims die.

Since climate models predict changes in both temperature and humidity, it's a simple matter to calculate the Heat Index. Figure 8.4 (see color insert) shows the Canadian Climate Centre's model's forecasts for the July average Heat Index increases across the continental United States by the year 2100. (More, *much* more, on this model beginning in Chapter 10, about the *U.S. National Assessment* of global warming.) Although it's not clear from the report, let's assume these apply by the year 2100. The most stunning aspect of this prediction is the projected increases of 25°F in July apparent temperatures across the southeastern United States. If these were realized, most of the region would see apparent temperatures of 120°F on an average July day. If that happened, a lot of people would die. Or wish they had.

Without equivocation, it is a 100 percent ironclad certainty that the Canadian Climate Centre's climate forecast is wrong. It's not often you hear such a bold statement about global warming, even in this book. But I make it with total confidence because some of the key physics that drive our climate are completely missing from the model that produced it. One impact of those omissions is ludicrously high maximum temperature projections.

Consider reality instead of the model. Globally, where do we see the highest maximum temperatures? In the subtropical deserts, of course, such as those in northern Africa and the Middle East. And what characterizes a desert? That's obvious. Dryness: It's hot in the desert because deserts are dry.

What controls maximum temperature? University of Virginia climatologist Bruce Hayden explored that question in a 1998 paper in *Philosophical Transactions of the Royal Society of London.* The average maximum temperature in the hottest time of the year in Manaus, Brazil, near the equator, is about 31°C (88°F), but the record high is only 35°C (95°F). How can a place near the equator that has plenty of direct sunlight never really get very hot? If the surface is wet, it takes about nine times more energy to evaporate water than to actually raise the temperature. In fact, if we look across the globe at data from weather stations in forested regions (which require plenty of precipitation over the long term for their sustenance), not a single forested landscape has average high temperatures much above 90°F.

Let's apply that knowledge to the Heat Index forecasts. Even if we assume atmospheric moisture levels will rise from increased future evaporation, those increases will be relatively small (a few percent in terms of the relative humidity values in Figure 8.3's Heat Index chart). The only way to really jack up the Heat Index is to raise temperatures. And to raise temperatures, we must decrease rainfall.

That's extremely difficult to do across the Southeast, with the Gulf of Mexico's limitless source of tropical moisture lurking nearby. So the only real way the Canadian Centre's apparent temperature forecasts could come true is if, by 2100, we drain and pave the Gulf of Mexico. Just imagine the environmental impact statement for that project!

Throughout the 20th century, precipitation has been increasing across the United States. At present, the models are incapable of forecasting future precipitation at a regional scale because they cannot reproduce current patterns. In a recent report for the Washington, D.C., Marshall Institute, University of Delaware climatologist David Legates reviews the precipitation forecasts in the U.S. National Assessment of climate change (see Chapter 10) and notes that errors in some regions equal more than double the mean annual precipitation. Legates concludes: "Anthropogenic climate change estimates are still uncertain (given the discrepancies between most models), and scenarios derived from still incomplete GCMs should not be used to assess future climate change or make national assessments."

In short, unless current rain stops falling over the southeastern United States over the next 100 years, future apparent temperatures will be only slightly higher than they are now.

Global Warming and Urban Mortality

According to the infamous *National Assessment* of global warming, "populations in urban areas are most vulnerable to adverse heat-related health outcomes. Heat indexes and heat-related mortality rates are higher in the urban core than in surrounding areas." That report, along with the United Nations statement on global warming and urban death, serves as our national and international authority on the relationship between heat and mortality, with the obvious implication that warming of our cities will lead to increasing heat-related death.

In reality, however, without assistance from the global warming phenomenon, our cities have been part of an experiment for decades as they warm up from the well-known "urban effect" on temperature: Bricks and buildings retain the heat of the day and impede ventilating winds. Most major urban core regions in the United States have warmed 1°C to 2°C (Washington, D.C., being a prime example) as a result of simple urbanization. Consequently, large North American cities are heat islands that allow us to test whether increased temperature does indeed create increased mortality.

On the surface, of course, the arguments of the *National Assessment* and the IPCC seem absurd, implying no compensatory adaptation fueled by changing technology, when humans have adapted marvelously to change, including climate change, for centuries. To test hypotheses about warming and urban mortality, my University of Virginia colleague Robert Davis and I examined changes in the

Figures 8.5a and 8.5b

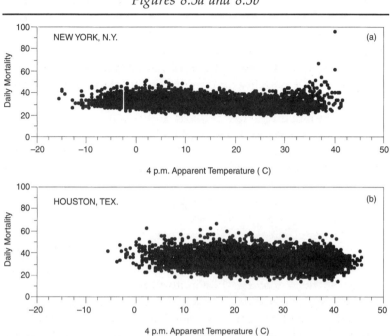

(a) Population-adjusted daily mortality vs. 4 p.m. apparent temperature for New York City; (b) same as in (a) except for Houston. Notice that on the hottest days, daily mortality in New York City rises rapidly, while there is no change in Houston.

SOURCE: Davis, University of Virginia, personal communication.

relationships between human mortality and hot, humid weather for 28 U.S. cities with populations greater than one million on a decadal time scale. Twenty-nine years of daily total mortality rates (1964–1998, with some years missing in the early 1970s) were standardized to account for changes in death rates related to inherent variations in the age of the population, and organized by decade for each city. Daily mortality rates were related to afternoon apparent temperatures. We calculated the annual excess mortality on days when apparent temperatures exceeded a threshold value for 28 major metropolitan areas in the United States.

Figure 8.5a shows daily mortality and apparent temperature for New York City. Although mortality actually declines with temperature rise, there are a number of clear excursions in death rates at the very highest temperatures. These were simply extrapolated by the *National Assessment* and the IPCC to form future mortality expectations.

Yet, at the same time, it is very clear that infrastructure is very important in determining heat-related mortality. Figure 8.5b shows the temperature-mortality relationship for Houston, a more modern city built near the very warm Gulf of Mexico. There is no excursion in the death rate on the hottest days.

Obviously, there is some personal and economic incentive to survive, so we hypothesized that adaptation should lead to a general decline in urban heat-related mortality, and this is what the data show.

Contrary to the implied hypothesis in the *National Assessment* and the explicit assertion by the United Nations IPCC, we found that heat-related mortality rates declined over time in 24 of the 28 cities (Figure 8.6). For the 28-city average, there were 41.0 excess heat-related deaths per year (per standard million population) in the 1960s–1970s, 17.3 in the 1980s, and 10.5 in the 1990s. In the 1960s–1970s, almost all study cities exhibited significantly above-normal death rates on hot and humid days. During the 1980s, many cities, particularly those in the southern United States, exhibited no excess mortality. In the 1990s, this effect spread northward across interior cities. Figure 8.6 shows trends in decadal mortality in major U.S. cities since the late 1960s. The overall negative tendency is obvious and especially marked in the old urban cores of the Northeast.

An interesting anomaly occurs in Seattle, which is the least air-conditioned major city in the United States. Although heat-related mortality figures are themselves very low (owing to the cool climate), there is an obvious rise in recent decades. There simply isn't enough incentive—in the form of number of deaths—to begin the adaptation process.

Also rather remarkable is the decline in mortality through the 1990s in Chicago, despite the approximately 500 deaths in the four-day heat wave of mid-July 1995. "Approximately" is appropriate because it is impossible to precisely capture all heat-related deaths, particularly in a massive incident such as this one. Actual estimates of the number range from 300 to 800, depending on the methodology used.

Figure 8.6

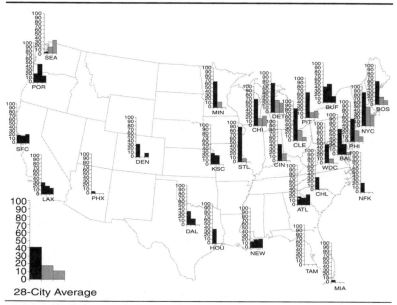

28-City Average

Decadal mortality since the late 1960s in major American cities. The overall decline is significant and contrary to projections from the United Nations and the *U.S. National Assessment* of global warming.

SOURCE: Davis et al., *Environmental Health Perspectives*, 2003.

The overall decadal decline in mortality in most cities is probably because of adaptations: increased air-conditioning usage, improved health care, and heightened public awareness of the biophysical impacts of heat exposure. This finding of a more muted mortality response of the U.S. populace to high apparent temperatures over time raises doubts about the validity of projections of future U.S. mortality increases linked to potential greenhouse warming.

What can explain such authoritative bodies such as the National Assessment "Synthesis Team" and the UN IPCC asserting "facts" on warming and urban-related death that turn out to be so obviously false? Clearly, something is very wrong in the scientific culture of global warming.

Conspicuously Absent Reporting

In September 2000, a major British journal cogently argues that there are tons more cold-weather-related deaths than those from

193

heat, and that warming the climate will reduce net deaths. *Not one news story followed.*

The study, by a research team led by W. R. Keatinge of Queen Mary and Westfield College in London, appeared in the September 16, 2000, edition of the *British Medical Journal*. The researchers examined daily mortality among the elderly and its relationship to temperature at a number of stations representing the climate extremes experienced throughout Europe.

They concentrated on people between 65 and 74 years of age because it is within that age group that the highest weather sensitivity is observed. On an annual basis in all regions, they found that cold-related mortality greatly exceeds heat-related mortality. On average, there were 2,003 deaths per million people between 65 and 74 as a result of cold and 217 deaths per million as a result of heat—nearly a 10:1 ratio of cold-related deaths compared with those caused by heat.

When considering the effects of climate warming in Europe, the authors note that the current population is well adjusted to a wide range of climate extremes, for example, the difference between the climate of northern Finland and that of Athens. On that basis, they conclude there is little reason to think that people would be unable to successfully adapt to a projected warm-up of several degrees during the next 50 years. However, the researchers assert that if a few, simple adaptive measures are taken, such as improving home ventilation and installing air conditioning in dwellings in which those within the vulnerable population are housed, the effect of temperature rise on heat-related deaths would be minimal. Warmer winter temperatures would lead to a decline in cold-related mortality. Winter is the season of the year when warming due to increases in the greenhouse effect is anticipated to be greatest.

The authors conclude—

> Our analysis indicates that in the regions we have studied the direct effect of the moderate warming predicted in the next fifty years would be to reduce, at least briefly, both winter mortality and total mortality. This could be continued into a large, sustained reduction in overall mortality if additional action is taken to prevent relaxation of protective measures against outdoor and indoor cold stress as winters become milder.

9. No Fact Checks, Please!

Our final collection of uncritical science revolves around claims of dramatically increasing temperatures and what appears to be "wishful science." Unfortunately, the incessant repetition of both creates political interest, which can create some pretty disastrous public policy.

9.1 Warmer and Warmer and Warmer?

Every December, the race is on to see who can publish the first article about how warm the previous year has been. As a consequence, its annual appearance makes the story appear a bit jaded. In 2002, a new twist was added: The rate of global warming is increasing dramatically!

In December of that year, Lisa McFarling reported in the *Los Angeles Times* that "groups that are concerned about climate change point out that the rate of warming is steeply increasing." The proof? McFarling quoted Lester Brown, author of the annual "State of the World" reports that impending ecological doom is at hand: "Studying these annual temperature data, one gets the unmistakable feeling that the temperature is rising and that the rise is gaining momentum," Brown says.

"Feelings" aren't a good metric either for science or reporting. In fact, it is easy to test whether the rate of warming is increasing or is constant. Most scientists believe that the earth's temperature turned a corner sometime in the mid- or late 1970s, when a three-decade cooling period ended abruptly and a warming began. So let's start the analysis in 1977. Figure 4.15 in Chapter 4 shows the average warming rate for successive periods beginning with the first five years (1977–1982), and incrementing year by year. If the *Los Angeles Times* and Lester Brown were right—and if the latter had really "studied" the data instead of relying on his "feelings"—he would have found *no significant trend whatsoever in the rate of warming*. Not even the huge El Niño of 1998 puts a false increase in the record in the last few years. Instead, the rise just hugs a constant 0.15°C (0.27°F) per decade.

Further, though he is characterized by the *Times* as a "respected authority," Brown seems remarkably out-of-step with global warming science, since the central tendency of most climate models is to produce constant—not exponential—rates of warming, something the observations bear out, and noted in the beginning of this book.

Have Brown and the *Los Angeles Times* discovered something new? Could it be that all that money got the mathematical form of future warming wrong? For the time being, according to Figure 4.15, the answer is a clear *no*.

9.2 A "Change Point"?

Even those of us jaded by glib assertions from within our government about the imminence of climate apocalypse were shocked by reports in the February 23, 2000, edition of the *Washington Post* and circulated on the Associated Press newswire describing a new study by federal climatologist Tom Karl. According to the *Post*,

> A new analysis of global temperature records since 1880 indicates that the spectacular warming of 1997 and 1998 may mark a "change point" at which the planet's surface suddenly began to heat up faster than in previous decades. The current pace of temperature rise is "consistent with a rate of 3 to 3.5 degrees Celsius per century," or 5.4 to 6.3 degrees Fahrenheit, said Thomas R. Karl, Director of the National Oceanic and Atmospheric Administration's National Climatic Data Center.

> "We're not claiming at this time that we're sure the rate has definitely climbed to that upper end of the scale," said Karl. But their statistical analysis indicates a good chance that it has.

What is a reader to take from that? Clearly, a major federal scientist now indicates that a rapid and sudden warming in two recent years is evidence for more rapid warming than is generally projected for the future. At least that's what a typical reader is going to take away from the words "good chance."

Using a newly developed temperature history from the U.S. National Climatic Data Center, Karl compared the results of climate model projections for the next century with the fact that 1997 and

1998 contained 16 consecutive months that were the "warmest" for that particular month. There was no press mention of the fact that only one among the 16 months was an all-time record temperature across all months.

The "central tendency" of all those climate model projections—based on the model intercomparison studies detailed earlier—is for around 2.0°C (3.6°F) of warming in the next century. The actual warming rate between 1975 and 2003 is 0.17°C per decade (0.31°F). As noted earlier, a mere 10 times this figure is a pretty good starting point for the best estimate for future warming, but for the purposes of argument (and given the fact that this is hardly exact science), this works out pretty close to the aforementioned two degrees Celsius.

Karl searched the statistics generated by those types of models and found that there was only a 5 percent chance that such an anomalous warming period as we have recently experienced would be accompanied by a mere 2°C per century warming. Instead, such an anomaly would approach 50 percent likelihood if the models had predicted 3°C warming in a century (his press quote centers higher, at the 3.0°C–3.5°C noted earlier). Karl called 1997–1998 a potential "change point" in the warming rate.

At first glance, this was doubtless the scariest global warming pronouncement yet made by a scientist of Karl's stature.

But a more detailed assessment finds major problems. The period Karl studied coincides exactly with 1997–1998's big El Niño. In fact, it was El Niño that caused the high temperatures. According to the weather satellites used to measure the temperature of the entire troposphere, that warm "blip" was long-gone by the time this news story appeared. In fact, globally averaged temperatures were below the average in the satellite record by February 2000.

Ditto for the temperatures measured by surface thermometers. By the time this article hit the news, they had also returned to where they were before the El Niño (see Figure 9.1). NASA's surface record had January 2000 below average. In fact, Karl's own record shows how temperatures have receded during the two years after the El Niño peak at exactly the same rate they rose as the El Niño began!

There's a further problem. Karl compared the output of climate models, in order to raise their forecast, because of what he is calling a "change point." But none of the climate models contains a change point! Instead, once models begin to show human warming, with few

Figure 9.1

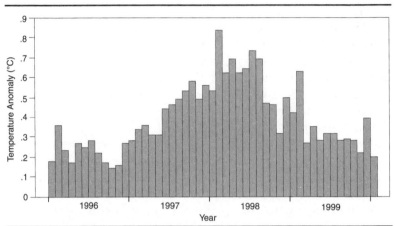

The 1997–1998 temperature rise that led Karl's research teams to conclude that a "change point" had occurred in the rate of global temperature increase was equaled by the temperature decline since then. As shown here, shortly before publication of the "change point" story, temperatures in January 2000 had returned to the level they were at in 1996 before the big El Niño of 1997–1998. This is the same record used in the "change point" study.

SOURCE: http://www.cru.uea.ac.uk.

exceptions, that warming continues at a constant rate, a phenomenon mentioned several times in this book.

Someone no less eminent than NASA scientist James Hansen reiterated that fact concerning the relative constancy of forecast warming when the *Post* staff writer asked him about Karl's new paper. Hansen told the *Post* he expected global temperatures in "the first decade of this century to be a couple of tenths of a degree higher" than the present. That sure sounds like 0.2°C to this reader, or the rounded rate of warming one gets from the argument of linear warming.

At the time of this report, there was one model that was a glaring exception, the Canadian Climate Centre model, which produces an ever-increasing rate of warming. Guess which model was featured in the subsequent *U.S. National Assessment* of global warming? But even that model doesn't exhibit a "change point."

9.3 Wishful Science?

Do climate scientists themselves—those responsible for taking the world's temperature—subliminally wish for global warming? An incident in 2002 sure points in that direction.

Usually it's some time close to the end of a year—say, October or November—before anyone ranks a year in relation to the warmest on record. But, in 2002, the British Meteorological Office simply couldn't wait and, on July 31, bet that the global temperature during the next five months had a very good chance of producing the warmest year on record. A cold analysis of the facts shows that the chance was indeed quite remote. Such facts are available to any climate scientist, and that they were ignored tells us much about the scientific dynamic of the global warming issue.

By the end of July 2002, all it had to go on was that the first six months of 2002 appeared to be the second-warmest on record. Then they somehow asserted that 2002 "may even break the record [for warmest year] set in 1998."

A betting man or woman would argue that "may" in a press release means there's a pretty good chance (and that's also what "may" generally means, as opposed to "might," which indicates a level of doubt). So, here's a little calculation, given the data through July 31, 2002, on the odds of that year being the warmest in the instrumental record, which goes back to 1856.

The temperature anomaly for the warmest year on record (as contained in the Met Office's own global temperature history since 1856) is 0.593°C above the 1961–1990 average, set in the El Niño-dominated 1998. And 1998 also holds the record for the greatest temperature anomaly during its first six months of 2002 at 0.657°C.

The Met Office had stated the first six months of 2002 were the second warmest on record with an anomaly of 0.570°C. That means the anomaly over the remaining six months would have to average 0.617°C above the 1961–1990 mean, or higher, for 2002 to break the 1998 record. Figure 9.2 shows what happened through June 30. The temperature departure from normal for each month is represented by the black bars. The average monthly anomaly that would have been required during the next six months to break the record is represented by the gray bars. Notice how the monthly temperature anomaly lessened from month to month as 2002 progressed (gray arrow). That should have been a red flag for the Met Office! In the

Figure 9.2

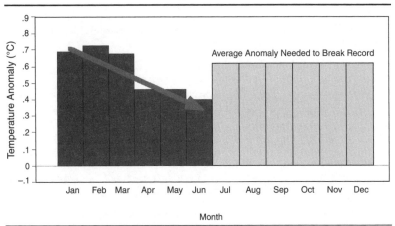

Temperature anomaly for the first six months of 2002 (black). Gray bars represent the average anomaly that was necessary in each of the remaining six months for 2002 to break the record for the warmest year set in 1998. Despite this glaring problem, the British Meteorogical Office produced a press release in July stating that 2002 "may" be the warmest year on record.
SOURCE: http://www.cru.uea.ac.uk.

absence of any special knowledge, the default climate forecast is always "persistence"; in other words, the assumption is that what has been happening will continue. Yet the Met Office waxed operatic about record-breaking temperatures for 1998—a situation that would have required a reversal of persistence, meaning a considerable string of warm months.

Figure 9.3 includes data from the 36 years in the entire (1856–2002) record in which the first six months were recorded to be warmer than the 1961–1990 reference average. It shows the difference in temperature when the average temperature anomaly of the first six months is subtracted from the average temperature anomaly in the second half of the year. The differences are ranked from lowest to highest.

When the black bars in Figure 9.3 are negative (below the zero line), the second half of the year was not as anomalously warm as the first half. When the bars are on the positive side of the line (above zero), the second half of the year had a greater temperature anomaly than experienced in the first months. For 2002 to break

Figure 9.3

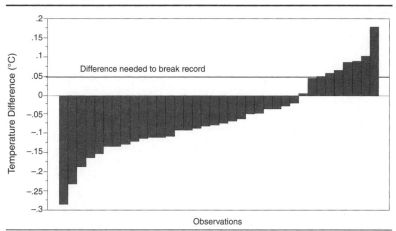

The temperature difference when the anomaly from the first half of the year is subtracted from the anomaly of the second half of the year during each year when the first half of the year was warmer than normal. A difference of 0.046°C is needed for 2002 to become the warmest year on record. That's happened only on 7 of 36 occasions.

SOURCE: http://www.cru.uea.ac.uk.

1998's record, July through December had to average 0.046°C above the departure from normal observed in the first six months.

Figure 9.3 shows that, out of the 36 recorded occasions when the first half of the year was warmer than the referenced average, only 7 times did the temperature anomaly of the years' second half exceed 0.046°C. That works out to a chance of 19.4 percent. On that basis, 2002 had little chance of becoming the warmest year in the record.

Perhaps the Met Office was thinking that a strong El Niño would develop in late 2002, which would have spiked temperatures. At the time of its statement, there was some preliminary information that an El Niño was brewing in the tropical Pacific, but it was characterized as "weak." According to the U.S. Climate Prediction Center (an organization that closely monitors El Niño activity), on July 11, 2002—

> The oceanic and atmospheric variables discussed above reflect the presence of El Niño conditions. Most coupled model and statistical model forecasts indicate that El Niño

201

conditions are likely to continue through the end of 2002 and into early 2003. Although there is considerable uncertainty in the forecasts about the timing and intensity of the peak of this warm episode, all of the forecasts indicate that it will be much weaker than the 1997–1998 El Niño. It is important to add that the global impacts of this warm episode should be correspondingly weaker than those observed during the very strong 1997–1998 El Niño.

Given all of this, why did the British Meteorological Office shinny so far out on such a thin limb? One reason might be that its press release resulted in the Reuters worldwide news service headline, "World Heads for Warmest Year Yet." Rest assured, that was not followed by a December 2002 or January 2003 headline "Forecast of Record Hot Year Wrong . . . Had Little Basis in History, Critics Say."

There's no excuse for such wishful science. But it is notable that, a mere month hence, in August 2002, the world's environmental ministers gathered in Johannesburg, South Africa, to celebrate the 10th anniversary of the Framework Convention on Climate Change (Rio Treaty), and the Met Office's story was everywhere at the meeting.

9.4 Toodle-oo, Tuvalu!

Talk about missing a fact check! The sad story of the putative sinking of the tropical island of Tuvalu takes the cake. But first, a little background.

In the early 1990s I founded a sassy quarterly publication called *World Climate Review* that compared scientific findings and facts with what was reported and touted—much as this book does. *World Climate Review* wasn't particularly shy about poking fun at media exaggerations of the climate story, and skated pretty close to the edge of what was legally permissible. In September 1995, it stepped over the line. The cover of the second issue, winter 1992–1993 (see Figure 9.4 in color insert), featured an obviously puerile satire of the *Washington Post*, depicting a satellite image of Earth and the headline, "The End Nears Again."

Post staffers didn't seem to appreciate our sense of humor. Their global warming writer, the estimable and gracious Boyce Rensberger, wrote that "the cover holds up my newspaper as an example of irrational alarmist reporting on global climate change." Another letter was less friendly and came from Jane Genster, Associate Counsel for the *Post,* who demanded that *World Climate Review* publish a statement that the *Post* had carried no such headline and no such story, which *World Climate Review* did.

Perhaps *World Climate Review* should have stalled for another nine years. Figure 9.4 (see color insert) reproduces the front page of Section E of the September 9, 2001, *Post.* The headline—"The End is Near"—is in umpteen-point type sinking into the ocean. It is followed by a remarkable four pages of climate gloom and doom.

The *Post* spared no rhetorical excess. The article began, "Now imagine your Chesapeake cabin flooded up to the bunk pillows by rising bay water. The Martinique hotel boarded up and forever closed due to record hurricanes."

Reality check: Most ocean- (or bay-) front homes are built on pillars based at around 10 feet above sea level. The space between the pillars and the bottom living space is usually an additional 8 feet or so for the inhabitants to walk around and park their SUVs (the ones with "Save the Bay" and decaying "Gore 00" bumper stickers). That means that the lowest "bunk" is somewhere around 20 feet above mean sea level.

Mike Tidwell's *Post* article cited the then-new "Third Scientific Assessment" of the UN Intergovernmental Panel on Climate Change. How much sea-level rise does it estimate for the next 100 years? Its median value is right around 1½ feet. That's about 18½ feet below Chesapeake Bay bunk level, and the IPCC estimate is almost certainly way too large because it predicts too much warming. Nothing at all to lose sleep over, is it?

At any rate, Tidwell wrote that sea-level rises so dramatic as to force everyone off, say, Tuvalu, will occur "as polar ice melts." In fact, the North Polar icecap is a floating mass, and melting that will have absolutely no effect on sea level; a glass of ice water does not rise when the cubes have melted. With regard to that other polar ice—Antarctica—most climate models predict little or no change. Greenland, as shown in Chapter 3, is also pretty neutral for ice, and in those places where ice is melting, temperatures have been observed to be cooling.

But on to Tuvalu, the tiny Central Pacific Island whose residents were, in 2001, clamoring for environmental refugee status in New Zealand. The genesis of the Tuvaluvian urban legend can only be somewhat documented. In the early 1990s, Tuvalu's prime minister started announcing that Tuvalu was "the world's first victim of climate change," and that "the greenhouse effect and sea-level rise threaten the very heart of our existence."

On October 29, 2001, London's *Guardian* joined the fray, right before the seventh UN "Conference of the Parties" (COP7) to the treaty that gave rise to the onerous Kyoto Protocol, held in Marrakech, Morocco. Dutifully repeating the Pacific agitprop, it described the plight of the Tuvalu residents who fear becoming "environmental refugees" as their homes are swallowed by a rapidly rising ocean, innocent victims of global warming caused by brutish nations thousands of miles away.

You would reasonably think things must be pretty bad in Tuvalu if the nation's leaders were planning to completely relocate the population of 10,991 souls, forcing them to abandon their homeland and way of life.

Well, things *are* bad on Tuvalu, but not because of rising seas. In fact, sea level in Tuvalu has been *falling*—and precipitously so—for decades.

Five days before the *Guardian* article—surely enough time for the editors to find out, and recent enough that they wouldn't have to strain their eyes searching back into the scientific archives for the fact-checking information they needed—the October 24 issue of *Science* contained an article examining the history of sea-level rise around the world. A team of French scientists led by Cecile Cabanes used data collected by altimeters aboard the TOPEX/Poseidon satellite—a cooperative mission between France and the United States that is designed to study the ocean's surface topology—to track changes in water level over time.

Oceans don't rise or fall uniformly around the globe. Instead they primarily respond to local changes in ocean temperature and winds. Figure 9.5 (see color insert) shows the rate of sea-level change in the world's oceans from 1993 (the first complete year of satellite data) to 1998. Tuvalu is at the epicenter of where sea level is *falling*.

Figure 9.6 (see color insert) shows sea-level changes since 1955. Cabanes and her colleagues generated these figures by matching the existing satellite data to a longer record of deep-ocean temperatures. Again, Tuvalu is located in a region where sea level has declined for nearly 50 years!

In spite of that fall in sea level, and ignoring the fact that local, not global, changes are most often to blame in such instances, the *Post* reported—

> Perhaps the most surreal indication of what might be in store comes from the idyllic, tourist-friendly nations of Tuvalu and Kiribati, in the South Pacific. Tuvalu is developing concrete emigration plans to evacuate its islands—perhaps entirely— in this century, migrating en masse to "host countries" like New Zealand. This is because *scientists say* sea-level rise could inundate Tuvalu and other low-lying countries almost entirely as polar ice melts and ocean water expands. [Emphasis added.]

Tuvaluans shouldn't be heading for New Zealand's hills because they think the ocean is rising around them, because, in fact, it's dropping. Even using the UN's probable overestimates of sea-level rise, combining Cabanes's results and observed changes in greenhouse gases suggests Tuvaluans won't see sea levels back up to where they were in 1950 until sometime around 2050!

So what's the problem, Tuvaluans? It's you yourselves. The real reason Tuvalu's population needs to relocate is that theirs is a nation without rivers and sources of potable groundwater. It's a place where beachheads erode because sand is removed for building material. Much of its vegetation has been cleared for fuel. Its soils are poor. There are no mineral deposits and not much to export. Modern Tuvalu is a place where a large percentage of its gross domestic product comes from the licensing of its area code for "900" lines and from the sale of its ".tv" Internet domain.

By early November 2001, it was all over the Internet that *Science* magazine had shown that the Tuvaluans were pulling a fast one on us industrialized dupes; nonetheless, the *Post* persisted:

> Maybe the Pacific island nation of Tuvalu isn't the best place to register your Internet domain name. Thanks to global warming, much of Tuvalu will soon be under water, said Lester Brown, president of the Earth Policy Institute.
>
> Last week, we noted a study by the Progress and Freedom Foundation that mentioned Tuvalu as a popular place for people to register their cyber-addresses. One problem: It seems the nine low-lying islands that comprise Tuvalu are slowly being inundated by the Pacific. The ocean rose about

eight to 12 inches during the last century in part because the warming climate has melted glaciers, Brown wrote.

Tuvalu has asked New Zealand and Australia to accept some of its 11,000 citizens. Australia has already said no.

On February 17, 2002, the following was in the second section of the *Post*: "Tuvalu is Really Going Places":

A guy on welfare finds a multimillion-dollar prize-winning lottery ticket lying on the sidewalk. Next morning Welfare Guy's doctor tells him he's got terminal cancer. That's the kind of good luck-bad luck pickle in which the South Pacific country of Tuvalu finds itself. . . . When Tuvalu was assigned the Internet domain suffix '.tv' in 1996, some cyber-savvy entrepreneurs in Canada and the United States took note and struck an exclusive deal with the Tuvalu government [agreeing] to pay the Tuvaluan government $50 million over a 10-year period [which] is a lot of coconuts for a country that counts dried coconut meat among its primary exports and whose annual operating budget is less than $15 million.

But, what the new Internet Age giveth, the old Industrial Age can taketh away. Tuvalu, which soars to a maximum elevation of 15 feet above sea level, tops many lists of countries . . . most threatened by global warming. Some doomsday climatologists predict that its ribbon-thin coral islands will be under water within 50 years. Dot-gone!

Tuvalu is still here. But who knows for how long? Anecdotal evidence keeps piling up that the climate-control engine has blown a gasket. In January, as the temperature soared to 77 degrees in Washington, snow was falling in Cairo. Crocuses and camels were confused. Meanwhile, passengers arriving on the two flights a week to Funafuti [Tuvalu's capital] airport can buy a rather telling souvenir: a poster showing the wide-open ocean, with a solitary pole sticking up on which a flag is flying. The flag reads "Tuvalu was here."

10. The "National Assessment" Disaster

Finally, we come to the capstone document resulting from the inevitable culture of global warming distortion (discussed extensively in Chapter 11), the *U.S. National Assessment of the Potential Consequences of Climate Variability and Change* (also known as the *U.S. National Assessment* and the USNA), published right around election time, 2000.

10.1 Overview of the "National Assessment of Climate Change"

The USNA began with a January 1998 letter to the National Science Foundation's Global Change Research Subcommittee chair from John Gibbons, Assistant to President Clinton for Science and Technology. Gibbons was a popular speaker on the university circuit, lecturing on the evils of rapid population growth, resource depletion, environmental degradation and, of course, global warming. His visual aids included outdated population and resource projections from Paul Ehrlich in which "affluence" was presented as the cause of environmental degradation, a notion that has been discredited for decades (after all, environmental protection and low population growth correlate highly with per capita income). Gibbons's material on climate change was also dated, assuming growth rates for carbon dioxide and other greenhouse gases that were known to many scientists to be gross overestimates at the time the USNA was in production (see Chapter 2).

In his capacity as the president's science adviser, Gibbons also led the National Science and Technology Council, which was established by President Clinton in November 1993. According to the USNA, "This cabinet-level council is the principal means for the President to coordinate science, space, and technology policies across the Federal Government." Further, "[M]embership consists of the Vice President [Al Gore], the Assistant to the President for Science and Technology [John Gibbons], Cabinet Secretaries and Agency Heads with significant science and technology responsibilities, and other senior White House officials." The Council is clearly a political body ("coordinating . . . policies"), and not a scientific one.

The National Science and Technology Council, in turn, is composed of several committees, including the Committee on Environment and Natural resources, chaired in 1998 by two political appointees, D. James Baker, the head of the National Oceanic and Atmospheric Administration, and Rosina Bierbaum, Associate Director of the Office of Science and Technology Policy. Baker then directed a subcommittee of his committee, the Subcommittee on Global Change Research, established by Congress in 1990 to "provide for the development . . . of a comprehensive and integrated United States research program which will assist the Nation and the world to understand, assess, predict and respond to human-induced and natural processes of global change." That subcommittee appointed the members of yet *another* committee, the National Assessment Working Group, which created the "National Assessment Steering Team."

This torturous bureaucracy was larded with political appointees at all levels and served to ensure that the proper individuals ultimately produced the USNA. Gibbons's letter didn't have to state the views of Clinton or Gore on global warming; the orders passed through so many political vettings that those who finally went to work on the USNA knew full well what was expected: Produce a document that pleases the council, which was led by none other than Vice President Gore. The resultant document was so subject to political pressure that it broke the cardinal ethic of science: that hypotheses must be consistent with facts.

As a prospective study of the impacts of climate changes caused by increasing human impact on atmospheric composition, the USNA was driven by forecasts of future temperature and rainfall made from general circulation models. But, *which* models?

As shown in Figures 10.1 (see color insert) and 10.2 (see color insert), the USNA team chose two models that were clearly the extreme outliers from the family of available models. The Canadian Climate Centre model (acronymed by the USNA as CGCM1) is one of the very few that produces a substantially exponential (rather than linear) change in temperature. The other model they used is known as the Hadley Centre Model (acronymed by the USNA as HadCM2), developed by the United Kingdom's Meteorological Office.

The CGCM1 model produces the most extreme temperature changes of *any* model that the USNA considered for inclusion, and the HadCM2 produces the most extreme precipitation changes.

The CGCM1 and the HadCM2 were not the only models considered by the USNA; others are included in Figures 10.1 and 10.2. The temperature rise predicted by CGCM1—4.5°C (8.1°F) over the United States between now and 2100—is more than twice the rise of 2.0°C (3.6°F) predicted by the HadCM2.

A close inspection of Figure 10.1 reveals that CGCM1 further "predicts" that the United States should have warmed 1.5°C (2.7°F) during the 20th century, but observed warming, according to the most recent analysis from the National Climatic Data Center, is 0.5°C (0.9°F). Thus CGCM1 is making a 300 percent error over the last 100 years.

Why select such an outlier model such as the CGCM1? Thomas Karl, Director of the National Climatic Data Center and cochair of the "Synthesis Team" that produced the report, told me that the CGCM1 was chosen because it was one of only two models (along with the HadCM2) that produced separate high and low daily temperatures, and that this level of detail was required for some of the USNA's analyses.

So, the most extreme temperature prediction model was chosen simply because it produced day and night temperatures. That should have been a red flag, screaming that the CGCM1 model was probably incapable of simulating observed temperatures. Michael Mac-Cracken, head of the National Assessment Coordination Office at the time the report was under review, supplied a different explanation, however, for the use of the CGCM1. He said USNA wanted an example of a "plausible worst-case" scenario for change in U.S. climate.

Whatever the reason, a very extreme model was chosen. All GCMs project changes in seasonal or annual temperatures. If those are unreliably extreme, then the smaller-scale values, such as daily or intraday values, are even more unreliable.

Basic scientific symmetry would have argued that USNA use an analogously cold model (such as the Community Climate Model from the U.S. National Center for Atmospheric Research) for all applications that didn't require daily data, such as mean seasonal or annual temperature or precipitation changes. But it did not.

The HadCM2 forecasts of precipitation changes are as extreme as those of the CGCM1 for temperature (Figure 10.2). Of all the models considered for the USNA, HadCM2 predicts more than twice the precipitation change of the next most extreme model (which is the CGCM1 model). The CGCM1 precipitation changes themselves are twice the average of the remaining unselected models.

The basic rule of science is that hypotheses must be verified by testing their predictions against observed data, and a climate model is nothing more than a series of hypotheses that result in prediction of future temperatures, or hindcasts of those that have already occurred. Any model that fails tests against reality should not be used as the basis for a "scientific" assessment of climate change, despite the prestige of the authors or the technical proficiency of the publication.

Both CGCM1 and HadCM2 make predictions of U.S. climate change on the basis of human alterations of the atmosphere. Those alterations have been going on for well over 100 years. Do the changes those models "predicted" resemble what actually occurred in the last century?

The answer is clearly *no*. In the review process, I compared observed U.S. annual temperature departures from the 20th century average with those generated by both the CGCM1 and HadCM2 models. In both cases I used 10-year running averages to minimize interannual noise.

This is a simple and common test. The modeled U.S. average temperature for 1991–2000 is compared with the observed value. Then the comparison period is backed up one year, to 1990–1999, and so on. That smoothes out the effect of single years that are unusually warm or cold, such as occurs in a strong El Niño year (e.g., 1998) or after a large volcanic eruption (1992).

I then examined the difference between the modeled and observed values for both the Canadian and British models versus the result that I would obtain if I simply used the average temperature for the 20th century from year to year. In fact, both models did worse than that base case. Statistically speaking, that means that both perform worse for the last 100 years than a table of random numbers applied to the U.S. temperatures.

On August 11, 2000, I sent this result as a formal comment to the U.S. National Assessment Team. Specifically, I wrote—

The essential problem with the USNA is that it is based largely on two climate models, neither one of which, when compared with the 10-year smoothed behavior of the lower 48 states (a very lenient comparison), reduces the residual variance below the raw variance of the data [this means that they did not perform better than a model that simply assumed the mean temperature of the 20th century]. The one that generates the most lurid warming scenarios—the Canadian Climate Centre [CGCM1] Model—also has a clear warm bias. [This] is a simple test of whether or not a model is valid . . . and both of these models fail. All implied effects, including the large temperature rise, are therefore based upon a multiple scientific failure. The USNA's continued use of those models and that approach is a willful choice to disregard the most fundamental of scientific rules. (And that they did not find and eliminate such an egregious error is astounding.) For that reason alone, the USNA should be withdrawn from the public sphere until it becomes scientifically based.

In its reply, USNA ignored my core argument:

When the observations of the full twentieth century in the U.S. are compared to the Hadley and Canadian model projections, comparable statistically significant warming is seen in all three.

That is not true. As shown earlier, the Canadian model predicts a rise of 1.5°C (2.7°F) in U.S. temperature in the 20th century, three times what was observed. Further, the USNA completely ignored the fact that the models were producing worse forecasts of temperature than would result from random variation around the mean U.S. temperature for the last 100 years. The USNA then replicated my calculation and found out virtually the same results! Thus the models failed an independent test designed to verify whether my original criticism—that the models were no better than "noise"—was correct.

The real reason for the models' failure can be found in a simple visual comparison between U.S. annual temperature departures from the long-term mean and modeled temperatures (see Figure 10.3 in color insert). The discrepancies result because—

(1) U.S. temperatures rose rapidly—approximately 0.7°C (1.2°F)—from about 1910 to 1930. The GCMs, which base their

predictions largely on changes in atmospheric carbon dioxide, miss this warming, as the greatest changes in carbon dioxide occur after this warming.

(2) U.S. temperature falls sharply—about 0.6°C (1.0°F)—from 1930 to 1975. That is the period in which the climate models begin to ramp up their warming.

(3) Temperatures rose again—the 0.6°C (1.0°F) lost between 1940 and 1975—from 1975 to 2000.

The summation is that most of the warming in the U.S. record took place before most of the greenhouse gas changes and, in fact, nearly half of the so-called "greenhouse era" of the 20th century was accompanied by falling temperatures.

Unless a climate model can explain the rapid run-up in U.S. temperatures in the early 20th century (and, perhaps, the subsequent 1930s Dust Bowl), and the succeeding fall to 1975, it is not an accurate guide to the future, because the most recent temperature rise in U.S. temperature is not yet greater than the one that ended more than 70 years ago.

Is the use of these models, demonstrated as failures, ethically correct? The answer is *no*. Using a model that is no better than random numbers is no better than prescribing a medication that demonstrably does not work. But that didn't stop the USNA from applying these models to a variety of related topics.

10.2 Assessment Spin-off: Upcoming Disaster in the Great Lakes

As shown earlier, before the *National Assessment* was released, the major media were already doing some pretty strident (and unwarranted) hype about climate change and the Great Lakes. Then came the *Assessment* in fall 2000, while much of the United States was in the thick of a four-year drought that began in the summer of 1998. Consequently, the *Assessment*'s prediction that Great Lake levels will drop by more than 6 feet during the next 100 years, largely as a result of increased evaporation from rising temperatures, received a lot of attention.

In 2002, the U.S. Environmental Protection Agency, the Fish and Wildlife Service, and the National Park Service all combined to produce "Climate Change, Wildlife, and Wild Lands—Case Study—Great Lakes—Upper Midwest" [sic]. Large sections were virtual lifts from the *Assessment*. Needless to say, most of the impacts were bad, caused by model-projected decreases in water availability across the region that will progressively worsen as the century drags on and humankind continues to rely on fossil fuels as our primary power source. As shown in the last section, those models don't work very well inasmuch as they can't simulate temperature over the United States (and therefore the Great Lakes) any better than a table of random numbers, when applied to the period in which the greenhouse effect has increased.

The EPA's "Case Study" predicted significantly lower water levels in the Great Lakes (affecting wetlands, water quality, recreation, shipping, and hydroelectric power generation), loss of breeding habitat for waterfowl in the prairie pothole region, alterations in the forest makeup, and some more nebulous notion that has something to do with change in the region's general character.

Despite all of this, there is absolutely no indication that the Great Lakes region is becoming drier. Rather, the opposite is occurring, with a long-term trend toward more annual precipitation (Figure 10.4), greater soil moisture (Figure 10.5), and increased stream flow (Figure 10.6).

For soil moisture, we use the well-known Palmer Drought Severity Index. As noted earlier, this is an integrated measure of overall hydrological status (and like just about every other integrated measure of anything, it has its problems), which objectively classifies both drought and wetness. When it's below -2.0, the indication is a moderate or worse drought. When above 2.0, the Palmer describes moderate or greater moisture excess. As is apparent from Figure 10.5, much of the greenhouse era of the last third of the 20th century has been unusually moist in the Great Lakes, not increasingly dry.

In other words, for the awful things predicted via the USNA to manifest themselves, current trends—established while the planet was warming and the greenhouse effect changing—would not merely have to stop. They would have to completely reverse!

But, that is not the way that future projections of climate work. As can be seen in our introductory sections, once greenhouse changes start to influence the climate, the path is quite well determined. In fact, the same models that project drier conditions for the future in the Great Lakes "hindcast" that drying should also have been taking place for decades.

Figure 10.4

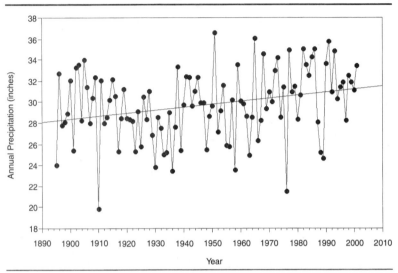

Great Lakes regional annual precipitation, 1895 to 2001.
SOURCE: http://www.ncdc.noaa.gov.

What should we believe: models that are wrong, or observations that are indisputable? Should we believe the *National Assessment*, or the EPA's resultant "Case Study," or should we believe reality?

10.3 USNA Horror Show in New England

> [The *National Assessment*] is an evangelistic statement about a coming apocalypse [and] not a scientific statement about the evolution of a complicated system with significant uncertainty.
>
> —Dr. John Christy, University of Alabama in Huntsville

As many people who follow this issue know, John Christy is the scientist responsible for the global satellite-based temperature record, and one of the most respected voices in this contentious field. What could prompt him to make such a statement about the USNA? Consider the "regional assessment" of New England.

Although the Synthesis Team that put together the USNA was told that the core models literally couldn't beat a table of random

214

Figure 10.5

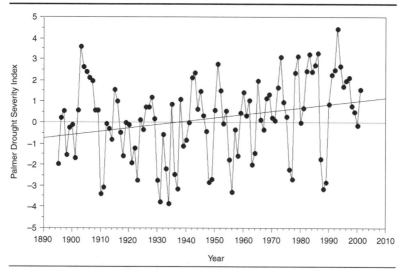

Moisture levels for the Great Lakes region, 1895–2001, as measured by the Palmer Drought Severity Index.

Source: http://www.ncdc.noaa.gov.

numbers when applied to 10-year average U.S. continental temperatures, that seemed to have little effect on USNA's claim that we could somehow "assess" future climate change at an even smaller level of resolution, such as a region like New England. The problem, as usual, starts with the core models noted in our overall summary of the USNA. In Figure 10.7 (see color insert), we show observed temperatures over the Northeast as well as the projections of the two core models.

In a sure sign that something is very wrong already, note that there is no significant warming trend in northeastern U.S. temperatures whatsoever during the last 100 years. Both of these models, and especially the Canadian one, "predict" that a substantial warming should already have happened. Inability to simulate the past guarantees that any future projection is simply not scientific.

The British model projects a rise of 2.8°C (5°F) in New England by the year 2100, and the Canadian climate model projects nearly double that amount! Those forecasts are not only quite different

215

Figure 10.6

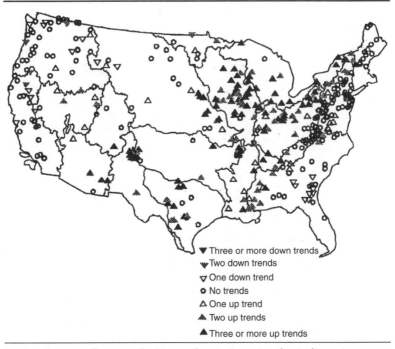

- ▼ Three or more down trends
- ⩔ Two down trends
- ▽ One down trend
- ○ No trends
- △ One up trend
- ⩗ Two up trends
- ▲ Three or more up trends

National stream flow trends. Upward pointing triangles indicate increases. Notice the plethora of stream flow increases in the Great Lakes Region.

SOURCE: Lins and Slack, 1999.

from each other, they are also clearly different from the past century's behavior.

Precipitation projections suffer from even greater problems. The observations show that during the last 100 years or so, there have been a variety of precipitation changes across the Northeast (see Figure 10.8 in color insert). Some areas have experienced moderate increases, others have experienced decreases, and some locations have seen no long-term trend at all. That patchwork of change is typical of observed climate.

As for what the next 100 years hold in store, however, the USNA models see things inconsistently. The Canadian model, on the one hand, predicts that during the next century, annual precipitation will decline by about 10 percent in the southern portions of the region, while expecting little change over the remainder of the Northeast (Figure 10.8, center). The British climate model, on the other hand, predicts that precipitation will increase by about 25 percent across the Northeast (Figure 10.8, right).

Both models predict that future precipitation trends will be nearly uniform across the region (as they do for temperature). That's because the models simply do not have the spatial resolution necessary to make projections on the same scale as the real world.

The Canadian model predicts future climate at points that are 3.8 degrees of latitude and longitude apart. In other words, that's the size of each "box" that it lays on a world map. That's about 52,750 square miles at latitude 40°. The combined area of the New England states (Pennsylvania, New Jersey, New York, Connecticut, Rhode Island, Massachusetts, and Maine) is only about three times larger than this. Needless to say, it's pretty hard to produce any variation in precipitation within that area when all the model can give you is three points for a region that size!

This didn't stop the USNA from making even much smaller-scale forecasts! Figure 10.9 (see color insert) shows the dominant forest type across the eastern United States projected by the USNA to be in place by the end of this century, based on Canadian model outputs.

Note that these are county-based forecasts. The average area of a county is about 1,000 square miles. So—believe it or not—the USNA is attempting to resolve the impact of climate change at 50 *times* less than the minimum resolution of its own models.

10.4 USNA Cooking Up Death in the Southeast

Remember our discussion of "apparent temperature," also known as the "Heat Index" in Section 8.3 ("We're All Gonna Die!")? That's an index that combines temperature and humidity to tell us all how miserable we are supposed to feel, despite the simple temperature.

The very hot Canadian model predicts tremendous warming in the Southeast. It projects year 2100 July apparent temperature *averages* of around 49°C (120°F) around the region (see Figure 10.10 in color insert and Figure 10.11). It is currently very rare for the Heat Index to exceed this value even on a single day. In the Southeast, moisture from the Gulf of Mexico makes it almost impossible to produce a temperature/humidity combination that yields a Heat Index much

Figure 10.11

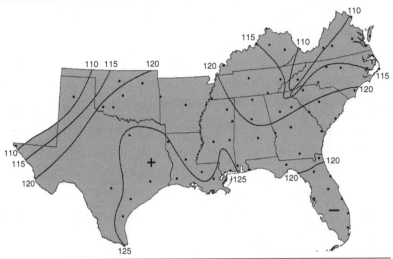

This preposterous scenario of average Heat Index values for the U.S. Southeast is what results from adding the USNA's projected changes in the Heat Index to actual values for today's climate.

above 49°C (120°F), because so much heat is used up in the process of evaporation rather than heating up the thermometer.

A recent study looking at heat index patterns across the United States found that even in the most uncomfortable locations in the Southeast, the Heat Index value, on average, only exceeds 41°C (105°F) on about 12 days per year. That fact just points to how ludicrous the notion is that the maximum daily Heat Index will average 49°C (120°F) in the summer.

The only place in the United States where it is not terribly unusual for the Heat Index on occasion to top 49°C (120°F) is in the desert Southwest, where it gets so high only because the air is so dry. In other words, we'll see Heat Index values projected by the USNA in the southeastern United States that resemble those in the desert Southwest as soon as the Gulf of Mexico dries up!

If we look elsewhere around the globe in search of a humid place where such conditions exist today, we have a difficult time finding even one. In steamy tropical locales, such as Manaus, Brazil, hard in the middle of the Amazon Rain Forest, so much water is available

218

that the daily maximum temperature doesn't get much above the low 90s. Coupled with the high humidity there, that average produces a heat index value that tops out around 41°C (105°F) to 43°C (110°F).

The only place on the planet that currently approaches the conditions forecast by the USNA for the southeastern United States is along the coast of the Arabian peninsula, where the warm waters of the Red Sea and the Persian Gulf supply moisture to the area, yet the weather patterns there are not conducive for rain. Therefore, you get a lot of sunshine and very hot, humid conditions. The Heat Index there averages nearly 120°F during the summer. Of course, there is no vegetation to speak of, because it never rains. No one, not even the USNA, will say that global warming will decrease rain in the Southeast, and just about everyone will tell you that it should increase precipitation there.

Undaunted, the USNA describes similarly oppressive conditions yet still maintains agriculture and forests (see the previous section). In other words, the USNA has produced a biophysical world that simply cannot exist on this earth, an entire new climate and ecosystem that is made up of a combination of things that simply cannot coexist.

11. The Predictable Distortion of Global Warming

Basic to any understanding of the dynamics of science is the concept of the paradigm, elucidated by Thomas Kuhn in a number of academic papers in the 1950s, and more comprehensively in the oft-quoted *The Structure of Scientific Revolutions*, first published in 1962 and a steady seller since then. (Indeed, more than 40 years later, it is still in print.)

But Kuhn's brilliant analysis of scientific behavior was developed at the same time that a remarkable shift took place in the public support of science. Thanks to its success, and thanks to the scientific bureaucracy that it engendered, the Manhattan Project, which coordinated American resources in a crash program to develop the atomic bomb, laid the groundwork for massive federalization of scientific research. Kuhn's work appeared before the impact of that federalization on his thesis could be assessed. Indeed, it makes Kuhn's view even stronger.

Kuhn defines science paradigms as bodies of knowledge that "define the legitimate problems and methods of a research field for succeeding generations of practitioners." Paradigms are fractal. They have the same dynamics whether they refer to an expansive notion, such as relativity, or a smaller one, such as the notion that we have the quantitative skills to confidently predict the future climate of the earth from first physical principals.

Some paradigms endure, others do not. Most are highly explanatory and only are replaced when fatal flaws are uncovered and a replacement paradigm exists. The physics of Isaac Newton will land you at a precise point on the moon, and will work just fine as long as your velocity is much less than the speed of light, whereas proper prediction and control require the newer paradigm of relativity. The Ptolemaic universe was quite adequate until Copernicus and Galileo blew it to bits. The flat earth couldn't survive the voyage that Magellan didn't survive.

Within climate science and its implied studies, it's reasonable to define this paradigm:

> The earth's surface temperature is influenced by human activity, and changes that are being measured today are largely consequences of that activity. We are developing the ability to quantify those changes from basic physical principles, and have determined that the major cause of recent climate change is the emission of carbon dioxide from the combustion of fossil fuel. Improved quantification of those changes will give policymakers improved guidance on what might be required to slow, stop, or reverse those changes.

That paradigm is under assault from a variety of sources, mainly nature itself. Because Kuhn observes that paradigms do not fall until there is a replacement, perhaps the new one needs a formal statement:

> The earth's surface temperature is influenced by human activity, and changes that are being measured today are largely consequences of that activity. We know, to a very small range of error, the amount of future climate change for the foreseeable future, and it is a modest value to which humans have adapted and will continue to adapt. There is no known, feasible policy that can stop or even slow these changes in a fashion that could be scientifically measured.

This book is about the resistance to this new paradigm. The implications of the current paradigm are important. Given some projection for future emissions of carbon dioxide, the existing paradigm says we can forecast the future mean temperature with some confidence, but not sufficient confidence to be definitive, unless a massive amount of future research is supported. Being in that gray zone, however, allows policymakers to have some information to begin to act on this issue.

This paradigm itself represents a remarkable shift that took nearly a hundred years. Despite the rather obvious evidence that large areas of the Northern Hemisphere were recently buried under kilometers of ice, climatology was traditionally uniformitarian, similar to many other sciences. "Weather changes from day-to-day but climate remains constant" reigned through at least the 1970s.

In response to the physical mensuration revolution of the late 19th century, physical scientists became interested in the absorption and transmission of solar energy through the earth-atmosphere system. Several gases, notably water vapor and carbon dioxide, were found to slow the release of heat through the atmosphere. At the same time, the earth was transitioning from animal power to fossil fuels, which were known to burn to carbon dioxide, a fairly stable compound whose atmospheric residence time turns out to be around 75 years. Svante Arrhenius published a paper in 1895 calculating how much those emissions might warm surface temperatures. It was a curiosity, not taken seriously. It was far outside of the uniformitarian paradigm.

It took another two-thirds of a century for enough reliable thermometric data to accrue to throw out the uniformitarian notion. There was undoubtedly a rapid warming of surface temperature in the early 20th century, followed by four decades of cooling. People began to seriously investigate whether human influence was involved. The reigning paradigm evolved.

Kuhn tells us that it's not surprising that such a change in worldview would take nearly a century. He writes—

> When, in the development of a natural science, an individual or a group first produces a synthesis able to attract most of the next generation's practitioners, the older schools gradually disappear. In part their disappearance is by their members' conversion to the new paradigm. But there are always some men who cling to one or another of the older views.

And,

> Paradigms gain their status because they are more successful than their competitors in solving a few problems that the group of practitioners has come to regard as acute.

But,

> The transition of allegiance from paradigm to paradigm is a conversion experience that cannot be forced. Lifelong resistance, particularly from those whose productive careers have committed them to an older tradition of normal science [Kuhn's term for the care and feeding of existing paradigms] is not a violation of scientific standards but an index to the nature of scientific research itself.

In climate science, the "acute problem" is the obvious nonstationarity of surface temperature, and the paradigm of human influence for changes in recent decades is simply more explanatory than other mechanisms. That does not prove it correct, however; it merely establishes it as the paradigm.

Established paradigms have lives of their own. The vast majority of scientists, Kuhn notes, do not question them, but rather, spend their time supporting them. As he succinctly states, "In science . . . novelty emerges only with difficulty, manifested by resistance, against a background provided by expectation."

Not long before Kuhn began his investigations, in 1944, President Roosevelt asked Vannevar Bush, an MIT engineer and director of the White House Office of Scientific Research and Development, to describe how the "unique experiment of teamwork and cooperation" that characterized the Manhattan Project could be continued after the war. Specifically, Roosevelt saw Manhattan's success as a marshaling of heretofore unexploited technical resources out of a preexisting scientific backwater, and he felt that a continued effort of such magnitude in the future could only serve to advance the technical knowledge (and therefore the security) of the nation.

Vannevar Bush teamed up with 50 of the nation's prominent scientists, and in 8 months they produced *Science: The Endless Frontier*, which, according to Claude Barfield, was "the conscious attempt by wartime science administrators such as Bush and leading science educators not only to create a new federal responsibility but also to set the terms and rules by which that responsibility would be carried out." After much wrangling about who would control what, President Truman finally signed into law a bill that placed what would become the National Science Foundation (NSF) under the authority of the president.

Thus began a brave new scientific world, at least in America, the only truly viable postwar economy at the time. Almost all the science Kuhn studied was practiced before *The Endless Frontier*, but Bush's paper only served to ultimately strengthen Kuhn's hypothesis.

In reality, Vannevar Bush got much more than he asked for. NSF is only one example of the massive federal reach into science, receiving about 15 percent of the current federal research outlay. The rest goes through major departments, such as the Department of Defense or the Department of Energy. It should be lost on no one that this latter department is an especially worn political football. President Nixon directed its predecessor, the Atomic Energy Commission, to carry out "project independence," through which he promised that in a mere 10 years we would be free of the need of any foreign oil. President Carter created the department and pushed synfuels, liquid fuel substitutes made from coal, and then nuclear power, because his Energy Secretary, James Schlesinger, became interested in global warming caused by the burning of fossil fuels. In the 1980s, Reagan's Energy Department took the lead in coordinating global warming science, and in the 1990s, the various Energy Department laboratories at Livermore, California, and Oak Ridge, Tennessee, were some of the most voluminous producers of global warming projections and research. The infamous *U.S. National Assessment* was co-coordinated by a Livermore scientist, as was the selective use of data in the famous 1996 *Nature* exchange (see p. 137).

Very few people should be surprised that Vannevar Bush's report was an advocacy document. It predicted cures for cancer and heart disease. It predicted a better world because of intensive federal involvement in science. There's truth in those predictions as well as self-interest. Handing any profession a pen and a paper and asking it to tell the government what it should do has a predictable outcome: "Give us money, and lots of it."

Already subject to "lifelong resistance" to change, did paradigms become even more insensitive with the federalization of science? Absent some change in financial incentive, Kuhn tells us that there's a lot of human psychology already involved:

> Individual scientists embrace a new paradigm for all sorts of reasons and usually for several at once. Some of these reasons—for example, the sun worship that helped make Kepler a Copernican—lie outside the sphere of science entirely.

Here, Kuhn is telling us that the personal philosophies of scientists indeed interact with the paradigms that they embrace.

When Vannevar Bush injected the political process into science, he therefore had to alter the dynamics of paradigm-shifting. Truman's successor, Dwight Eisenhower, sensed the danger in that. The portion of his Farewell Address in which he worries about the possibility of a "Military-Industrial Complex" is often quoted, but he had the same worries about science. Eisenhower said: "The prospect of domination of the nation's scholars by Federal employment, project allocations, and the power of money is ever present—and is gravely to be regarded. Yet, holding scientific research and discovery in respect, as we should, we must always be alert to the equal and opposite danger that public policy could itself become a captive of a scientific-technological elite."

But the community that was served by the federalization of science isn't the purely logical, linearly progressing, impersonal enterprise that Bush or Eisenhower may have thought it was. It was a community that parsed itself into paradigms.

The science structure that ultimately evolved served paradigms more than individuals. For example, although the National Science Foundation works primarily through individual awards, each of those individuals applies under a specific program, such as "environmental biology" or "climate dynamics." The programs are defined by their respective paradigms, and the individual scientists, as Kuhn repeatedly notes, are likely to devote their careers to the care and feeding of those paradigms.

At the agency level, the interaction of politics and science is more direct. It's interesting to run a thought scenario demonstrating the logic and the inevitability of this dynamic. Some examples are brutal and blatant, some more subtle. In late winter, 2004, *Fortune* magazine trumpeted an illogical study of an extreme-case climate change scenario published by two Pentagon contractors, Peter Schwartz and Douglas Randall, with little experience in climate science and no track record of scientific publication in the field. The report, titled "An Abrupt Climate Change Scenario and Its Implications for United States National Security," made little sense. *Fortune* wrote about the climate of Great Britain possibly becoming like "Siberia" in 15 years. That's simply impossible. Siberia is extremely cold in the winter because it is the center of a huge land basin, with considerable mountains on three sides and the North Pole on the other. The snow-covered land radiates outward into the long winter nights, and the resultant cold air is trapped by the mountains, forming a deeper and deeper pile. For England to become Siberia, then, it is necessary to drain the Atlantic Ocean for thousands of miles around London. Then some considerable mountains need to build up on the edges of this dry basin. That might take a few dozen million years, not a dozen single ones.

But the report received considerable coverage, which put it in the political sphere. Within a month the Senate Committee on Commerce, Science and Transportation, under the direction of John

McCain (R-Ariz.), Susan Collins (R-Maine), Olympia Snowe (R-Maine), and Ted Stevens (R-Ark.), approved legislation creating a $60 million study of the impact of "abrupt climate change" on federal property. That's a small example of a pretty gross scientific excess. Other excesses are more subtle, expensive, and pervasive, and demonstrate how paradigms create funding.

Consider the larger picture. A Lexis-Nexis search reveals literally hundreds of news articles in the last year on the perils of climate change. Those stories create public concern. Politicians are under pressure to act. The reigning paradigm is that we are in the process of developing, via the first principle of physics, quantitative methods that can inform public policy on climate change.

Now, imagine yourself as, say, the administrator of NASA, or EPA, or any one of dozens of federal entities that expect budgetary gains from global warming research funds. Imagine yourself as the principal witness at a hearing on funding for climate change research. Can you see yourself telling McCain's committee that your agency really doesn't need any additional climate change funding? To do so would deny the paradigm, which holds that, while we are in the process of increasing understanding of climate change, much more research is required to provide quantitative guidance for the policy process.

Anyone in that position who states that his agency doesn't need the funding is committing professional suicide, for two reasons: denial of the paradigm and denial of the opportunity of employment and advancement of the agency professionals. In fact, after the hearing, after receiving congratulations from all who would have risen up had you refused the money, you turn to your colleagues and tell them you need a report, within two months, about how your agency will effectively spend however many millions or billions of dollars the taxpayers just dropped off on you. Don't expect that any of your senior administrators are going to tell you they don't want the funding. Because they are now competing with each other for shares of this new pie. So, as soon as they can, they will e-mail their working scientists demanding research proposals designed to spend all of this money. Those administrators who produce the best proposals will receive the most funding.

What worker-bee scientist is going to write a proposal saying that global warming is exaggerated and he doesn't need the money?

Certainly no one wanting advancement in the agency! There is no alternative to this process when paradigms compete with each other for finite funding. In this competitive environment, paradigms are advantaged when they are backgrounded by lurid threats. Further, such threats provide justification for the outlay of taxpayer dollars. Politicians can then claim, with the backing of the nation's most serious scientists, that their activities are saving us from certain peril. All of this calamity-hyping, perfectly rational on the part of all the participants, sells newspapers and television time, which only serves to recycle the political importance of climate change.

The "paradigm-political" process is a classic example of a positive feedback loop. As Kuhn notes, most of the rank and file, now funded for more research, will devote that research to the care and feeding of the reigning paradigm. So, when that funding finally does produce research, the ultimate outcome will be a manuscript sent to a major journal such as *Science* or *Nature*. Who are going to be the peer reviewers? The people journal editors pick for peer review have to have established a reputation in the field—that is, to have published a lot. Which means, inevitably, that there is a high probability that they are recipients of the same funding stream that the manuscript writer is, and therefore that that they, too, are devoted to the paradigm. Which means, inevitably, that any manuscript arguing that global warming is exaggerated is going to have, to put it mildly, a very low chance of acceptance. To reiterate Kuhn: "Novelty emerges only with difficulty, manifested by resistance, against a background provided by expectation."

The body of scientific writing that makes up the peer-reviewed literature defines the canon of science. It holds more weight than anything else when presented in public, whether by the *New York Times* or to a Senate Committee debating a bill on global warming. The way we fund science practically guarantees that this literature *must* be biased toward the reigning paradigm. There's no other way out, ever since Kuhn's paradigms and Vannevar Bush's federalized science were married.

The paradigm-political interaction also determines who ultimately makes the team and who gets cut. That decision occurs at the crisis-time in the life of most university faculty—the six-year review for promotion from assistant to associate professor, which almost always is coincident with the granting of tenure, or a contract "without term."

228

There are several criteria for the dubious benefits of lifetime employment at a university. Most important for scientists is the number and quality of publications in the refereed scientific literature, which we have already demonstrated must necessarily be biased toward the view that global warming is a problem so important that it merits massive taxpayer funding.

At promotion time, a professor's contribution to that literature is judged by outside reviewers, all of whom, like the reviewers in the refereed literature itself, have acquired expert status by repeated publication in that literature. In Kuhn's analysis, those people are almost always going to be supporters of the extant paradigm. So the candidate who is on record as working against the paradigm is profoundly disadvantaged.

So tenure is largely granted to supporters of the paradigm. Now *they* are the middle managers, the principal investigators, the literature reviewers, and those who sit in judgment of the next group of candidates for tenure. That does not guarantee a monolithic paradigm, but it surely increases its probabilities. Further, the interaction with the political/funding process makes existing paradigms even more entrenched. It's no wonder that, in general, academics don't speak against the reigning paradigm, because tenure has had the exact *opposite* effect as to its stated goal of diversifying free expression. Instead, it stifles free speech in the formative years of a scientist's academic career, and all but requires a track record in support of paradigms that may have outgrown their usefulness.

But what of Kuhn's notion about personal biases? It should come as no surprise that many environmental scientists go into their field because of a concern for the environment.

That's no different from what happens in another field of applied science: medicine. People become doctors because of (among other reasons) concern for others' well-being. In that light, the following statement by Stanford University's Stephen Schneider becomes completely logical for a paradigm-supporting scientist:

> We are ethically bound to the scientific method, in effect promising to tell the truth, the whole truth, and nothing but. . . .

> On the other hand, we are not just scientists, but human beings as well. And like most people we'd like to see the world a better place, which in this context translates into our

> working to reduce the risk of potentially disastrous climate change. To do that we have to get some broad-based public support, to capture the public's imagination. That, of course, entails getting loads of media coverage. So we have to offer up scary scenarios, make simplified, dramatic statements, and make little mention of any doubts we might have. This "double ethical bind" that we frequently find ourselves in cannot be solved by any formula. Each of us has to decide what the right balance is between being effective and being honest. I hope that means being both.

If that statement were philosophically divergent from the paradigm-supporting rank and file in climate science, it would surely have harmed Schneider. Instead, it enhanced his reputation, and established him as a leading defender of the paradigm. Thirteen years later, Bjorn Lomborg published *The Skeptical Environmentalist*, a compendium arguing that the specter of ecological gloom and doom is highly exaggerated. Lomborg's book is especially anti-paradigmatic with its claim that the body of scientific evidence has already determined that global warming is likely to be modest (which is formally expressed in our "counter-paradigm"). *Scientific American* recruited Schneider to knock Lomborg down. It is hard to argue that there is a more paradigm-centered publication in world science than *Scientific American*.

Self-interest is another parameter that Kuhn repeatedly claims is involved in the maintenance of paradigms. A good definition of self-interest is behavior that promotes what a person perceives as success, which may be personally equated with virtue. Schneider defines his particular version of success as achieving certain environmental policies. That's a value system that is perfectly acceptable and logical. There are other definitions of scientific success, also perfectly logical. They include promotion and advancement, either in the university or in government laboratories.

To use Schneider's words, that creates another "double ethical bind." To him, the belief system of the paradigm-keepers is one in which future climate change is minimized. (It must be noted that there has never been any formal study to determine the degree to which this is true. But Schneider's accelerated prominence after his statement is some supporting evidence.)

There were other changes in science occurring as Kuhn was writing. As a result of Vannevar Bush's success, large amounts of money began to flow to American scientists. Whenever this happens because of any legislative or executive activity, powerful lobbying interests appear on behalf of the recipients. Before Vannevar Bush, the American Association for the Advancement of Science (AAAS) was mainly known as the publisher of *Science* magazine. Now it's our lobbying organization, headquartered in a fancy building on New York Avenue in Washington, not far from the National Association of Homebuilders' "National Housing Center," the Air Line Pilots Association, and the American Society of Association Executives, a lobby that could *only* have a home in Washington.

According to National Oceanic and Atmospheric Administration Deputy Secretary for Oceans and Atmosphere James Mahoney, taxpayers have already disbursed $20 billion at the scientific community for global warming work since 1990. That money would not have arrived if AAAS promoted either the notion that climate change was likely modest or claimed that we knew enough about it that little further research is needed.

Rather, it has demonstrably done the opposite in *Science*, arguably the most prestigious scientific journal in the world. *Science* publishes a section called "Compass" that includes perspectives and commentaries, which are subject to peer review. Since 2000, roughly 75 of those commentaries have been consistent with the view that global warming is a serious problem requiring a massive solution. Not one has emphasized the obvious truth, detailed throughout this book, that warming in the next 50 and 100 years is already known to a rather small range of error and that it is likely to be very modest. But the bias is obvious and understandable. It is what climate scientists expect. Their lobby exists to support research that supports the paradigm that is increasingly commingled with the political process. Britain's *Nature* is similar, with five recent "opinion" pieces editorializing about the perils of warming and the need to do something about it, plus one "editorial" and one "insight" on the same. Nothing whatsoever on the other side. Again, nothing here is illogical, nor is it particularly nefarious. Rather, it is predictably human. What is illogical is a belief that science and scientists would behave in any other way given the nature of science and the world in which it is enmeshed.

Kuhn is careful to note that paradigms do not change all at once. In the face of anomalous data, certain scientists are "converted" before others:

> Still, to say that resistance is inevitable and legitimate, that
> paradigm change cannot be justified by proof, is not to say
> that no arguments are relevant or that scientists cannot be
> persuaded to change their minds. Though a generation is
> sometimes required to effect the change, scientific communi-
> ties have again and again been converted to new paradigms.
> . . . Though some scientists, particularly the older and more
> experienced ones, may resist indefinitely, most can be
> reached in one way or another.

NASA scientist James Hansen is an interesting example of this process. He's often called the "Father of Global Warming" because of his congressional testimony on June 23, 1988, that there was a "cause and effect relationship" between "the current climate" (then horribly hot and dry in the East and the Midwest) and "human alteration of the atmosphere"; in other words, global warming from human beings was creating a climate hell in the United States. More than any other single event, Hansen's testimony turned on the $20 billion spigot, resulting in the currently intransigent paradigm.

On February 11, 1989, Hansen wrote in the *Washington Post* that he felt it was his duty to call the issue to the attention of the political process. By 2001, however, he had turned against the paradigm of insufficient knowledge, stating that we know future warming "to a very small range of error," and citing a figure very close to what was originally published in my 2000 book *The Satanic Gases*. In a subsequent 2003 publication in the journal *Natural Science*, Hansen seemed to reflect the belief system that Schneider feels is characteris- tic of those espousing the original paradigm, saying that "emphasis on extreme scenarios may have been appropriate at one time, when the public and decision makers were relatively unaware of the global warming issue." That isn't very far from Schneider's statement that drawing attention to global warming required "getting loads of media coverage. So, we have to offer up scary scenarios, make simpli- fied, dramatic statements, and make little mention of any doubts we might have." All of these processes are a formula for science that's going to bias in the direction of a paradigm, and that most certainly will give rise to quite a bit of distorted reporting in the press.

In the press, many of the same dynamics operate that encourage people to select environmental science as a career. People gravitate toward environmental journalism in no small part because they are concerned about the environment, just as doctors are concerned about people. The Society of Environmental Journalists numbers more than 2,000 members, and a constant topic of discussion at their annual meetings concerns the ethics of environmental advocacy in journalistic reporting.

One measure of the leanings of that society is given by the titles of books currently published by its members. Here's a smattering:

Asphalt Nation: How the Automobile Took Over America and How We Can Take It Back

Beyond Earth Day: Fulfilling the Promise

Blue Frontier—Saving America's Living Seas

Eco-Economy: Building an Economy for the Earth

Environmental Education & Communication for a Sustainable World: Handbook for International Practitioners

The Greenhouse Trap: What We're Doing to the Atmosphere and How We Can Slow Global Warming

And finally, *Toxic Deception: How the Chemical Industry Manipulates Science, Bends the Law, and Endangers Your Health*, a title that was sufficient to get its author, Dan Fagin, elected president of the society.

However journalists may strive (or claim to strive) for objectivity, there's an additional group that makes use of the primary science and science reporting with no pretense for the same: environmentalist organizations that are very effective at promoting their agendas. Those include the Sierra Club, the National Resources Defense Council, the Union of Concerned Scientists, and the World Wildlife Fund, all of which are highly accomplished at weaving the most lurid aspects of global change research and global change reporting into a very alarming cloth. That, of course, spurs contributions, which increase their political clout—which feeds back into the federal paradigm-science structure.

Even without scientific distortion, raising the specter of disastrous climate change is an easy sell by any demagogue. The United States is home to some of the planet's most violent weather. Tornadoes? We have 10 times more per square mile than our closest competitor, Australia. Hurricanes? A mere repeat of a storm that hit Florida in

1926 would produce $70 billion of damage today. El Niño? Any climate demagogue can associate global warming with any kind of weather, and El Niños have been blamed from everything, from precocious cherry bloom in Washington, D.C., to bubonic plague in Los Angeles.

How about drought? After the end of the big wet El Niño of 1998, the U.S. East Coast entered a four-year on-and-off drought, epicentered right on the Washington Monument. Despite there having been a very similar drought of the same proportion in the mid-1960s in the mid-Atlantic, and much worse drought pandemics in much of the nation in the 1930s, people were happy to associate the last one with global warming. A Google search under "2002 drought global warming" yields 48,100 hits. (The big 2002 *flood* in Europe, despite multiple precedents, yields a similar result: 43,400 hits.)

In summary, the nature of paradigm science, leavened by a political process that pits paradigms against each other in competition for funding, produces a climate of sensationalized reporting, which, unfortunately, can lead to an inevitable policy spiral. The political process responds to threat and takes advantage of "saving" us. The review process in the scientific literature and the judgment for academic tenure are heavily biased toward the paradigm model. The environmental media, while claiming objectivity, have left a voluminous trail of advocacy books. Environmental organizations pick and choose from an already biased set of information, political pressure builds, and finally Congress passes a disastrously unwarranted law limiting carbon dioxide emissions and trashing our economy. Not a pretty picture, but pretty inevitable, and a virtual template for what has been happening with S. 139, the McCain-Lieberman bill to limit our greenhouse emissions, which, as of this writing, is only six senators short of passage.

This concatenation from competing paradigms in a political environment to ultimate policy proposals guarantees global warming will figure in the 2004 campaign. Indeed, Washington political consultant Dick Morris has been pleading for years with the Democrats to pick up the global warming flag, a fact noted in Chapter 1 of my 2000 book *The Satanic Gases*. Morris has since published his own book, *Power Plays*, in which he argues that if Gore had pursued the issue of climate change, which is the reason he wants to be president to begin with, he would have won in 2000. The Democrats see their opportunity coming. In fall 2002, the Democratic Leadership Council (DLC) issued a broadside entitled "Turn Up the Heat on Climate Change"—spoiling for a fight on global warming in the 2003 legislative season, which ultimately resulted in the floor vote on S. 139.

At any rate, predicting the course of politics six months in advance of a presidential election is about as reliable as estimating the weather in New York on Election Day in 2100. But as the coming election engages the climate issue, no one should expect a lack of spin. This book describes the inevitable misconceptions and misperceptions of climate change that have intruded into the public discourse as a result of the logical and predictable behavior of scientists, those who report science, and those who use science in a taxpayer-funded world.

12. Breaking the Cycle

This book details a natural process. As explained in Chapter 11, scientific paradigms compete with each other for a finite outlay of taxpayer funding. Paradigms, resistant to change to begin with, become even more calcified by the support structure that has evolved for science, largely a consequence of the federalization of science created by Vannevar Bush's *Science: The Endless Frontier* published in 1946. In this environment, scientists are rewarded and promoted in the academy largely on the basis of research productivity that must be funded from within existing paradigms. Those who do not support the existing paradigm are therefore not likely to be funded sufficiently for promotion. Scientific papers are reviewed by scientific peers, who are functioning within the same dynamic. The canon of science, as represented by the refereed scientific literature, becomes increasingly skewed and resistant.

Some will take offense with this argument, but the phenomenon is real and inescapable given the way that we do science. There are simply too many stories in this book that fit so neatly into this paradigm, with direct reference and discussion of dozens of important articles in top-line scientific journals implying peril from global warming and containing egregious errors that should have been caught in the peer-review process. There are also dozens of instances in which prominent scientists gave alarmist quotes to the press that were far beyond the scope of the scientific publication to which that coverage referred. And there is a *National Assessment* of global warming based on models that can't simulate the climate of the nation. As a result of all of this, in the last five years, there are more than 50 examples in which the pioneer media uncritically accepted or embellished the vision of climate doom and gloom. There is simply no analogous balance on the side of moderation despite the fact that moderate climate change is much more likely in the foreseeable future than anything extreme.

How do we stop this spiral of exaggeration?

1. Break the Government Monopoly

Environmental science funding should not derive from a single provider, but such a monopoly will inevitably develop as long as the political process provides the vast share of scientific largesse. In this environment, private sources, meaning individuals and foundations, have little incentive to fund basic science. Why should a shareholder-owned corporation dilute its resources to support research with little or no direct financial gain for the company when that burden can be spread across the entire population?

One solution to the dilemma of predictable exaggeration is to take advantage of the relationship between science and its funders, recognizing that nothing is free. There is clearly a broad spectrum of interests on climate change, ranging from those who are threatened by regulations to those who will thrive from them. These interests are sometimes not intuitively obvious.

For example, some sectors of the fossil-fuel industry, particularly those associated with natural gas, are quite positively disposed toward carbon dioxide restrictions. Enron Corp., which both marketed gas and wanted to broker "permits" that industries could trade for the right to some limited emissions, repeatedly petitioned both the Clinton and George W. Bush administrations to promote some Kyoto-like regulation. Some coal producers may view regulations as a threat, while others see global warming as a vehicle to create "clean coal" technologies. Those technologies attempt to sequester or remove carbon dioxide from the effluent of power production. While producing much less carbon dioxide, these technologies will almost certainly be much less energy-efficient, requiring an increase in the combustion of coal for an equivalent amount of electricity. As long as that keeps coal competitive with natural gas (which will also lose efficiency with this technology), why would coal oppose such regulation? However, if "clean coal" technology is economically disadvantageous, obviously that industry will remain opposed to regulation.

The list goes on. Some automakers, notably Honda and Toyota, see advantage in front-loading technologies that would be economically advantageous in a Kyoto-like environment. Consequently, they have led in developing hybrid gas-electric automobiles, which enjoy an efficiency premium over pure-gasoline cars. American automakers see their own advantage in producing high-margin SUVs and aren't as likely to welcome emissions restrictions.

Obviously these competing interests have different hopes for global warming science. Why, then, constrain the base-of-bias to Washington, where lurid views and consequently expensive policy proposals are an inevitability of the way we do and fund science?

There is no way that science will ever be pure. Steven Schneider is right. Scientists are "human beings as well," and the way to take advantage of our humanity is simply to offer a wider choice of bias. That approach may not be pretty, but it is realistic.

2. Change the Peer-Review Structure

It is very clear from several examples in this book that there can be extremely cursory peer review in the scientific literature and that the review process itself must be biased in the directions predicted by the current dynamic of science. Destroying the federal monopoly is a prerequisite to a fundamental change in the review process.

Here's the modest proposal. Drop secrecy from peer review. Rather, at the end of each article, the reviewer names and institutions should be prominently featured, as well as highlights (just a few sentences) from the reviews. Right now the opposite situation persists. Not only are reviews secret, but also some academic journals are so bold that they will allow an author to submit a list of reviewers that he or she *would not want* the article sent to, although editors are not bound to abide by their wishes.

Why not simply publish the names of the reviewers and their reviews? That makes it easy for the journal to defend itself against the charge of cursory review as well as making the reviewers themselves a bit more circumspect. In addition, editors would no longer be subject to the criticism that they ignored critical reviews out of a desire to see a certain article get published.

Of course, this would be a dangerous practice and would certainly serve to intimidate reviewers if the funding bias remained as the current monopoly. But creating a larger bias base obviates this concern as each mutual interest is likely to be strengthened by a free exchange of information. The worst that could happen is that one group (or the authors) would be enraged by a review while others might be pleased, making this largely a zero-sum game for the reviewer but a clear net-positive for the scientific journal.

3. Abolish Academic Tenure

Academic tenure—lifetime employment granted after six years at most colleges and universities—was originally designed to protect academic freedom. The purpose was to prevent the arbitrary political dismissal of university professors, who, at public universities, are employees of their respective states. Without such protection, professors are subject to summary dismissal for airing unpopular views.

Given the nature of modern science and its attendant biases, a person might be tempted to argue for strengthening the tenure system to protect individuals who may call attention to these issues. But that paradigm, too, has changed. The fact of the matter is that the academic world has increasingly evolved in a diverse fashion, with the proliferation of a large number of university-like environments of various philosophical hues. These include the plethora of think tanks that pride themselves on academic research, ranging in Washington from very liberal to very conservative, as well as "neither," which is to say libertarian (such as the Cato Institute, the publisher of this book). The scholar is now much freer to choose than he once was.

More important, however, is that the tenure process in fact stifles dissent. Promotion and tenure are largely determined by academic publications that require massive research support, which mires the young scientist in the paradigm-political process. As long as the primary funding source remains a necessarily politicized federal monopoly, a lack of scientific diversity and a biasing in the lurid direction become predictable and unavoidable.

Just as important as academic publication are outside evaluations from senior figures established in one's field of study. As demonstrated repeatedly, the same biasing process that results from the current scientific process is likely to be active here. Consequently, the young scientist will rightfully avoid any research or scholarship that will offend either the funding apparatus or those who have already benefited from it by gaining lifetime employment.

There is an additional salutary effect of abolishing tenure: Professors will make more money. With everyone employed for life, there is little ability for lateral movement (and large pay raises) between universities. Abolishing of tenure will create a much more fluid market at the senior level, but more significant than that, it will free academics from the necessity of establishing a career of compliance in order to receive a promotion.

The costs of inaction will be dear. Vannevar Bush's legacy is that science issues tend to be distorted by competition for a single federal source of funds. The resultant exaggerations become tiresome, and life goes on. Decades of doomsaying about global warming collide with decades of prosperity. People notice and increasingly disregard science and scientists, a process that has already invaded several aspects of our lives. That is the ultimate tragedy that this predictable distortion of global warming causes: A society that can no longer rely on the wisdom of science can only be governed by irrationality and fear.

Afterword: Composite Campaign Speech on Global Warming

On October 30, 2003, for the first time ever, the U.S. Senate voted on a bill, S. 139, to restrict our energy use to slow global warming. Sponsored by John McCain (R-Ariz.) and Joseph Lieberman (D-Conn.), it went on to defeat, 55–43.

The narrow margin of defeat for S. 139 guarantees three things: global warming is politically hot, President Bush's environmental record will be an important part of the 2004 campaign for his defeat, and S. 139 will never go away. On Halloween 2003, McCain vowed to reintroduce the bill in 2004, promising a year-over-year fight until it passes, just as he did with his "Campaign Finance Reform" legislation.

In preparation for the vote on S. 139, and for years previous, McCain and others concerned about global warming assembled a written record in numerous House and Senate hearings on the subject, and in other venues. So much so, that a pretty decent campaign speech could be constructed by merely concatenating the recorded wisdom of our Solons on the subject of global warming. Think of the following as a generic campaign speech in the 2004 election cycle. (Each of the following statements is a direct quote from the sources noted.)

Global warming is a serious threat. There is overwhelming evidence that increasing amounts of carbon dioxide and other greenhouse gases are heating up the earth's climate and that inaction could be disastrous (1).

President Bush speaks of an axis of terror, but there is another axis of evil in the world: poverty and ignorance, disease and environmental disorder (2). The Bush Administration ignores the terror of environmental peril and denies the reality of 2,500 United Nations scientists who tell us that unless we find ways to stop global warming, sea levels could swell up to 35 feet, submerging millions of homes under our present day oceans (3). The crisis in climate change is like the crisis in Social Security. Today, the problem is manageable, tomorrow, it will be overwhelming (4). This is not an academic debate—not any more. It's time for President Bush to wake up and smell the carbon. It's time for him to show some leadership (5). Ignoring global warming threatens our environment, our economy, and our international credibility (6).

But I know changes are taking place. The storms are more violent. The floods are more frequent. The droughts are more severe, with far more costly results and more often. The winters have changed. No longer do I experience the snows that I experienced as a boy. The ice masses at the two poles to the north and the south are diminishing. They are melting. The seas grow higher (7). Islands in the Pacific are seeing the water rising. Meteorological changes suggest that global climate change is here to stay. My candidacy steps forward and says, "Hey, stop! Hold it!!" (8).

In Massachusetts, we always looked forward to fall because the ponds froze over and we could play hockey. Today you are lucky if the ponds freeze in northern New Hampshire. Up there, I used to freeze and wear a coat when we were campaigning in the morning. I do not wear a coat until after November now. Anybody who does not see the impact of these changes is putting their head in the sand (9). The great ice cover that stretches across the top of the globe is about 40% thinner than it was just 2 to 4 decades ago. We find that through our data from nuclear submarines that have been plying the Arctic Ocean (10). This summer the North Pole was water for the first time in recorded history (11). In 1995, after a period of unusual warming, a 48-by-22-mile chunk of the Larsen Ice Shelf in Antarctica collapsed, and in subsequent years we have seen remarkable sizes of ice falling off (12). We've seen the destruction of heat-sensitive coral reefs, the melting of glaciers at unprecedented levels, the increase of wildfires, and the spreading of diseases (13). The end result of these changes could be substantial ecological disruption, local losses in wildlife, and extinction of certain species (14).

This morning reminded me of a sultry summer in Vermont. I was hiking in the Green Mountains. I could barely see across the great lake, Lake Champlain. My friends in the area tell me that the fishing permits came with an advisory about mercury. And they are concerned that sugar maples are being affected by acid rain and global warming. Christmas tree growers are worried about the acid rain's impact on tree health and vitality. These are important businesses, and these are big concerns for Vermonters (15).

Scientific models further project a rise in sea levels of a foot and a half by the year 2100. This projected rise is two to five times faster than the rise experienced over the past century. The impact of such movement on our coastal communities and businesses, such as fisheries, agriculture, and tourism, is unknown, but the consequences could be serious considering that half of the U.S. population lives in the coastal communities (16). Coastal states such as Alaska will see massive impact, including flooding of coastal villages. Brook trout may lose 50% of their habitat. Drought will be pervasive. Heat-related deaths will increase 100% in cities such as New York, Philadelphia, Cleveland, Los Angeles, and others (17). Among the top environmental concerns of New Yorkers is global warming (18).

Florida is a land that we call paradise, but it happens to be a peninsula sticking down into the middle of something known as Hurricane Highway. Hurricanes are a part of our life, and global warming foretells, for us, an increased intensity of hurricanes and an increased frequency of hurricanes (19). Diseases such as malaria and dengue fever will spread at an accelerated pace (20).

We know that human activity obviously has a significant impact on climate change. Why not take steps, like closing the loophole on SUVs (21)? The Japanese and others are moving rapidly to provide hybrid automobiles that get up to 70–80 miles per gallon very quickly (22). Fuel cell technology which would make zero emissions vehicles is just a few years away (23).

I am not a scientist, but virtually every study I've seen leaves little doubt that global warming is a serious, mounting problem that must be addressed. Yet the United States is disengaged, disconnected, and without a voice or even a position at the negotiating table. German Environment Minister Juergen Trittin told our delegation that an aloof United States could devastate U.S.-European relations. I'm afraid he was right (24).

In town after town, young Americans have asked me, "Senator McCain, what is your position on global warming?" "What is your plan?" is the question that is asked. I do not have a plan (25).

The United States is responsible for 25 percent of the worldwide greenhouse gas emissions. It's time for the United States to do its part to address this global problem. (26). We need to ratify the Kyoto

Protocol. There should be no misleading bookkeeping counting the production of nuclear power plants (27). Without nuclear power we will be increasing, not decreasing our greenhouse gas emissions (28). We do know the emission of greenhouse gases is not healthy for the environment. As many of the top scientists throughout the world have stated, the sooner we start to reduce these emissions, the better off we will be in the future (29). Reduction in fossil fuel use is the only honest way. We've completely ruled out new taxes of any kind as a means of meeting our obligations under this treaty (30).

We must take another look at the Kyoto Protocol to find ways to cooperate with other countries instead of opposing them on issues as monumentally important to the earth's future as global warming (31). The Kyoto climate change treaty is urgent. The U.S. *has* to recognize the interconnectedness, interdependence of the world. We're not doing it (32).

Global warming is one of the most serious challenges facing the world in the 21st century and its impact on our children and future generations cannot be overstated. President Bush has gone back on his promise to reduce greenhouse emissions, a broken promise and a bad omen for our children, our environment, and America's position of leadership in the world (33). For the earth is in the balance. Save it we can, and save it we must—for this is the great responsibility of our generation (34).

It is my hope that *Meltdown* will serve as the reality check for the material in this speech.

References

(1) Sen. John McCain 1/8/03
(2) Al Gore 2/12/02
(3) Sen. Joe Lieberman 8/3/01
(4) Sen. Joe Lieberman 2/20/02
(5) Sen. Joe Lieberman 2/20/02
(6) Sen. John McCain 1/8/03
(7) Sen. Robert Byrd 6/8/01
(8) Rep. Dennis Kucinich 4/03
(9) Sen. John Kerry 5/17/00
(10) Sen. John Kerry 5/17/00
(11) Sen. John Kerry 5/1/01
(12) Sen. John Kerry 5/1/01
(13) Sen. John McCain 1/8/03
(14) Sen. John McCain 1/8/03

(15) Sen. James Jeffords 8/1/01
(16) Sen. John McCain 5/17/00
(17) Sen. James Jeffords 2/14/02
(18) Sen. Hillary Clinton 4/22/01
(19) Sen. Bill Nelson 6/8/01
(20) Sen. Joe Lieberman 4/26/01
(21) Sen. Olympia Snowe 5/10/01
(22) Sen. John Kerry 5/10/01
(23) Sen. Dianne Feinstein 5/1/01
(24) Rep. Richard Gephardt 8/2/01
(25) Sen. John McCain 5/17/00
(26) Sen. John McCain 1/8/03
(27) Ralph Nader (undated)
(28) Sen. Bob Graham 3/9/00
(29) Sen. John McCain 1/8/03
(30) Al Gore 12/11/97
(31) Gov. Howard Dean (undated)
(32) Rep. Dennis Kucinich (undated)
(33) Sen. Hillary Clinton 3/14/01
(34) Al Gore 4/21/01

References

Ainley, D. G., et al., 2003. Adélie penguins and environmental change. *Science* 300: 429–30.

Anderson, D. M., et al. 2002. Increase in the Asian southwest monsoon during the past four centuries. *Science* 297: 596–99.

Angell, J. K. 1994. Global, hemispheric, and zonal temperature anomalies derived from radiosonde records. pp. 636–72. In *Trends '93: A compendium of data on global change*, ed. T. A. Boden, D. P. Kaiser, R. J. Sepanski, and F. W. Stoss, 636–72. ORNL/CDIAC-65. Carbon Dioxide Information Analysis Center, Oak Ridge National Laboratory, Oak Ridge, Tenn.

Aubrey, D. G., and K. O. Emery. 1991. *Sea levels, land levels, and tide gauges.* New York: Springer-Verlag.

Bad news for third world: Warming will cut rice yields. 2000. Daily University Science News. December 4. http://unisci.com/stories/20004/1204005.htm.

Barbraud, C., and H. Weimerskirch. 2001. Emperor penguins and climate change. *Nature:* 411, 183–86.

Barfield, C. E., ed. 1997. *Science for the twenty-first century: The Bush report revisited.* Washington, D.C.: AEI Press.

Boer, G. J., et al. 2000. A transient climate change simulation with historical and projected greenhouse gas and aerosol forcing: Experimental design and comparison with the instrumental record for the 20th century. *Climate Dynamics* 16: 405–25.

Boville, B. A., and P. R. Gent. 1998. The NCAR climate system model, version one. *Journal of Climate* 11: 1115–30.

Cabanes, C., et al. 2001. Sea level rise during the past 40 years determined from satellite and in situ observations. *Science* 294: 840–42.

Castles, I., and D. Henderson. 2003. Hot potato: The Intergovernmental Panel on Climate Change had better check its calculations. *The Economist,* February 13.

Changnon, S. A. 1999. Impacts of the 1997–1998 El Niño–generated weather in the United States. *Bulletin of the American Meteorological Society* 80: 1819–28.

CIA World Factbook. 2001. http://www.cia.gov/cia/publications/factbook/geos/tv.html.

Crowley, T. J. 2000. Causes of climate change over the past 1000 years. *Science* 289: 270–77.

Croxall, J. P., P. N. Trathan, and E. J. Murphy. 2002. Environmental change in Antarctic seabird populations. *Science* 297: 1510–14.

Dai, A., et al. 2001. Climates of the twentieth and twenty-first centuries simulated by the NCAR climate system model. *Journal of Climate* 14: 485–519.

Davis R. E., et al. 2002. Decadal changes in heat-related human mortality in the eastern United States. *Climate Research,* 22: 175–84.

Davis R. E., et al. 2003a. Decadal changes in heat-related human mortality in the eastern United States. *International Journal of Biometeorology* 47: 166–75.

Davis R. E., et al. 2003b. Changing heat-related mortality in the United States. *Environmental Health Perspectives*, in review.

Doran, P. T., et al. 2002. Antarctic climate cooling and terrestrial ecosystem response. *Nature* advance online publication.

Dybas, C. L. 2002. Jellyfish "blooms" could be sign of ailing seas. *Washington Post*, May 6, p. A9.

Easterling, D. R. 2002. Recent change in frost days and the frost-free season in the United States. *Bulletin of the American Meteorological Society* 83: 1327–32.

El Niño and global warming: What's the connection? *UCAR Quarterly* 24, Winter 1997.

Epstein, P. R. 2000. West Nile: It's not just local. It's global. *Washington Post*, October 8.

Fisheries and Oceans Canada. 2001. Is Arctic sea ice rapidly vanishing? http://www-sci.pac.dfompo.qu.ca/osap/projects/ipod/projects/arc_thin/thin1.htm.

Frauenfeld, O. W., and R. E. Davis. 2002. Midlatitude circulation patterns associated with decadal and interannual Pacific Ocean variability. *Geophysical Research Letters* 29, DOI: 10.1029/2002GL015743.

Gibbs, J., and A. Breisch. 2001. Climate warming and calling phenology of frogs near Ithaca, New York, 1900–1999. *Conservation Biology* 15: 1175–78.

Goldenberg, S., et al. 2001. The recent increase in Atlantic hurricane activity: Causes and implications. *Science* 293: 474–79.

Gould, S. J. 1981. *The Mismeasure of man.* New York: W. W. Norton & Co.

Hanna, E., and J. Cappelen. 2003. Recent cooling in coastal southern Greenland and relation with the North Atlantic oscillation. *Geophysical Research Letters* 30: 32-1–32-3.

Hansen, J. E. 2003. Can we defuse the global warming time bomb? *Natural Science*. http://naturalscience.com/ns/article/10-16/ns_jeh.html.

Hansen, J. E., et al. 1998. A common-sense climate index: Is climate changing noticeably? *Proceedings of the National Academy of Sciences* 95: 4113–20.

Hansen, J. E., and M. Sato. 2001. Trends of measured climate forcing agents. *Proceedings of the National Academy of Sciences* 98: 14778–83.

Harvell, C. D., et al. 2002. Climate warming and disease risks for terrestrial and marine biota. *Science* 296: 2158–62.

Hay, S. I., et al. 2002. Climate change and the resurgence of malaria in the East African highlands. *Nature* 415: 905–09.

Hayden, B. P. 1998. Ecosystem feedbacks on climate at the landscape scale. *Philosophical Transactions of the Royal Society of London B* 353: 5–18.

Hilmer, M. A model study of Arctic sea ice variability. Ph.D. thesis, No. 320, Institut für Meereskunde, University of Kiel, Kiel, Germany.

Hoerling, M., and A. Kumar. 2003. The perfect ocean for drought. *Science* 299: 691–94.

Holloway, G., and T. Sou. 2002. Has Arctic sea ice rapidly thinned? *Journal of Climate* 15: 1691–1701.

Houghton, J. T., et al. 1996. *Climate change 1995: The science of climate change.* Contribution of WGI to the *Second Assessment Report* on the Intergovernmental Panel on Climate Change. Cambridge: Cambridge University Press.

Houghton, J. T., et al., eds. 2001. *Climate change 2001: The scientific basis.* Contribution of Working Group I to the *Third Assessment Report* of the Intergovernmental Panel on Climate Change. Cambridge University Press.

Johns, T. C., et al. 1997. The second Hadley Center coupled ocean-atmosphere GCM: Model description, spinup, and validation. *Climate Dynamics* 13: 103–34.

Johnson, K. 2002. When good winters go bad. *New York Times*, March 10.

Jones, P. D. 1995. Recent variations in mean temperature and the diurnal temperature range in the Antarctic. *Geophysical Research Letters* 20: 1345–48.

Jones, P. D., T. M. L. Wigley, and K. R. Briffa. 1994 (and updates). In *Trends '93: A compendium of data on global climate change*. U.S. Department of Energy.

Joughin, I., and S. Tulaczyk. 2002. Positive mass balance of the Ross Ice Streams, West Antarctica. *Science* 295: 476–80.

Kahl, J. D., et al. 1993. Absence of evidence for greenhouse warming over the Arctic Ocean in the past 40 years. *Nature* 361: 335–37.

Karl, T. R., et al. 1995. Indices of climate change for the United States. *Bulletin of the American Meteorological Society* 77: 279–92.

Karl, T. R., et al. 1995. Trends in high-frequency climate variability in the twentieth century. *Nature* 377: 217–20.

Keatinge, W. R., et al. 2000. Heat-related mortality in warm and cold regions of Europe: Observational study. *British Medical Journal* 321: 670–73.

Kerr, R. A. 1997. Model gets it right—Without fudge factors. *Science* 276: 1041.

Kerr, R. A. 2003. A perfect ocean for four years of globe-girdling drought. *Science* 299: 636.

Kiesecker, J. M., A. R. Blaustein, and L. K. Belden. 2001. Complex causes of amphibian population declines. *Nature* 410: 681–84.

Knappenberger, P. C., et al. 2001. Nature of observed temperature changes across the United States during the 20th century. *Climate Research* 17: 45–53.

Krabill, W., et al. 2000. Greenland ice sheet: High elevation balance and peripheral thinning. *Science* 289: 428–30.

Kuhn, T. S. 1962. *The structure of scientific revolutions*. Chicago: University of Chicago Press.

Ladruie, E. L. 1988 (Reissue date). *Times of feast, times of famine: A history of climate since the year 1000*. Noonday Press.

Landsea, C. W., et al. 1996. Downward trends in the frequency of intense Atlantic hurricanes during the past five decades. *Geophysical Research Letters* 23: 1697–1700.

Lawton, R. O., et al. 2001. Climatic impact of tropical lowland deforestation on nearby montane cloud forests. *Science* 294: 584–87.

Lean, J., and D. Rind. 1998. Climate forcing by changing solar radiation. *Journal of Climate* 11: 3069–94.

Legates, D. R. 2000. *A climate model and the national assessment*. Washington: George Marshall Institute.

Legates, D. R. 2001. Climate models and the National Assessment: Report to the George C. Marshall Institute. http://www.marshall.org/Legatesclimatemodels.htm.

Lins, H. F., and J. R. Slack. 1999. Stream flow trends in the United States. *Geophysical Research Letters* 26: 227–30.

Lomborg, B. 2001. *The skeptical environmentalist*. Cambridge: Cambridge University Press.

Los Angeles Times. 1996. August 29.

Los Angeles Times. 2002. December 8.

Manley, B. 1974. Central England temperatures: Monthly means 1659 to 1973. *Quarterly Journal of the Royal Meteorological Society* 100: 389–405.

Mayeux, H. S., et al. 1991. Global change and vegetation dynamics. In *Noxious range weeds*, ed. F. J. James, et al. Boulder: Westview Press, pp. 62–74.

McCabe, G. J., and D. M. Wolock. 2002. Trends in temperature sensitivity of moisture conditions in the conterminous United States. *Climate Research* 20: 19–29.

Meehl, G., et al. 2000. The coupled model intercomparison project. *Bulletin of the American Meteorological Society* 81: 313–18. (See also http://www-pcmdi.llnl.gov/cmip/cmiphome.html.)

Michaels, P. J., et al. 2000. Observed warming in cold anticyclones. *Climate Research* 14: 1–6.

Michaels, P. J., et al. 2001. Integrated projections of future warming based upon observed climate during the attenuating greenhouse enhancement. *Proceedings of the 1st International Conference on Global Warming and the Next Ice Age*, American Meteorological Society, pp. 162–67.

Michaels, P. J., et al. 2002. Revised 21st-century temperature projections. *Climate Research* 23: 1–9.

Michaels, P. J., et al. 2002. Rational analysis of trends in extreme temperature and precipitation. *Proceedings of the 13th conference on applied climatology*, May 13–16. Portland, Oregon, 153–58.

Michaels, P. J., and P. C. Knappenberger, 1996. Human effect on global climate 7. *Nature* 384: 522–23.

Morris, D. 2002. *Power plays: Win or lose—How history's great political leaders play the game.* Regan.

Myneni, R. B., et al. 1997. Increased plant growth in the northern high latitudes from 1981 to 1991. *Nature* 386: 698–702.

National Assessment Synthesis Team. 2000. *Climate change impacts on the United States: The potential consequences of climate variability and change.* Washington, D.C.: U.S. Global Change Research Program.

National Climatic Data Center. www.ncdc.noaa.gov/ol/climate/climatedata.html.

New York Times. 1996. September 3.

New York Times. 2002. August 28.

New York Times. 2002. December 8.

Noren, A. J., et al. 2002. Millennial-scale storminess variability in the northeastern United States during the Holocene epoch. *Nature* 419: 821–24.

Norris, S., L. Rosenstrater, and P. Martin. 2002. *Polar bears at risk.* WWF International Arctic Programme. http://www.worldwildlife.org/climate/polar_bears.pdf.

Otterman, J., et al. 2002. North Atlantic surface winds examined as the source of winter warming in Europe. *Geophysical Research Letters* 29: 18-1–18-4.

Parmesan, C. 1996. Climate and species' range. *Nature* 382: 765–66.

Parmesan, C., et al. 1999. Poleward shifts in geographical ranges of butterfly species associated with regional warming. *Nature* 399: 579–80.

Parmesan, C., and G. Yohe. 2003. A globally coherent fingerprint of climate change impacts across natural systems. *Nature* 421: 37–42.

Polykov, I. V., et al. 2002. Trends and variations in arctic climate systems. EOS, Transactions, American Geophysical Union 83: 547–48.

Polykov, I. V., and M. A. Johnson. 2000. Arctic decadal and interdecadal variability. *Geophysical Research Letters* 27: 4097–4100.

Popper, K. R. 1963. *Conjectures and refutations: The growth of scientific knowledge.* London: Routledge & Kegan Paul.

Pounds, J. A., et al. 1999. Biological response to climate change on a tropical mountain. *Nature* 398: 611–15.

Powell, M. 2001. Northeast seen getting balmier. *Washington Post,* December 17.

Pryzbylak, R. 2000. Temporal and spatial variation of surface air temperature over the period of instrumental observations in the arctic. *International Journal of Climatology* 20: 587–614.

Quayle, W. C., et al. 2002. Extreme responses to climate change in Antarctic lakes. *Science* 295: 645.

Reiter, P. 2001. Climate change and mosquito-borne disease. *Environmental Health Perspectives* 109: 141–61.

Robeson, S. M. 2002. Increasing growing season length in Illinois during the 20th century. *Climatic Change* 52: 219–38.

Root, T. L., et al. 2003. Fingerprints of global warming on wild animals and plants. *Nature* 421: 57–60.

Rothrock, D. A., Y. Yu, and G. A. Maykut. 1999. Thinning of the Arctic sea-ice cover. *Geophysical Research Letters,* 26: 3469–72.

Sansom, J., 1989. Antarctic surface temperature time series. *Journal of Climate* 2: 1164–72.

Santer, B. D., et al., 1996. A search for human influences on the thermal structure of the atmosphere. *Nature* 382: 39–46.

Schneider, S. H. 2001. What is "dangerous" climate change? *Nature* 411, 17–19.

Schneider, S. H., et al. 2002. Misleading math about the earth. *Scientific American,* January.

Serreze, M. C., et al. 1997. Icelandic low cyclone activity: Climatological features, linkages with the NAO, and relationships with recent changes in the Northern Hemisphere circulation. *Journal of Climate* 10: 453–64.

Serreze, M. C., et al. 2000. Observational evidence of recent change in the northern high-latitude environment. *Climatic Change* 46: 159–207.

Spencer, R. T., and J. L. Christy. 1990. Precise monitoring of global temperature trends from satellites. *Science* 247: 1558–62 (and updates).

Still, C. J., et al. 1999. Simulating the effects of climate change on tropical montane cloud forests. *Nature* 398: 608–10.

Thomas, A. 2000. Climate changes in yield index and soil water deficit trends in China. *Agricultural and Forest Meteorology* 102: 71–81.

Thomas, C. D., et al. 2004. Feeling the heat: Climate change and biodiversity loss. *Nature* 427: 145–48.

Thomas, R., et al. 2000. Mass balance of the Greenland ice sheet at high elevations. *Science* 289: 428–30.

Thompson, L. G., et al. 2002. Kilimanjaro ice core records: Evidence of holocene climate change in tropical Africa. *Science* 298: 589–93.

Transcript, June 23, 1988. Hearing before the Senate Committee on Energy and Natural Resources.

Transcript, May 17, 2000. Hearing before the Senate Committee on Commerce, Science, and Transportation.

Trenberth, K. E., and D. P. Stepaniak. 2001. Indices of El Niño evolution. *Journal of Climate* 14: 1697–1701.

UN Intergovernmental Panel on Climate Change. 1996. *Climate change 1995: The science of climate change.* Cambridge: Cambridge University Press.

U.S. Army Corps of Engineers, Great Lakes update. http://huron.lre.usace.army.mil/levels/update143.pdf.

U.S. Environmental Protection Agency et al. 2002. Climate change, wildlife, and wild lands—Case study—Great Lakes—Upper Midwest. http://www.epa.gov/globalwarming/impacts/water/cs_glum1.html.

Vinnikov, K. Y., and A. Robock. 2002. Trends in moments of climatic indices. *Geophysical Research Letters* 29, 10.1029/2001GL014025.

Wadhams, P., and N. R. Davis. 2000. Further evidence of ice thinning in the Arctic Ocean. *Geophysical Research Letters* 27: 3973–76.

Winsor, P. 2001. Arctic sea ice thickness remained constant during the 1990s. *Geophysical Research Letters* 28: 1039–41.

Wittwer, S. H. 1995. *Food, climate, and carbon dioxide. The global environment and world food production.* Boca Raton: CRC Press.

World Climate Review. http://co2andclimate.org/wcr.html.

Ziska, L. H., and F. A. Caulfield. 2000. Rising atmospheric carbon dioxide and ragweed pollen production: Implications for public health. *Australian Journal of Plant Physiology* 27: 893–98.

Ziska, L. H., J. A. Bunce, and F. A. Caulfield. 1998. Intraspecific variation in seed yield of soybean in response to increased atmospheric carbon dioxide. *Australian Journal of Plant Physiology* 25: 801–07.

Index

Articles, papers, and reports are indexed by primary author(s) cited in text and under the source of the article by title (if given) or topic.

ABC News with Peter Jennings, melting alpine glaciers reporting, 61–63
Abies balsamea (balsam fir), 108
Academic journal publishing
  changing peer review structure, 239
  peer review problems, 5, 22, 96, 137–42, 228, 229, 234
  See also specific journals by name
Adaptation to climate
  human, 109, 146–47, 192, 193, 194
  Inuits, 66–67
  penguins, 100–102
  plants and animals, 102–3, 105
  wildlife species, 84. *See also specific species*
Aedes aegypti, 185–86
Aedes albopictus, 185–86
Africa
  climate change and malaria, 179–80
  tropical rainforests, 128
"Aggregate weather," climate models and, 17–18
Agriculture
  growing seasons, 6, 15, 163, 170
  increased soil-moisture level and, 137
Ainley, D. G., rebuttal of Croxall arguments, 101–2
Air conditioning, spread of disease and, 185
Alicia, Hurricane, 115
Allen, Hurricane, 115
American Association for the Advancement of Science (AAAS), 94, 231
American Bird Conservancy, 82
Amphibians. *See* Toads and frogs
Anderson, David, on Indian monsoon, 148
Andrew, Hurricane, 111

Angell, Jim, arctic record comparisons, 46–47
Antarctica, 33, 51, 63–66, 203
  ecotourism, 96
  penguins, 96–102
Anthropogenic global warming, 36–37, 60
  factors humans can/cannot change or influence, 1–2
  Hansen on, 232
  initial interest in and beginnings of climatology, 222–26
  reprieve from blame for hurricanes, 122–23
  variability of storminess and, 151
AP. *See* Associated Press (AP)
"Apparent temperature," 188–89, 217–19
Arctic climate
  Arctic warming models, 95
  Greenpeace press release on threat to polar bears and, 93–94
  high-latitude temperature studies, 45–46, 94
  New York Times article(s), 5, 42–46
  "source region," 47–48
  temperature records, 46–47, 94, 95–96
Arctic Ocean, 44–45, 48–54
  See also North Polar icecap
Arctic winds and wind patterns, 51
  ice movement and, 54, 95
Argentière, Switzerland, 61–63
Arrhenius, Svante, 14, 223
"Artificial" genetic diversity, 109
"Asian Brown Cloud" (ABC), 147–49
Asian monsoon, 147, 148
Assessments, 21–26, 74
  1996 *Assessment (Third Assessment Report)*, 22–23, 51–54, 60–61, 64, 100–101, 106, 107, 127, 148–49, 190
  USNA. *See U.S. National Assessment of the Potential Consequences of Climate Variability and Change*
Associated Press, reporting on Karl's climate projections and "change point," 196–98

Cato Institute

Founded in 1977, the Cato Institute is a public policy research foundation dedicated to broadening the parameters of policy debate to allow consideration of more options that are consistent with the traditional American principles of limited government, individual liberty, and peace. To that end, the Institute strives to achieve greater involvement of the intelligent, concerned lay public in questions of policy and the proper role of government.

The Institute is named for *Cato's Letters*, libertarian pamphlets that were widely read in the American Colonies in the early 18th century and played a major role in laying the philosophical foundation for the American Revolution.

Despite the achievement of the nation's Founders, today virtually no aspect of life is free from government encroachment. A pervasive intolerance for individual rights is shown by government's arbitrary intrusions into private economic transactions and its disregard for civil liberties.

To counter that trend, the Cato Institute undertakes an extensive publications program that addresses the complete spectrum of policy issues. Books, monographs, and shorter studies are commissioned to examine federal budget, Social Security, regulation, military spending, international trade, and myriad other issues. Major policy conferences are held throughout the year, from which papers are published thrice yearly in the *Cato Journal*. The Institute also publishes the quarterly magazine *Regulation*.

In order to maintain its independence, the Cato Institute accepts no government funding. Contributions are received from foundations, corporations, and individuals, and other revenue is generated from the sale of publications. The Institute is a nonprofit, tax-exempt, educational foundation under Section 501(c)3 of the Internal Revenue Code.

CATO INSTITUTE
1000 Massachusetts Ave., N.W.
Washington, D.C. 20001
www.cato.org

Figure 2.3

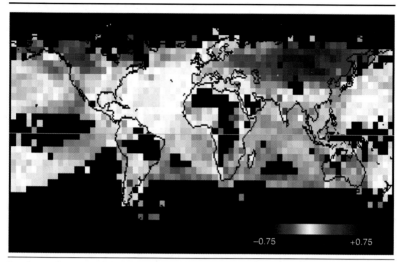

−0.75 +0.75

In the cold half-year, warming since the mid-20th century is greatest in Siberia, as predicted by greenhouse theory.

SOURCE: http://www.cru.uea.ac.uk.

Figure 2.5

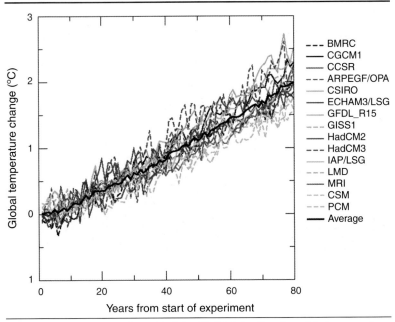

Clearly, the "central tendency" of the CMIP-I family of models is to produce a constant rate of warming once human-induced warming starts. That behavior ultimately allows a much more confident forecast of global warming.

SOURCE: http://www-pcmdi.llnl.gov/cmip/cmiphome.htm.

Figure 2.6

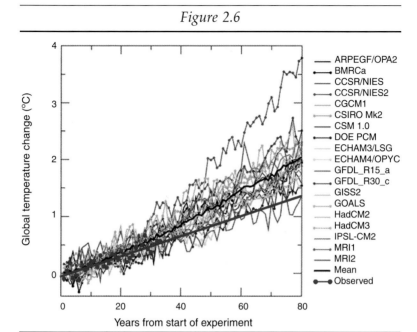

The central linear tendency allows us to compare reality with the suite of models. This study includes more models than Figure 2.5, but retains the same mean character. Clearly, models predicting the slowest rates of warming are the most realistic.

SOURCE: Meehl et al., 2000.

Figure 2.7

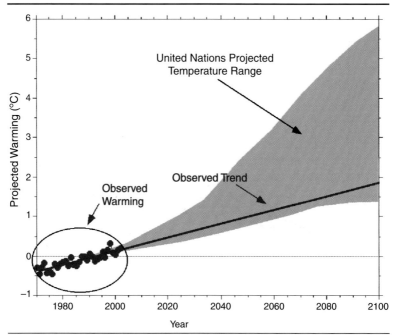

Scientists now know global warming is likely to be very modest, based on the linearity argument. Note how this "reality-based" argument varies from the large warmings projected by the United Nations.

SOURCES: IPCC *Third Assessment Report* (forecasts) and www.cru.uea.ac.uk (temperature data).

Figure 2.8

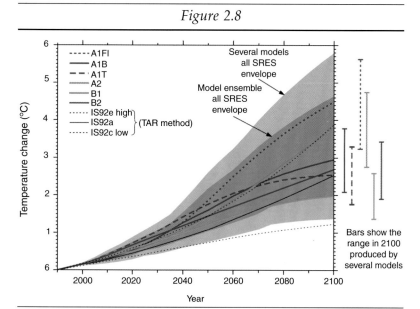

Range of temperature estimates from the UN based on its "storylines" (SRES) and various climate models.

SOURCE: IPCC *Third Assessment Report.*

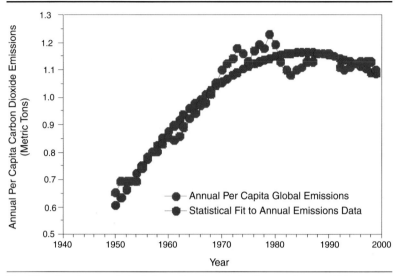

Figure 2.10

The blue line is a statistical fit to the data. It indicates about a 99.5 percent likelihood that emissions are truly in decline.

SOURCE: Carbon dioxide data are from the U.S. Energy Information Administration.

Figure 2.12

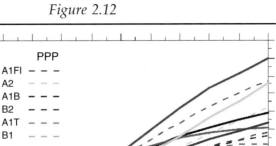

The dotted lines show the effect on global temperature projections for the various UN "storylines" using purchasing price parity-based (PPP-based) comparisons of economies rather than the outdated method of using market exchange (MEX) rates. The resulting declines in warming average 15 percent.

Figure 3.2

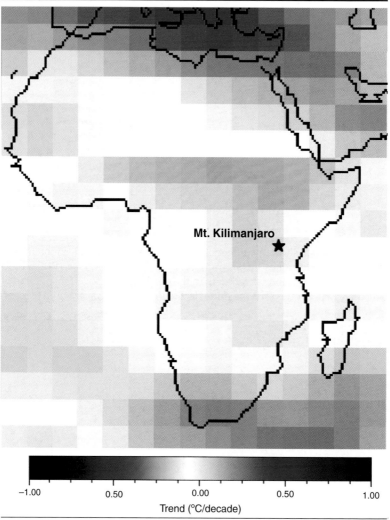

Trend (°C/decade)

Temperatures monitored by satellite for the Kilimanjaro region. The satellite record begins in January 1979 and shows a cooling of 0.22°C (0.40°F) for the region—at a rate of 0.09°C or 0.17°F per decade.

SOURCE: http://vortex.nsstc.uah.edu.

Figure 3.12

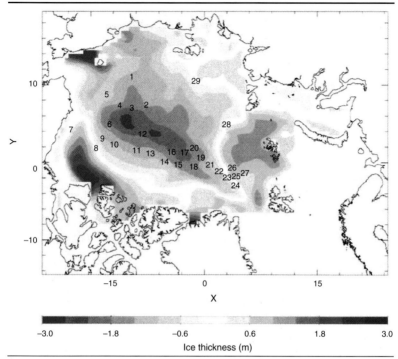

Modeled change in ice thickness (red = thinning, blue = thickening) between 1990s record and 1950s–1970s records for the 29 locations where Rothrock took measurements.

SOURCE: Holloway and Sou, 2001.

Figure 3.19

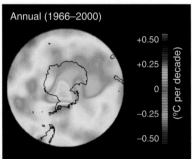

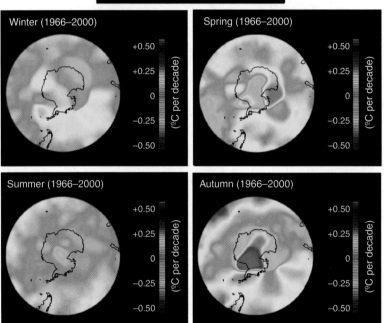

Antarctic temperature histories.

SOURCE: Doran et al. 2002.

Figure 3.20

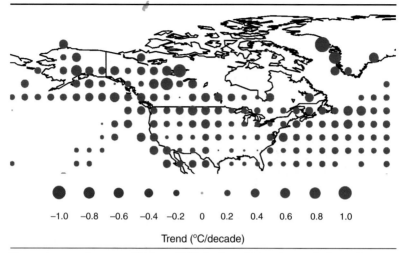

Temperature changes, 1910 to 1945, before the major emission of green-house gases.

SOURCE: http://www.cru.uea.ac.uk.

Figure 3.21

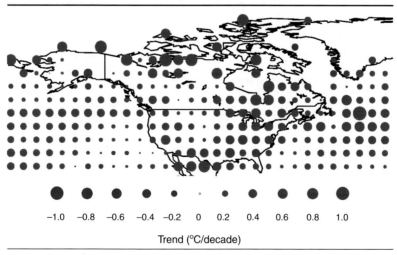

Temperature changes, 1976 to 2000, concurrent with the major emission of greenhouse gases.

Figure 3.22

The cover of the January 22, 1996, issue of *Newsweek* marked the start of reporter Sharon Begley's perseveration on the notion that warming will cause an ice age in just a few years.

Figure 4.4

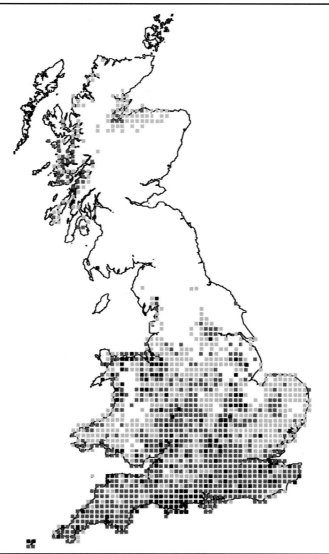

Range changes for Great Britain's butterflies, 1915 to 1997. (Black squares show butterfly populations in 1915–1939; red squares, 1940–1969; blue squares, 1970–1997.) What may at first look like a northward expansion is in fact an expansion of butterflies throughout the island.

SOURCE: Parmesan, *Nature*, 1999.

Figure 4.10

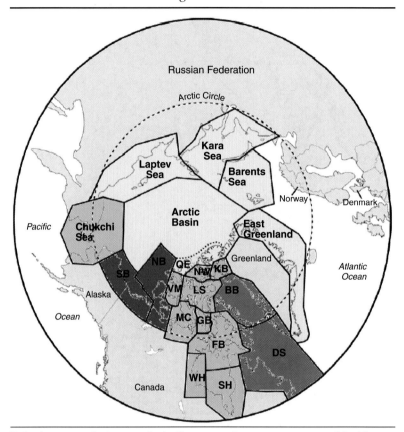

Polar bear population trends (yellow = unknown; green = stable; blue = decreasing; red = increasing).

SOURCE: 2001 World Wildlife Fund report, *Polar Bears at Risk*.

Figure 4.11

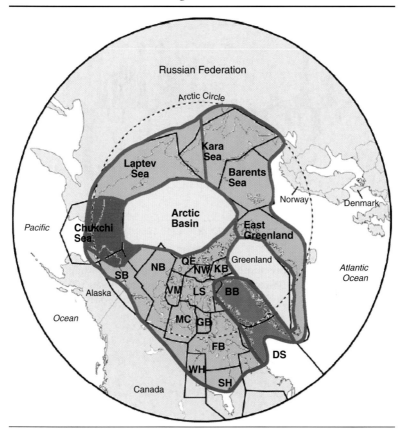

Temperature trend, 1950 to 1995, for subregions of the Arctic (outlined in pink) as determined in a recent study of Arctic temperature trends by Rajmund Przybylak (blue = cooling; red = warming; yellow = no data; green = no significant change).

Figure 5.6

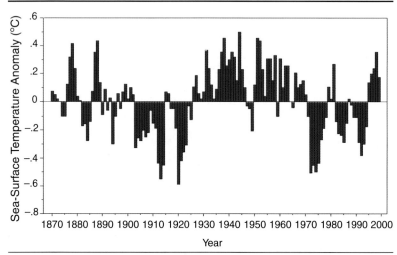

Sea-surface temperature anomalies in the Atlantic Ocean's main hurricane development region. Warm anomalies (red) are associated with increased major hurricane activity; cold anomalies (blue) with suppressed activity.

SOURCE: Goldenberg, *Science*, 2001.

Figure 6.6

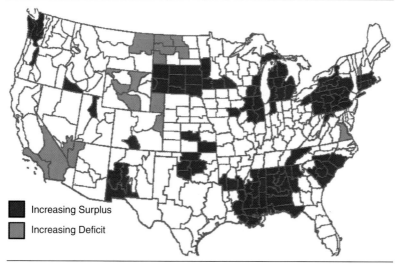

The green areas are regions where the moisture surplus has significantly increased during the 20th century, while the red areas are regions where the annual moisture deficit has grown significantly larger. The green regions represent 25 percent of the country, while the red regions make up only 8 percent.

SOURCE: McCabe and Wolock, 2002.

Figure 6.16

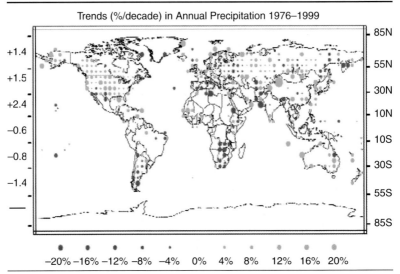

Trends (%/decade) in Annual Precipitation 1976–1999

Changes in precipitation in the last quarter-century (changes by latitude band are indicated on the vertical axis). Despite the UN's pronouncement, there are no systematic changes congruent with the Asian Brown Cloud.

Source: Intergovernmental Panel on Climate Change, *Third Assessment Report*.

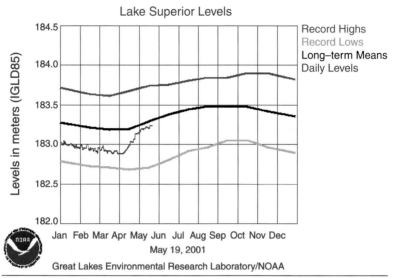

Figure 6.24

Lake Superior Levels

Great Lakes Environmental Research Laboratory/NOAA

The daily water levels of Lake Superior (blue line) compared with the average (black line), record high (red line), and record low (green line). Notice the sharp recovery from April to May 2001.

SOURCE: http://www.glerl.noaa.gov.

Figure 6.25

Crop Moisture Index

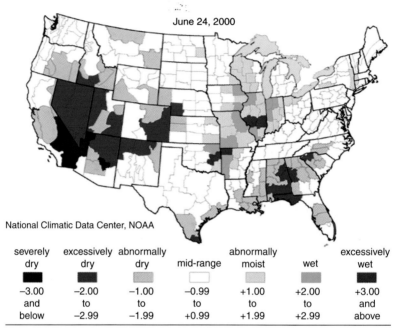

June 24, 2000

National Climatic Data Center, NOAA

severely dry	excessively dry	abnormally dry	mid-range	abnormally moist	wet	excessively wet
■	■	▦	□	▨	▨	■
−3.00 and below	−2.00 to −2.99	−1.00 to −1.99	−0.99 to +0.99	+1.00 to +1.99	+2.00 to +2.99	+3.00 and above

The Crop Moisture Index, a measure of shallow-soil moisture content, shows that for most of the U.S. Midwest, there was plenty of available moisture for crops during what Rather called an "ultra-drought" building in the Midwest.

SOURCE: http://www.cpc.noaa.gov.

Figure 7.2

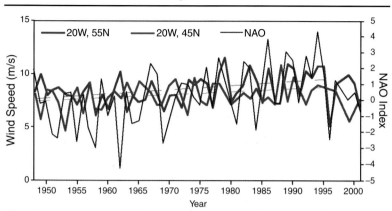

The strength of westerly wind flow (blue and red lines), and the North Atlantic Oscillation (black line), 1948 to 1995. Note that the trend toward stronger westerlies and a positive NAO falls apart after 1995.

SOURCE: Otterman, 2002.

Figure 7.3

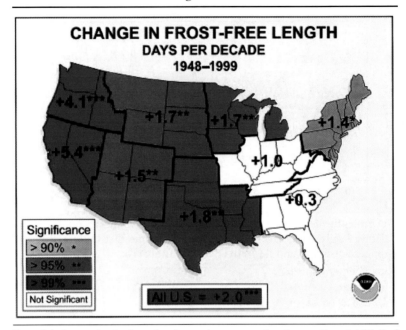

Decadal change in the length of growing season for the continental United States, 1940 to 1999.

SOURCE: Easterling, 2002.

Figure 8.3

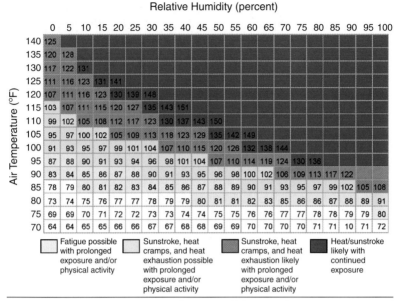

Apparent temperatures are a combination of the actual air temperature and the relative humidity. For example, an air temperature of 100°F coupled with a relative humidity of 45 percent makes it feel like 115°F to a human.

SOURCE: http://www.nws.noaa.gov.

Figure 8.4

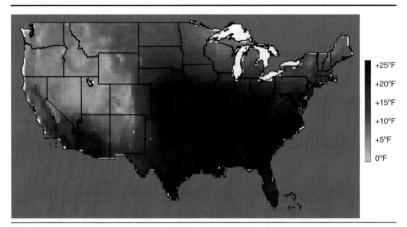

The change in the July apparent temperature by the year 2100, as depicted by the Canadian Climate Centre's climate model.

SOURCE: *Climate Change Impacts on the United States (National Assessment).*

Figure 9.4

A 1992 issue of the slick science capsulizer, *World Climate Review*, published an illustration that mocked the *Washington Post's*, much to that newspaper's vocalized consternation. Nine years later they chose to return the compliment, promising the end of the world on September 9, 2001.

Figure 9.5

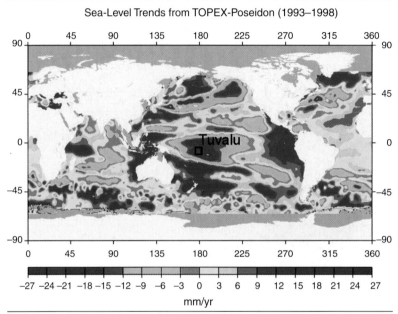

Sea-Level Trends from TOPEX-Poseidon (1993–1998)

mm/yr

The rates of sea-level rise during 1993 to 1998 as measured by the TOPEX/ Poseidon satellite. The Tuvalu Islands are located smack in the middle of the area of the most rapid sea-level *decline*. During these six years alone, the sea level has become 99 mm (3.9 inches) lower.

<small>Source:</small> Cabanes et al., *Science*, 2001.

Figure 9.6

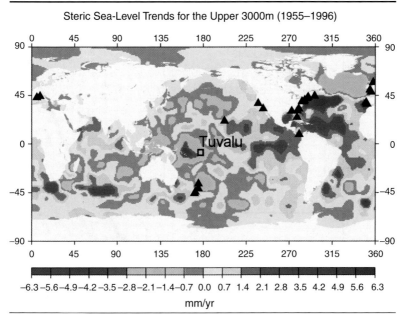

Steric Sea-Level Trends for the Upper 3000m (1955–1996)

mm/yr

If rates of sea-level change are examined over a longer period (1955 to 1996), the record shows that sea level has been falling at Tuvalu at a rate of about 2.5 mm per year (0.1 inches per year) for a total drop during this time period of 105 mm (4.1 in.).

Source: Cabanes, *Science*, 2001.

Figure 10.1

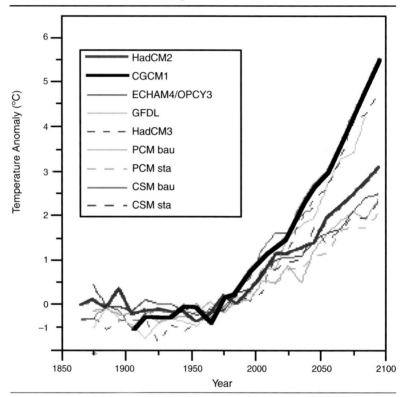

The temperature increase for the United States as forecast by the climate models considered for inclusion in the *U.S. National Assessment*. Notice that the Canadian Climate Model (CGCM1, heavy black line) produces the most extreme temperature rise.

Source: *U.S. National Assessment of the Potential Consequences of Climate Variability and Change.*

Figure 10.2

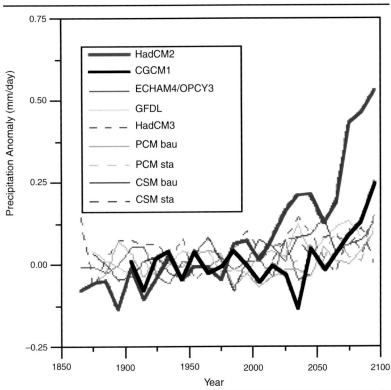

The precipitation change for the United States as forecast by the climate models considered for inclusion in the *U.S. National Assessment*. Notice that the Hadley Centre Climate Model (HadCM2, heavy red line) produces the most extreme precipitation increase, while the Canadian Climate Model (CGCM1, heavy black line) produces the second largest increase.

SOURCE: *U.S. National Assessment of the Potential Consequences of Climate Variability and Change.*

Figure 10.3

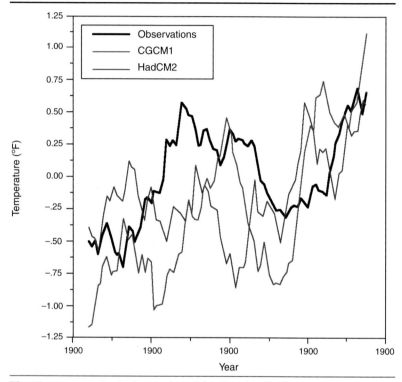

The 10-year smoothed, observed, and predicted annual average temperature for the United States during the 20th century by the two models used in the USNA.

SOURCE: *U.S. National Assessment of the Potential Consequences of Climate Variability and Change.*

Figure 10.7

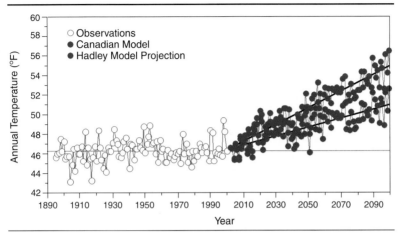

Observed Northeast U.S. temperature from 1895 to 2000, and typical forecast temperatures from 2000 to 2100 from the USNA climate models for that region.

SOURCE: For observed data: http://www.ncdc.noaa.gov. Model results from the *National Assessment*.

Figure 10.8

The observed precipitation trends during the past 100 years in the Northeast (left) exhibit a varied pattern of change as the planet warmed. The USNA forecasts for the next 100 years, based on output from two climate models, show nearly uniform, but opposite changes over the region. Either one or neither of these models is correct.

SOURCE: *National Assessment*.

Figure 10.9

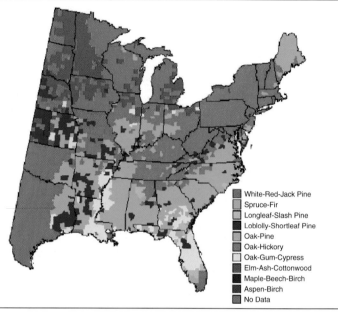

White-Red-Jack Pine
Spruce-Fir
Longleaf-Slash Pine
Loblolly-Shortleaf Pine
Oak-Pine
Oak-Hickory
Oak-Gum-Cypress
Elm-Ash-Cottonwood
Maple-Beech-Birch
Aspen-Birch
No Data

Dominant forest type by the period 2070–2100 was predicted on a county-by-county basis, 50 times smaller than the resolution level of the Canadian model upon which this forecast is based.

SOURCE: *National Assessment.*

Figure 10.10

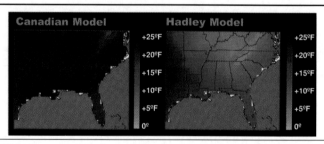

The USNA's projected changes in the southeastern Heat Index for the year 2100.